THEN A SOLDIER
A JEWISH ODYSSEY

RICHARD G. KURTZ

Then a Soldier: A Jewish Odyssey

© 2016

Richard G. Kurtz

ISBN: 978-1-629670-62-1 (Paperback)
ISBN: 978-1-629671-82-6 (Hardcover)

Revised Edition 2026

No portion of this book may be reproduced
without written permission
of the author.

Warwick House Publishers
1318 Church Street
Lynchburg, Virginia 24504

All the world's a stage,
And all the men and women merely players;
They have their exits and their entrances;
And one man in his time plays many parts...
At first the infant...
And then the whining school-boy...
And then the lover...
Then a soldier,
Full of strange oaths, and bearded like the pard,
Jealous in honour, sudden and quick in quarrel,
Seeking the bubble reputation
Even in the cannon's mouth...

WILLIAM SHAKESPEARE
AS YOU LIKE IT

CONTENTS

About the Author vii
Acknowledgments ix
Introduction—Why? xi
How Army Units Are Named xiv
Chapter 1   June 1
Chapter 2   Parkchester 8
Chapter 3   Ancestry 20
Chapter 4   CCNY: Harvard-Adjacent 28
Chapter 5   Fitting in 48
Chapter 6   Europe 60
Chapter 7   For Tin and Tungsten 74
Chapter 8   The FO and the Artillery Kill Chain 80
Chapter 9   Company Town 86
Chapter 10   Company Men 92
Chapter 11   Loc Ninh 102
Chapter 12   The Captain 114
Chapter 13   And God Laughs 121
Chapter 14   Running into Burning Buildings 135
Chapter 15   Respite 149
Chapter 16   Meaning Making 152
Chapter 17   Getting to Know You 162
Chapter 18   Bong Trang 172
Chapter 19   Making Monkeys 193
Chapter 20   Change 200
Chapter 21   "Servabo Fidem" 208
Chapter 22   Prek Klok II 215
Chapter 23   Chickens, Pigs, and Bicycles 220
Epilogue   Moving On Down the Road 223
Afterword   The New Antisemitism 245
Glossary   277
Index   287

ABOUT THE AUTHOR

Richard Gary Kurtz served thirty years in the US Army, retiring as a Colonel. Almost ten of those years were spent overseas, including two years in Vietnam with the 1st Infantry and 101st Airborne Divisions. He was later a battalion and brigade commander and served two tours as a Pentagon staff officer. He then worked as a consultant to the Department of Defense on missile defense issues. Mr. Kurtz has a BS from the City College of New York (CCNY) and an MS from the University of Texas at El Paso and Salve Regina University in Newport RI. He lives with his wife, Carol, in Alexandria, Virginia. They have three children and seven grandchildren. His hobbies include fly fishing, hiking, weight training, and gardening.

ACKNOWLEDGMENTS

The battles of Hill 150 and Bong Trang were historically insignificant but, nonetheless, lethal, difficult, and confusing. Attempting to describe them made me think of the proverbial problem faced by two blind-folded men touching different parts of an elephant, trying to reach a consensus on how it might look—the man at the tail having a wholly different opinion than the man at the trunk.

Several men helped me portray that elephant. Major Ray Blanford (Retired) and Mr. Richard Meadows added clarity and coherence to my initial description of the fight for Hill 150. Brigadier General Bill Mullen (Retired) and Mr. Tom Galvin provided a broad, overarching appreciation of the battle of Bong Trang, far beyond the narrow "soda straw view" I had observed.

My wife, Carol, kept my experiences in perspective and executed her wifely duty to keep my hat size in check. She was an army nurse during the late 1960s, working in a stateside hospital. Caring for long-term injured soldiers, she knew the difference between their extensive injuries and my one-week vacation in a field hospital in Saigon.

In addition to this, she knew firsthand the sad emptiness resulting from the death of the young men who served in that war. Her high school days had been filled with the laughter and exuberance of two of her classmates, sons of senior Fort Benning officer families. And then they were gone, their budding lives extinguished by a war that quickly grew unpopular.

Professor Yohanan Petrovsky-Shtern of Northwestern University enabled a vastly expanded understanding of my ancestry within the context of my choice to make the military a career.

His book, *Jews in the Russian Army, 1827-1917*, is a meticulously researched account of a relatively undocumented segment of the Russian society where my grandfather lived and in whose army he served before immigrating to America.

The late Ms. Joyce Maddox of Warwick House Publishing did yeoman's work in producing the first edition of this book; Ms. Amy Moore did the same in creating this revised edition. I am grateful to both for making this book possible.

My last acknowledgment is not to an individual but to the collective spirit of thousands. The 1st Infantry Division was the most difficult and transformative of all my life experiences. It was the no-nonsense, no-excuses, get-it-done school of war. The men in its ranks were imbued with the ethos of veterans of World Wars I and II. They all, both the current and past soldiers, taught me how to be a man, and that was a lifetime gift.

INTRODUCTION

WHY?

"We have some impulse within us that makes us want to explain ourselves to other human beings."
MAYA ANGELOU, AUTHOR

The Vietnam War, which defined my generation, is almost ancient history. Its veterans are entering the age of irrelevance. They exist on the periphery of a culture obsessed with youth and relatively ill-informed on history. No one dreams these aging veterans were ever warriors. I want my readers to know these men as the vibrant teenagers they were, the men they quickly became, and explain how the war they fought came to be.

This memoir covers my first year in Vietnam and the events leading to it. It accounts for only a fraction of my life. Friends have asked why such a narrow focus. I tell them my one year in combat with the 1st Infantry Division defined me; it constitutes all I know about being a soldier. It was the most honest work I ever did.

I also wish to portray combat in a realistic, non-glamorized manner. My war was an industrialized process, often described as a "kill chain," wherein each soldier has a specific function to produce the required lethal effect. I was part of that kill chain. Accordingly, I present my view of war in a dispassionate, factual, and unromantic manner. This book will, therefore, not serve as a script for a dramatic war movie, and I never intended it to be so.

War is not heroic; the soldiers are. And not necessarily because they might lead a bayonet charge, but because they endure. I want my readers to understand the quiet dignity and courage of soldiers in combat. They face danger repeatedly and steadfastly. They must control all impulses for self-preservation and subordinate their survival instincts for the good of the group with whom they serve. This altruism is a virtue too few Americans know. Hopefully, this book will remedy that deficit.

Søren Kierkegaard tells us we live life going forward but understand it by looking backward. This memoir was written long after my last battle in Vietnam. Had I written it then, it might well have sounded bombastic and adolescent. Telling my story now benefits from looking back on the experiences that led me to Vietnam, what happened there, and why. And the telling is more mellow and reflective.

My post-combat experiences contain enough *sturm und drang* to populate several memoirs or afternoon television soap operas. They include my second tour in Vietnam, battalion and brigade command, six years in the Pentagon, and two weeks on special assignment in Beirut after Hezbollah terrorists bombed our embassy. I can add to that marriage, fatherhood and grandfatherhood. Also, work as a military contractor in the DC area and Israel, helping prepare US and Israeli forces to meet a ballistic missile attack, which they successfully did in 2024 and 2025. Additionally, I have strong opinions about the two armies in which I served—a draft military connected to society and a professional one that is not. Though the volunteer force is more effective and efficient, I favor universal service, as the embodiment of citizenship and application of the Ephebic Oath.[1] But I am not inclined to elaborate on life after Vietnam, save for some abbreviated mention in the Epilogue. These years are certainly not irrelevant; but for the purpose of this memoir, their main function is to have paved the long road from which I can look back and understand Vietnam and place it in context.

---

[1] Oath taken in Athens, by 18-year-olds upon graduating the Ephebic College military academy. It conferred citizenship and demanded loyalty to the city, its laws, fellow soldiers, and a promise to leave Athens a better place than the one inherited.

INTRODUCTION—WHY?

This story is about me and my war. I am Jewish, so it contains things Jewish as well as things martial. My ancestry, my experiences with childhood antisemitism, and the Holocaust influenced my choosing the profession of arms. Thus, these topics are relevant to my presence in Vietnam, and are, therefore, discussed in some detail. Some have suggested that this "non-war" content detracts from the focus on Vietnam. I acknowledge that criticism but ask my readers to abide by this necessary detour before getting to "the mud and the blood."

And the present suddenly intruded and influenced my assessment of past experiences with things Jewish. On October 7, 2023, Hamas unleashed a terror attack on Israel involving, murder, rape, and mutilation which was more than sufficient to garner the world's condemnation.[2] Yet, Israel's legitimate response quickly turned world opinion against it. The associated explosion of antisemitism on American college campuses, the role of the news and social media in inciting and accelerating this animus, and its lethal and violent projection into American life made whatever antisemitism I had heretofore experienced miniscule and inconsequential in comparison. I am, therefore, compelled, as a matter of honor, to address this matter in an Afterword at the end of the book.

Returning to my life's military theme, a few years ago, one of my former lieutenants, then promoted to colonel, related that my officers used to joke that the Army should build a glass case on the E Ring (senior Army leadership suites in the Pentagon), put Colonel Kurtz in it, and affix a sign reading, "In case of war, break glass." That is the lens through which this memoir is best read and understood.

---

[2] Isaac Chotiner, "How Hamas Used Sexual Violence on 7 October," The New Yorker, December 10, 2023, https://www.newyorker.com/news/q-and-a/how-hamas-used-sexual-violence-on-october-7th.

HOW ARMY UNITS ARE NAMED

"Is it any wonder that I love my regiment?"
THEODORE ROOSEVELT, *THE ROUGH RIDERS*

Later in this memoir, you will encounter US Army unit designations of seemingly meaningless letters and numbers. This short primer explains the "unit naming" convention and enables the reader to focus on the narratives in which unit designations are embedded.

You will read in Chapter 9 that I was assigned to Charlie Battery, 2d Battalion, 33d Artillery, with duty in Alpha Company, 2d Battalion, 28th Infantry, abbreviated as C-2-33 Artillery and A-2-28 Infantry. Let's "unpack" these alpha-numeric sequences and learn what they mean.

Each unit in the US Army is given a unique alpha-numeric designator, or in civilian terms, a "name." It is like the combination of our first, middle, and last names and our birthday or Social Security number to identify each of us, uniquely, for legal or financial purposes. In the military, this uniqueness is paramount in a time of war during which orders are issued to specific units to accomplish specific missions at particular times and places. There is no room for error in the wrong unit receiving an order not intended for it. Or, in an operations center or command posts, tracking unit locations and progress, there must be no confusion over which unit is being reported.

This convention abbreviated my "home address" in combat as A-2-28 Infantry. The first letter, pronounced "Alpha," in the military phonetic alphabet system, represents the rifle company in which I served. The other rifle companies in my battalion were designated "Bravo" and "Charlie." We were assigned to the 2nd battalion, thus the number "2." All combat units are named after a famous or notable ancestor, just like people are. This unit ancestor is a regiment that can trace its history or lineage back in time. Thus, the final number, "28," indicating that our battalion is affiliated with and named after the 28th Regiment of Infantry, which was made famous in combat in France in WWI. When referring to the battalion as a whole, without regard to the individual companies, the designation is 2-28 Infantry.

Again, for simplicity, consider these alpha-numeric designators similar to people's first, middle, and last names associated with famous ancestors.

CHAPTER 1

JUNE

*"Men love war…it's the only thing that
stops women from laughing at them."*
JOHN FOWLES

A terse radio report by the point squad announces that they "have a situation"—a deliberately understated military term for a problem requiring more senior leadership than is already at the scene. When we cross over to the reverse slope of the hill, I see bodies lying along the bank of a drainage ditch. One figure looks familiar. As we get closer, I know it is the teacher from the village, even before I see her face. Her dress is distinctive. I had seen her in it a few days earlier.

Each step forward reveals more detail. She lies next to her father. Her upper arms are bound behind her with the all-purpose, thin, black, plastic-clad copper-steel wire we use to connect our field telephones. It is ubiquitous and in plentiful supply. Everyone uses it as a binding material. Then I notice her elbows. They are almost touching, with her forearms splayed out at a forty-five-degree angle. Out of curiosity, I sling my M-16 rifle across my chest and force my elbows back toward each other, trying inanely to replicate her posture. I cannot; the gap is considerable.

Next, the back of her head appears covered with rice. At first, I do not comprehend. Then, instinctively, I do. My stomach turns. I gag and try hard not to let it show. What at first looked like little white seeds is the Tropics' version of the circle of life trick, whereby a formerly complex life form is transformed into a more primitive one. They are fly eggs, soon-to-be maggots that will feed on the open gunshot wound to the back of her head. She serves now as a commissary for blowflies.

The peasant women in the Loc Ninh Rubber Plantation dressed in black, pajama-type garb, just like the men. Their femininity was well hidden. The teacher, however, wore a simple but flattering long, cream-colored dress called an Ao-Dai. Her attractiveness was out of place but certainly welcomed by the soldiers. She was the closest thing to the "girl back home" any of us would see for the rest of the year.

We, her formerly appreciative audience, are the men of an infantry rifle company. I am the forward observer. My military function is to provide artillery fire support. At the moment, that is the total of any thought I am capable of.

I had not seen combat when I first met the teacher a few days earlier. Between then and now, I have been in battle. I am exposed. The dead and the wounded are no longer novel; they have become the backdrop of war. Nonetheless, as I begin the slow realization of the circumstances of her death, my emotions build and then drain out of me, unexpressed. I am numb. I do not know what to say. It is the same with the others. They cannot verbalize their shock. The young soldiers around me are silent, their faces blank. They light up cigarettes and stare into the landscape.

Looking through the gray haze of the resultant smoke from a dozen soldiers, I try to take in the meaning of the teacher's death. It is a painful thought process. My brain goes into overdrive to structure a memory of the past week's events for clues to my possible causation of her death.

We had patrolled through her village about seven days earlier. She watched us with uncertainty, like we were a militarized biker gang from a far place that had to be placated and then hurried on its way.

But my ego was soaring. I was two weeks a soldier. So far, war has been a great and non-lethal adventure. We had neither yet met the enemy nor suffered any casualties. I was full of youthful enthusiasm and feeling particularly "in role" as a combat officer. I wanted her to notice me; I wanted her to like me. Since we were in a French rubber plantation under French management, I assumed she spoke French. While our company commander, Captain Ray Blanford, spoke with her father, the village elder, using our Vietnamese interpreter, I engaged her in the best of my college French, which was never that good and certainly had gotten no better after three years of only sporadic use.

Cumulatively, we spoke for no more than fifteen minutes as I struggled to construct the simplest of sentences and fumbled for the French translation of military terms not contained in my college readings of Verlaine and Rimbaud. I must have sounded comedic. I asked what she had seen that might interest us and what she thought of the Americans compared with the French. I imagine she understood enough of what came so clumsily from my mouth because she answered, speaking too rapidly for me to understand. I responded, asking her to please speak more slowly. She smiled, and we both knew that I had overplayed my hand in trying to engage her in conversation. At any rate, her answer amounted to her knowing nothing about anything. She didn't even ask where I had learned to babble in French. It was a dead-end conversation; it went nowhere.

Worse still, out of the corner of my eye, I had noticed some of our soldiers nudging each other as they watched the new lieutenant putting the moves on the best-looking girl for many miles around. She was not exactly dismissive. True to what one expects of a beautiful woman upon whom all other favorable attributes are automatically bestowed, she showed her classiness in letting me off the hook by excusing herself to attend to her duties. When we left the village, having accomplished nothing of military value other than to show our presence, Blanford asked, in perfect deadpan, "Did you get her number?" Stung by his sarcasm, I made a mental note to redeem myself the next time we passed through her village.

The next time came this past Saturday. The village was deserted, and gunfire filled the air. We were in the battle for Hill 150.[3]

---

[3] I believe the teacher and the other executed villagers were taken hostage early Saturday morning and judged and executed several hours later. The remaining villagers probably fled after realizing that they were caught between us and their teacher's executioners.

Afterward, Sunday was gifted to us as a twenty-four-hour stand down. There was no grief counseling; the term had not yet been invented. Instead, we cleaned ourselves and our weapons. It was, in effect, a ritualistic washing away the preceding day's unpleasantness. A new company commander, Captain John Hutcheson, was sent down from brigade staff to replace Blanford, whose right eye was shot out in the initial assault on the hill. Nine new replacements also arrived as partial compensation for our twelve dead and wounded in the fight.

Today's operation, Monday, 13 June 1966, was a "tune-up patrol" with our new commander and the replacement infantrymen. It was supposed to be "routine," just something to get us back in the swing of things. We had not expected to find the murdered village schoolteacher.

The men around me finish their smokes and drift back into patrol formation. I consider, briefly, the possibility that the teacher was killed because she had been seen talking to me and because the battle that soon followed went badly for the enemy. That thought bathes me in guilt. It makes me wish I were somewhere else, doing something else. That, of course, is not possible. Besides, there are other villagers along that ditch, and I had not spoken with any of them, yet they, too, were executed. Reflexively, I shift my focus to the role of the enemy. Years will pass before I allow myself the luxury to consider more carefully my part, if any, in causing her execution. For now, I see the enemy's cruelty and culpability as predominant.

The teacher's execution is the work of the Viet Cong, the communist insurgent movement assisted by North Vietnam, whose objective is to "unify" South Vietnam with its neighbor to the north. The United States, as part of its national strategy to contain communism, is "assisting" South Vietnam in resisting this unification. Our rifle company is a minor instrument in this struggle, and the teacher and the other villagers in the drainage ditch are the scrap work of the unification process.

The name we give our enemy reflects their place in the wider, on-going global conflict. Viet Cong is Vietnamese for "Vietnamese Communist." It was developed as a pejorative term by the US

Information Agency, circa 1957, to discredit the Vietnamese forces opposing the government favored by the US. It leveraged the fear of communism that peaked during the Cold War. The Viet Cong were known to themselves as the "Viet Minh"—the League for the Independence of Vietnam. This group was founded by Ho Chi Minh, their Vietnamese communist leader who fought the French, Japanese, and Americans for independence, before, during, and after WWII. In the US Army phonetic alphabet, the term "VC" is spoken as Victor Charlie, and our apolitical but "hip" soldiers refer to the Viet Cong as just "Charlie."

I deflect further thought of the schoolteacher by turning my attention to the broken typewriter. It is an old one, full size. It, too, lies by the drainage ditch. At first, I assume it was part of the VC battalion headquarters, used to type orders and such, and left there when they retreated in haste after the battle turned against them. Then I realize it is too large for use by a mobile combat unit. Eventually, I conclude it belonged to the village and was seized and made inoperable for the same reason the teacher was killed. In the rural margins, a typed notice represented something official, something authoritative. It connoted orderliness. The typewriter was a token of governance, which was the basis of its death warrant and the teacher's.

The strategy of insurgency is purely utilitarian. All is permissible so long as it is effective. And if you are lucky or brutal enough to win, you will control all moral judgments. No more typed notices for the villagers to read means no more governmental authority. Children sitting in an empty classroom knowing that their teacher was cruelly executed will not miss the point—the VC are the real authority and are to be feared more than the Americans. But it was an unnecessary lesson. The teacher had avoided contact with us as she carefully navigated through a VC dominated environment. The village understood who wielded the enduring power long before their teacher, her father, and other local "officials" were executed.

If we were living in movieland, we would carry her body back to the village and lay her to rest alongside her ancestors. I would say a few words, finally, in flawless French. Then, we would hunt down her killers and dispatch them without mercy. However, it is nothing like that. We are sickened by what we find and anxious to put it behind us. We report by radio and resume our patrol, assuming conveniently that the teacher and the other villagers will be properly buried.

The remainder of our patrol is uneventful. On our return leg, I ask Hutcheson if we could make a minor diversion in our route so that we cross Hill 150. I tell him I will point out, on the ground, where it all happened. We approach the hill in a direction different from which we attacked forty-eight hours earlier. Somehow, this disorients me. Nothing looks the same.

I search for landmarks in the military world of the millimeter, a measurement unit abbreviated as mm, with about twenty-five millimeters equaling one inch. I seek out the shell craters along the trench line that the VC had occupied and on which I had directed 105mm howitzer fire. I find none. I look for the broken treetops in which some of our 81mm mortars had prematurely detonated. I see none. I jump into the trench line and search for the 7.92mm shell casings from the German World War II MG-34 machine gun we had captured. There are none. Tellingly, there are no enemy corpses. I had counted upwards of ten dead enemy soldiers two days earlier. Now, there is no trace, begging the dual questions of who cleans up battlefields after a fight and why the VC dead were recovered but not the teacher and other villagers. In this case, it looks like the work of a local VC support unit; the only evidence left to be found, for shock value, would be the dead villagers.

I turn to my Radio Telephone Operator (RTO), Specialist Four (Corporal) Robert Dooley, a tough, eighteen-year-old Irish draftee from Detroit, who carries, in addition to his load, a twenty-six-pound battery-powered, PRC-25 field radio that we use to call for artillery support. He was by my side during the entire fight and guided me through my first taste of combat. Trying not to look the fool, I whisper, "Dooley, this is the place, isn't it?"

But Dooley is preoccupied. Before departing on the patrol this morning, he had "mass-produced" letters to three different girlfriends and placed them in the company mail sack. Around mid-patrol, he experienced a frightful flashback, leading him to believe that he might have stuffed the letters into the wrong envelopes in his haste. He has since been eager to return to base and retrieve the letters before they are flown out on the evening re-supply helicopter.

I, personally, am in a romantic hiatus. My on-again-off-again high school summer love, now in medical school, has recently married. Adding to that, my friends have written that my college ex-soulmate for life was serving as a front-line soldier in the "sexual revolution," doing the work of three or four. Rounding out my misfortune is the fact that my girlfriend in Germany prematurely adapted to my forthcoming transfer. I was "gone" before I ever got on the airplane. In response to my question, as if confirming the disparities in our problems, Dooley takes a desultory look around, pretends to consider the terrain, and then shrugs.

His gesture sums up my immediate future. This, the third June since college graduation, is an anomaly. June used to be the best month of the year for me. I especially remember grade school Junes: the last day of the school year, turning in textbooks, and then absolute freedom for the ten weeks of summer. My two previous Junes in West Germany were cheerful enough: they marked the first noticeable transition from wet, cold, gray winters to something that looked and felt like spring. But this is a different June. Almost the entire month is spent on patrol, living outdoors, and sleeping on the ground. The meals are mostly cold and from a can. There is no running water. It is a hobo existence, with the added possibility of death or injury by gunfire. The tour of duty in Vietnam is one year unless seriously wounded. If I stay lucky, I will be here until the next June.

A number of the men around can rightfully blame others for sending them here. They are entitled to have murder in their hearts for the members of their draft boards or the recruiters who told them everything about army life, save this. My case is different. This morning, I got a good look at the person responsible for my being here. He was staring at me from the mirrored surface of my artillery compass as I shaved, using my helmet as a basin. I am here by my own choice and because I am Jewish, and that requires some explanation.

CHAPTER 2

PARKCHESTER

"Other people have a nationality.
The Irish and the Jews have a psychosis."
BRENDAN BEHAN

The trail that led me to an infantry rifle company in Vietnam began in the Bronx, a borough of New York City, in a large-scale apartment complex called Parkchester. Childhood experiences there became enduring and shaped my future in ways that were then unpredictable.

Parkchester was a private venture, owned and operated by the Metropolitan Life Insurance Company, designed to provide affordable housing for working and middle-class families. It operated under rent control regulation, thus, in 1950, we paid $80.00 for our two-bedroom apartment. Adjusted for inflation, this equals $1,100.00 in 2025 dollars. The current Parkchester web site lists average rents for a similar apartment at closer to $3,000, so it was quite the bargain in my time.

Construction began in 1938 on the former grounds of the New York Catholic Protectory, a trade school and farm established in 1865 for youth placed in court-ordered custodial care. The name derived from two communities adjacent to the farmland: *Park* Versailles and Wes*tchester* Heights. My parents arrived in 1941, and I was born the following year.

In the time before "helicopter parents," Parkchester youth self-organized their play and got to where they had to be via foot, roller-skate, or bicycle. In the summer, kids left their apartments after breakfast and did not return until dinner. All

Grounds of Catholic Protectory before Parkchester. View is along Unionport Road. Photo from Bronx County Historical Society Archives.

activities—roller-skating, shooting marbles, flag football, jump rope, punchball, and softball were synchronized, done "in season," in unison. In the play areas, we learned self-regulation, teamwork, and self-direction. Fair play and being picked for teams based on skill was the law of the land.

Parkchester was meticulously regulated and maintained; it was an aberrational oasis in the otherwise freewheeling, teeming,

*Parkchester under construction, 1940.
Photo from Bronx County Historical Society Archives.*

hectic Bronx. It defined what "right" should look like. Weekdays were a beehive of organized activity. Dozens of men in working khakis painted the outside metal works, mowed the lawns, tended the flower beds, and trimmed the hedges. After winter snowfalls, they shoveled the sidewalks clean. Each building had an assigned "porter" to maintain cleanliness, including polishing the brass mailboxes in the lobby. Plumbers and electricians, with their toolboxes, kept all in good repair. Other men in blue uniforms patrolled the streets and raised and lowered the American flag at dawn and sunset.

The development encompassed 129 acres and was about eight hundred yards, or almost a half mile, on edge. It was large enough to have its own post office and zip code. The 171 red-brick building complexes housed 12,273 families. The floor plans consisted

Aerial photograph of Parkchester in 1955. Two major roadways, Unionport Road running northwest to southeast, and Metropolitan Avenue running northeast to southwest, crossing at Metropolitan Oval, divide Parkchester into four quadrants.
Photo from Bronx County Historical Society Archives.

*Parkchester stoves to be installed, 1940.
Photo from Bronx County Historical Society Archives.*

*View along East Avenue, 1940. My building is at head of street to the
left. Photo from Bronx County Historical Society Archives.*

Metropolitan Oval, circa 1940s. My building is in center background. Photo courtesy of Parkchester South Condominiums archives.

Another view of Metropolitan Oval, circa 1940s. Photo courtesy of Parkchester South Condominiums archives.

Parkchester, circa 1940s.
Photo courtesy of Parkchester South Condominiums archives.

of one, two, and three-bedroom apartments, all with only a single bathroom. The kitchens were small but functional, with metal cabinetry. There was room for a washing machine if one of the cabinets was removed. Damp clothing was hung in the single, small bathroom. The buildings had elevators, incinerators, and centralized hot water heat, but no air conditioning. The remedies for the hot, humid summers were fans and a prized architectural feature known as "cross-ventilation," bedrooms with windows on two adjacent walls.

The landscaping was, as the name suggests, park-like. There were gardens, fountains, playgrounds, and a singular preoccupation with "grass," the type you look at rather than smoke. The management treated grass like people at that time treated the front parlor—to be admired but not used. It was a severe infraction of the rules to be caught by the Parkchester Police playing on the grass. This infraction often resulted in our names being "taken" and a follow-up letter to our parents summarizing the offense. Too many such letters could endanger the renewal of the rental lease.

Parkchester was 100 percent Caucasian. There was a waiting list to live there. The application process required photographs of the prospective tenants and in-home interviews by Metropolitan Life Insurance agents to assess suitability for residence in the new development. In this manner, no African American families were admitted. To keep this onerous policy in perspective, racial segregation was practiced in many other Bronx neighborhoods, where individual realtors, rental agents, and building managers were responsible, as opposed to a single, identifiable, corporate entity. Ultimately, this segregation was reversed, with unintended consequences. As a result of the 1954 Supreme Court *Brown v. The Board of Education of Topeka* ruling, children from predominantly African American, low-performing grade schools were bused into the Parkchester public schools. The hope was that these children would thrive once enrolled in a better school. Instead, the busing policy was a significant factor in inspiring "white flight" to the suburbs. Finally, in the late 1960s, Parkchester was integrated.

The majority population segment was Irish Catholic. In terms of today's diversity paradigm, the Jewish population was underrepresented. In the 1950s, the Bronx was approximately 35 percent Jewish. Parkchester had a population of forty thousand, of which no more than 15 percent was Jewish. It was commonly believed, but not documented or proven, that the Metropolitan Life Insurance Company imposed an unofficial "gentleman's agreement" type quota on Jewish tenants, very much like those set by private colleges. However, some attribute this statistical anomaly to Jewish ethnocentricity—a desire to remain in Jewish neighborhoods.

Pre-school kids usually played together. However, at age five, the Jewish and Irish youth gravitated into two worlds. Jewish children and most of the small minority of Protestant children attended public schools and wore regular clothing. Most of the more numerous Irish Catholics attended parochial schools, the closest being Saint Helena's, which was tuition-free. They wore a uniform consisting of a dark blue suit, a white shirt, and a dark blue tie for the boys, and a blue jumper with a white blouse for the girls.

CHAPTER 2—PARKCHESTER

Playground, circa 1950s.
Photo courtesy of Parkchester South Condominiums archives.

Good Humor ice cream man, in white uniform.
Photo courtesy of Parkchester South Condominiums archives.

*East Quadrant basketball courts, circa 1950s.
Photo courtesy of Parkchester South Condominiums archives.*

The Jews and the Irish stood out like two distinct tribes. Anyone, and everyone, could immediately discern who was what.

In addition to separate schools, Parkchester was divided by geography and cultural affiliation. Its two main, intersecting roadways sectioned it into four "quadrants," North, South, East, and West. Each had a playground, mini-park, and flagpole, like a small city-state. The Jewish and Irish kids "hung out" separately. The South was traditional Irish territory. The West was Jewish. The North had the only ball fields. It attracted both Jewish and Irish youth. The same was true of the East quadrant, except there it was a matter of basketball courts.

The Parkchester police, when not inanely preoccupied with keeping kids off the grass, were charged by the management with preserving order and safety. The primary thrust was to keep outside youth gangs off the premises, which they did well. Absent external threats, Parkchester youth were free to look inward for enemies. Unfortunately, a few defined these enemies as the Jewish kids.

For the most part, our parents either interacted favorably or ignored each other without incident. For example, my father belonged to a shuffleboard club with equal numbers of Jewish, Protestant, and Irish members. The club hosted an annual secular Christmas party for the members' pre-school children, which I eagerly attended.

But it could be different with teenagers. The actual antisemitic incidents were not frequent or experienced by all. You had to be in the right place and time to find it, usually on the athletic fields. Most non-Jewish kids abstained from this behavior, and I got along well with the Irish kids in my building. I would guess that a small fraction of the Irish accounted for the antisemitic incidents I knew of.

The antisemitism I experienced on occasion was direct and unambiguous. There is no subtlety in being called a "Dirty Jew" or the fistfight deriving from that. For example, early in my sophomore year in high school, when I felt particularly grown-up and tough, two friends and I were playing basketball in the East Quadrant. When our ball rolled onto an adjacent court where Irish kids were, they cussed us out. Naturally, I returned the compliment.

Words evolved to shoves and, finally, the main event. To speed up the tick-tock of the story, I faced ten of them, itching for a fight. I was terrified. The actual fight was fair, one-on-one, and not much by movie standards. We pushed each other several times and then grappled and boxed poorly. "Technically," I lost—I had a bloody nose; my opponent did not.

In retrospect, fights like that were relatively trivial, especially compared to the existential events I experienced in Vietnam. Nonetheless, they left lasting impressions because they touched on personal freedom and safety. Being targeted for your religion left no remedy. There was nothing I could or should change in my behavior. Should I have avoided all future opportunities to use the athletic fields? Should I have changed or denied my religion? Should I have run from the fights? Should I have adopted a cringing and obsequious demeanor to defuse those situations? I felt vulnerable to the whim of others. Other kids, other times, to paraphrase Freud, a rolling basketball could be just a rolling basketball.

I viewed these incidents as interrelated with the history of Jewish oppression. I read all I could in the public library on anti-semitism, trying to understand its basis. The Holocaust made the biggest impression. I could not fathom either the oppressor's barbarity or the victims' seeming passivity. Once slaughter became the known end state, why not die fighting? That seemed better than dying doing nothing. And there was a personal dimension. I was a three-year-old child when World War II ended. Children my age were gassed up to the very end, and I would have been swept up in the slaughter had my grandparents not left Eastern Europe a few decades earlier.

A particular documentary about the Holocaust shook me to my core. Based on captured German film, it depicted Lithuanian Jews

Lithuanian militiamen at execution site in Pajouste Forest, 1941. Jewish women in background are being forced to strip naked before being shot. Photo from the United States Holocaust Memorial Museum archives. The views or opinions expressed in this book and the context in which the image is used do not necessarily reflect the views or policy of, nor imply approval or endorsement by, the US Holocaust Memorial Museum.

being stripped naked, shot, and dumped into mass graves in late summer and fall of 1941 by Lithuanian collaborators.[4] A recently published history establishes, based on a firsthand account, that the Lithuanian savagery offended even German Army sensibilities.[5]

My mind placed my mother in those scenes—her family came from Lithuania. I wondered who would have been there to save her and her sister had her parents not immigrated to America in the late 1890s.

The total of all my reflections, from fist fights to the Holocaust, made me resolve to learn how to fight and be strong.[6] That translated into karate classes, ROTC in college, and Army Airborne School at Fort Benning, Georgia. And eventually, when war came, I went—I needed to know.

Parkchester also heightened my awareness of political and social power, who had it and who did not, and its relationship to opportunity. The Irish had it in Parkchester and in the Bronx at large. I was also vaguely aware, in a very simplistic manner, that people known as Episcopalians ran vast parts of America and controlled the presidency. At the same time, the Baptists ruled in the South and the Mormons in Utah. My people, the Jews, wielded no such political power. Others determined where we were welcome, what we could be, and what we could not be. All of this was based on ancestry: those who had the right kind and those who did not. My future seemed bound by my ancestry, and that troubled me.

---

[4] British Broadcasting Corporation, *The Nazis: A Warning from History*, 1997, Disc 2.
[5] Richard J. Evans, *The Third Reich At War* (New York: The Penguin Press, 2009), 217-218.
[6] For a long time, I thought this motivating factor was unique to me. Later, I met several tough, professional, Jewish officers, some children of Holocaust survivors, who related the same motivating factor, in as many words.

CHAPTER 3

ANCESTRY

"Whoever serves his country well has no need of ancestors."
VOLTAIRE

*"We all grow up with the weight of history on us.
Our ancestors dwell in the attics of our brains…"*
SHIRLEY ABBOTT, AUTHOR

It is challenging to characterize the ancestry-based societal barriers of my youth in the 1950s as they appear in the context of today's accepting and diverse environment, unimaginable and almost un-American. Ethnicity was not in vogue. The Madison Avenue advertising profession, the movies, television, and *Playboy* and *Esquire* magazines defined American beauty and style. It was a world where people lived in single-family homes on tree-lined streets, had last names for their first, and wore coats, ties, and crinoline-lined dresses at home. Children had cute nicknames like "Buffy," attended elite prep schools and colleges, spoke well, and exuded perfect manners. Indeed, our grade school reading text, *Fun With Dick and Jane*, portrayed this magical world—Dick, Jane, Baby Sally, Mother, Father, and their dog, Spot, living and playing in suburbia whilst we lived in tall brick apartment buildings, played on concrete, and were not allowed dogs as pets. I wanted to climb into those book pictures and be of that world.

In the 1950s, religion and family provenance, over which we exercised no control, defined and limited our career and social aspirations. The Jewish people were the consummate Caucasian "outsiders" of that time. We were consigned to a societal ghetto, allowed to prosper and excel within our sphere with our kind. Jewish doctors had Jewish patients, held privileges at Jewish hospitals, belonged to Jewish country and social clubs, and resided in non-exclusive neighborhoods. Jewish bankers worked for Jewish banking houses and had Jewish clients. The same applied to Jewish lawyers and businessmen. This condition did not rest easily with me. I wanted what others deemed I should not have: entrance to the elite segment of "their" society.

Resistance to this type of discrimination and the use of judicial and legislative processes as a remedy were still several years away. My generation did not fight unfair rejection; instead, we sought to make ourselves more worthy of acceptance. Diversity, as we know it today, was neither desired nor celebrated. Assimilation and adherence to the norms of society were the operative behavioral models. To me, assimilation did not mean desertion of the Jewish religion. I was born Jewish, and that was fine with me. I would remain Jewish, but I wanted to escape from my perception of the confines of Jewishness. I wanted an adventurous life outside the norms of the prevalent Jewish culture. I wanted to do what Jews were not supposed to do and go where Jews were not supposed to go, but I would do so as a Jew.

My family was lower-middle-class. They could not afford to send me to a traditional college with the associated social networks to move up in society. That is how the US Army entered my thought process as a vehicle to project me into an otherwise forbidden orbit. The Army promised adventure, and from movies and novels, I understood that military officers lived in a universe of clubs, golf courses, stables, and formal events. The civilian etiquette guides of the time equated military officers with governmental dignitaries, not doctors, lawyers, or engineers.

My teenage brain began to develop a conceptual plan whereby I would enter military society as "an officer and a gentleman," do well, and earn my place. I would live within the sphere of military culture and, at the same time, intersect with and have certain entrance rights into the world of civilian higher society. Thus, in a time when we were relatively at peace, a military career seemed both a viable and desirable trajectory to enter the world of the insiders and allow me, as an individual, to inject at least one more Jew into a physical and martial environment. Fortunately, my youth conferred a degree of immunity against a complete understanding of mortality and danger. The danger inherent in my choice excited me, and I brushed over the existential threat my strategy presented. Nor did I analyze the ethical issues associated with my choice, though, when I entered college to begin implementing my plan, I realized that the military profession was incompatible with an idealized, intellectualized concept of a warless society. Even more so, I was often reminded by friends and relatives that a long-term military commitment lay far outside the values, habits, and expectations of American-Jewish culture and the extended historical family in which I was raised.

Most American Jews are descendants of East European immigrants. Almost all the adults of my parents' generation were party to a national, almost Biblical, Exodus-like escape epic, true or otherwise, of having used all manner of subterfuge to flee the Russian empire to avoid being drafted into its army. It mattered little that facts conflicted with this escape epic. Statistically speaking, the Jews did not escape military service. They were drafted into the Russian Army, served in excess of their representation in the population, and were predominately posted to combat units.[7] It is further postulated that this exposure had a nominal and unintended benefit of propelling the Jews into modernity.[8] Nevertheless, the Jewish escape narrative resonated with the single-purposed "strategic message" that the military was bad for the Jews. And that message defined the tension between my ancestry and my decision to become a professional soldier. Accordingly, it is worth a few seemingly-extra pages to trace the history of Jewish military service in the Russian empire, and its practical outcomes, because it has many parallel themes with my decision to voluntarily enter the US military and use it as a means to propel and assimilate

---

[7] Yohanan Petrovsky-Shtern, *Jews in the Russian Army, 1827-1917* (New York: Cambridge University Press, 2009), 184-203.
[8] Petrovsky-Shtern, *Jews in the Russian Army*, 270.

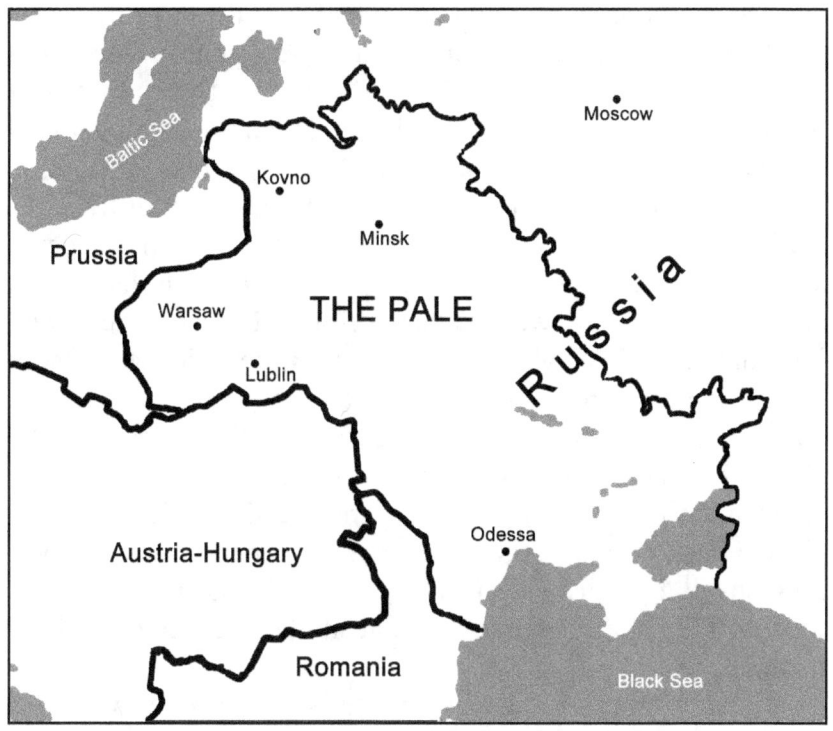

The Pale of Settlement. Adapted by Amy Moore.

myself into a different, and to my mind, preferred, culture and lifestyle.

Within Tsarist Russia was an area known as the Pale of Settlement, covering southwest Russia, Lithuania, and Eastern Poland. It was a sizeable geographic ghetto in which over 90 percent of the Jews in the Russian empire were required to live. Both sets of my grandparents came to America from the Pale, and it is there that my personal and collective ancestries originate.

The Russian government had initially imposed this geographic restriction as a punitive measure, but an unintended consequence was that the Jewish communities became more insular and less "Russian" than desired. To remedy this, from 1827 to 1857, Tsar Nicholas enacted a law imposing a disproportionate levy of Jewish males for periods of military service, initially set at twenty-five years and later reduced to fifteen.[9] Because of the low life expectancy of most Russian soldiers, even in peacetime, conscription into the military was essentially a life sentence. The ultimate aim of this draft was to force the assimilation of religious Jews into the Russian culture and, to an extent, the Russian Orthodox Church.

The law presented a paradox across the spectrum of Russian-Jewish society. Before 1827, Jews were denied the privilege of serving in the army. This restriction was most keenly felt by the secular Jews who viewed exclusion from military service as an impediment to integration into Russian society. Some of these highly assimilated Jews, serving as an advisory group to Nicholas, petitioned for the draft as a means to bring "enlightenment" to the Jews.[10] The more numerous religious Jews, living either in small self-contained communities[11] or separate sections of larger ones, did not seek military service, as it was incompatible with their religious obligations and dietary restrictions. But it was toward them that the draft laws were specifically targeted, and they bore its full brunt.

The draft quotas allowed youths to be recruited at twelve for service (although some were taken as young as eight), first in Cantons or military schools, and thence to the army (the years in the Cantons did not count toward the twenty-five-year term). These Jewish youths were targeted, to varying extents, for conversion, as they were deemed more impressionable and held more significant potential for assimilation than those selected at an older age. Conversion to Christianity may not have been a prime factor, but it did occur. Larry Domnitch's The Cantonists summarizes numerous accounts of the brutalization and regular beatings inflicted on these youths to "encourage" their "voluntary" conversion to Christianity. The conversion success rate is questionable. Self-serving bureaucratic reports addressing Jewish, Lutheran, and Roman Catholic converts indicate a maximum of about 33 percent of a given "Jewish" cohort baptized. Other such reports

---

[9] Petrovsky-Shtern, *Jews in the Russian Army*, 55.
[10] Petrovsky-Shtern, *Jews in the Russian Army*, 36-43.
[11] Evyatar Friesel, *Atlas of Modern Jewish History* (New York: Oxford University Press, 1990), 30-33.

indicate less—the aggregate figures for 1842 and 1843 show about 5 percent and 2 percent conversion rates, respectively.[12]

By the late nineteenth century, there were approximately 5.2 million Russian Jews. Almost 4.9 million lived within the Pale. Nearly half lived in small, mixed Russian-Jewish communities, or Shtetl, in Yiddish, comprising less than five thousand Jews each. On average, the Jews constituted about 50 percent of the total population in these communities.[13] The Jewish constituencies were relatively self-governing at the local level, and the method for meeting the draft quotas was left to the resident Jewish community councils (Kahal, singular in Yiddish), often led by a rabbi.

A failure to meet the prescribed draft quota led to a higher quota the next year or the forced enlistment of selected council members or their children. Placing responsibility for meeting the draft quotas on the local Kahal, and the draconian punishments for failure to do so fractured the cohesion and moral basis for leadership in the affected communities. The draft wreaked havoc on families and individuals and set Jew against Jew. It brought out the worst of human nature both in those who enforced it and in those who avoided it by guile or treachery, often at risk to others.[14] The choice of the Jewish leadership to trade morality for practicality in preserving the vitality and functionality of their communities while providing men for the draft spawned a large part of the cultural message that military service was terrible for the Jews.

The situation improved somewhat under the more enlightened reign of Tsar Alexander II. By 1874, the Jews were subject to a universal, equitable, and more significant draft. As modified over the next twenty-five years, it required a nominal six-year term of active-duty service and nine in the reserves. The age of draft vulnerability was set at eighteen to twenty-five, and selection from the pool of the registered eligible was by lottery. Failure to meet draft quotas was still met with severe repercussions.[15]

---

[12] Larry Domnitch, *The Cantonists* (Devora Publishing, New York, 2003), 44-129; Petrovsky-Shtern, *Jews in the Russian Army,* 94-99.
[13] Friesel, *Atlas of Modern Jewish History,* 33.
[14] Domnitch, *Cantonists,* 9-43.
[15] Petrovsky-Shtern, *Jews in the Russian Army,* 129-136.

The draft was not the only problem. Alexander II was assassinated in 1881. The successor government sought to retard reform and punish Jewish involvement in organizing labor and trade unions and spreading Socialist dogma. It enacted the May Laws of 1882, which shifted the focus from assimilating the Jews to encouraging their emigration. Further restrictions were placed on where Jews could live, the trades in which they could engage, and quotas set on their access to secular education.

The year 1882 also gave rise to a series of pogroms or spontaneous rampages against Jewish communities, resulting primarily in arson and thievery. These pogroms spread from the Ukraine to Poland and into the Baltic States. More serious pogroms occurred in 1903 and 1906, this time with suspected government encouragement and larger-scale acts of assault, murder, and rape, as well as attacks on property.

This period was further framed by economic and political turmoil. Demographics also played a role. Due to rising birth rates, the Jewish population increased and outpaced available/allowed housing and employment opportunities.

Emigration was the most viable solution to facing the threat of the pogroms, the draft, population pressures, and economic dislocation. During the period that favored emigration to relieve internal pressures within Russia and provide for cheap labor in America, about one-third of the East European Jewish population departed. Between 1881 and 1910, approximately 1.1 million Russian Jews migrated to the United States.[16] My grandparents were part of those. One family was not affected by the draft; the other was.

My maternal grandfather, Max Friedman, was born in Lithuania in 1865. He became draft-eligible upon reaching his eighteenth birthday in 1883 and remained so until his twenty-fifth in 1890. He married in 1882 and lived with his wife Mammie in the Kovno region. He was not selected for induction by the lottery and immigrated to America in 1890.

---

[16] Friesel, *Atlas*, 13-15, 133-134. Samuel Joseph, *Jewish Immigration to the United States From 1881-1910*, (New York: Columbia University Press, 1914), 98-99.

My paternal grandfather, Isidore, was drafted. He came from a simple, subsistence farming family that lived in a cluster of small farms near the village of Stoczek in Eastern Poland. The family had at least one cow, one horse, and a chicken or two, because they sold eggs and butter at the local market, and travelled by horse. Accordingly, since he knew horses, when he was drafted, he served in the Russian cavalry, or perhaps more likely as a dragoon—mounted infantry—and fought in Manchuria during the 1904-1905 Russo-Japanese War. His military service is supported by a six-year gap between the births of his first son in 1899 and the second in 1905. That gap is not explained by infant mortality but is suggestive of the then-standard six-year obligation for draftees.

In 1905, in the face of a humiliating defeat by the Japanese and a rising left-wing political awareness by the working class and intelligentsia, Russia was beset by turmoil, such as the previously mentioned pogroms. Further complicating this situation was the fact that my grandfather was not the first-born son and, by Biblical tradition, could not inherit the family farm. All this probably signaled to him it was a good time to leave Poland. Accordingly, in early 1907, he emigrated to New York City and saved enough money by 1910 to send for the rest of his family, including my three-year-old father. I was told by my much older cousins that my grandfather often expressed pride in having been a cavalryman and a soldier in wartime.

Thus, my early view of a military career as a passport to move up in society was bounded by two conflicting but true propositions—there was a Jewish narrative that military service was bad, contradicted by the historical record that Jews did serve in the army of the Russian empire, as exemplified by my grandfather, who was proud to have done so.

CHAPTER 4

CCNY: HARVARD-ADJACENT

"We have three cats. It's like having three children, but there is no tuition involved."
RONALD REAGAN, 40TH PRESIDENT

I entered college in the fall of 1959 at the age of seventeen. The headline for this chapter is that I received a tuition-free, world-class education, did not encounter the classical college experience, and was positively acculturated to a military career.

A college of choice it was not. It was a decision that had been made for me, much like the one for my childhood dental care. As I began to discover girls and obsess over my looks, I noticed that my lower front teeth overlapped. I asked our family dentist if I needed braces. The dentist, a self-made, up-from-poverty man, studied my lower jaw. Then, he answered a question different from the one I had posed. He replied, "Your family cannot *afford* braces."

Nor could my family afford college. In 1959, the national median income was $5,417.00 for an average family of 3.67 individuals.[17] Before taxes, my father earned $5,200.00 a year, and we were a family of five. Additionally, I was one of three brothers, and we all had to be able to attend college. My younger brother was only two years behind me, and our college costs would overlap; I could not take too big a bite from the family budget. At the time, my leaving home to work through college seemed a bridge too far for me and my parents.

---

[17] US Bureau of Census, *Current Population Reports, Consumer Income, Series, NO.35, P-60*, (Washington: Government Printing Office, 1961), 4.

My situation was repeated hundreds of times in many households all over New York. In an era pre-dating government-backed student loans, too many like me needed financial aid to attend college. I had won a New York State Regents scholarship, which would have covered some of my tuition at an in-state college, but my family could not afford room and board.

High school guidance counselors were overwhelmed with the problem of finding a college home for too many bright but not wealthy students, like me. The fairest and most straightforward thing for them to do was to batch-process us to the most practical and affordable default college options. For the girls, it was Hunter College, a women's New York State teachers' college in Manhattan. For the boys, it was the City College of New York, known in shorthand as CCNY, a tuition-free college on the upper west side of Manhattan, less than eight miles straight-line distance from Parkchester.

CCNY was a first-rate academic institution open to all with the requisite high school grade point average in a specified core curriculum. It was founded in 1847 to provide a college education to the sons of immigrants so that they might improve their life and contribute to society meaningfully.

The college had a long list of distinguished alums. Jonas Salk, who developed the first polio vaccine, was a graduate. George Goethals, the chief engineer for the Panama Canal, attended for three years before being admitted to West Point. From 1933 to 1953, the college produced eight Nobel Prize winners.

But it was also a college of necessity. People did not move to New York City, so they or their children might attend. Youngsters did not dream of going to CCNY in a way they might have yearned to attend an Ivy League, or a Division I football college. Alums did not have to pull strings to get their children admitted there because they usually had better plans for their offspring.

CCNY had no dormitories; it was a commuter college in the Harlem section of Manhattan. I would spend about one-and-a-half hours a day on the subway, getting from home to class and back. As such, it was a bit like high school on steroids. Additionally, the opportunities for social growth and enrichment were limited.

I would attend college with many kids I had known since kindergarten. I would sleep in the same bedroom I had for the past ten years, sharing it with a brother in high school and another still in grade school.

Sports played a strong role in defining colleges, but not CCNY. In 1950, the school had won both the NCAA and NIT basketball championships. However, that enormous achievement ended in disaster after it was revealed that several players were involved in a nationwide point-shaving scandal for an organized crime gambling syndicate. After that, the school was relegated to Division III, banned from playing at Madison Square Garden, and the college de-emphasized all sports, further separating the school from a mainstream college experience.

The college also had a residual left-wing political reputation from the 1920s and 1930s. The newspaper magnate William Randolph Hearst had dubbed it "The Little Red Schoolhouse." During the heyday of the 1950s Cold War, that reputation did little to improve the credentials of its graduates in the more politically conservative and less tolerant atmosphere that prevailed outside of New York City. A more flattering sobriquet, in acknowledgment of the school's high academic standards and devotion to learning, was "The Harvard of the Proletariat," but even this compliment was problematic. The proletariat is a Greek word meaning the lowest, poorest class of society, whose only wealth is its children. However, Karl Marx had co-opted that term to describe the working class of society exploited by the capitalists and for whom communism was the only salvation. Thus, even this tribute to the school's academic excellence unintentionally alluded to communism. Nonetheless, it did make my education Harvard-adjacent.

Jewishness was a dominant dimension of the college's culture and sociology. As a tuition-free institution, the college had always represented the population of New York City. In its first fifty years, the college reflected the Anglo-Saxon, Dutch, and Huguenot cultures and society of New York. Its first two presidents were West Point graduates who understandably transposed their college experience and values onto the campus culture.

Evolving patterns of immigration reshaped the content of the college's student body as the Irish and then German Jews arrived in New York. These waves were followed by large numbers of impoverished and, compared with their German cousins, unsophisticated East European Jewry. By 1918, the CCNY student body, although small in size, had become almost 80 percent East-European Jewish, and that percentage prevailed over the next two decades.[18]

This figure represented a significant over-concentration of Jewish students. The Jewish population across all of New York City peaked at about 27 percent, signifying that Jews were present in the student body at almost three times their representation in the population at large. Some of this over-representation was explained by the tendency for Jewish families to send their children to college at twice the national rate: two out of every three eligible versus one out of three.[19]

A quota system also played a role. In the 1920s and 1930s, some elite East Coast private colleges established a gentlemen's agreement limiting the admittance of Jewish students. The quota arose from a belief that their campuses were becoming overgrown by a Jewish presence whose culture they believed detracted from the atmosphere the colleges should foster. The tipping point that led to the imposition of this quota was when certain colleges experienced a Jewish student load of 30 percent. This quota system drove many Jewish applicants to the doorstep of CCNY.[20]

When I entered in September 1959, the Jewish student numbers had declined from its previous high, probably resulting from factors, neither of which affected me. First, in the late 1950s, the quota system was relaxed or abandoned, allowing more Jews to attend formerly restricted colleges. Also, as Jewish families

---

[18] Study by Alfred Jospe, *Jewish Students and Student Services at American Universities* (Washington, D.C.: B'nai B'rith Hillel Foundations, 1963), Table 1, Number and Percentage of Jewish Students in 106 Institutions, 7.
[19] Jospe, *Jewish Students and Student Services at American Universities*, 13.
[20] Steven Steinberg, "How Jewish Quotas Began," *Commentary*, September 1971, https://www.commentary.org/articles/stephen-steinberg/how-jewish-quotas-began/.

accumulated sufficient wealth, they migrated to the suburbs, reducing the size of the potential applicant pool.

Nonetheless, the Jewish student population was at least twice that which spawned the Jewish quota system at the private colleges. By this standard, CCNY should have imposed such a quota on itself. That notion is not as cynical as it sounds. Some notable Jewish faculty members despaired the college had become overly Jewish and drifted too far from a more diverse student body that would have yielded a mutual benefit for all the students. In 1938, Morris Raphael Cohen, a renowned professor of philosophy at the school and a CCNY alumnus of the Jewish faith, mused that it was not good that the school had become predominately Jewish because it caused a lack of critical, inter-religion social connections that were essential in developing employment opportunities for the graduates.[21]

All that aside, I received an excellent education. I was one of about fifteen hundred entering freshmen. Accordingly, my classes were large, and personal contact with my professors was minimal. On the more positive side, my Bachelor of Science curriculum closely approximated a classical education. In addition to math and science, I took required courses in French, history, English, economics, political science, geology, logic, art, music, and physical education. Even my gym courses were demanding. I had to swim one mile in a crowded indoor pool by going around the borders without touching any edge and avoiding collisions with my classmates. The one-mile swim was not a trivial aerobic event but a high athletic bar. I swallowed my chlorine-flavored puke, gasping for breath, before I dragged my body out of the pool with a passing grade. That was followed by a semester of wrestling, which made the swim class seem easy.

The campus covered 35 acres, close to one-fourth the size of Parkchester. It was divided into a north campus devoted primarily to science and engineering classes and a south campus dedicated to liberal arts courses. Five main buildings formed the heart of the north campus at Saint Nicholas Terrace. They were massive

---

[21] S. Willis Rudy, *The College of the City of New York*, (New York: Arno Press, 1977), 399.

CHAPTER 4—CCNY: HARVARD-ADJACENT

Shepard Hall, the flagship structure on the North Campus. Photo from City University of New York archives.

gray-blue stone neo-Gothic structures that, ironically, could be iconic of the East Coast colleges that had adopted the quota system restricting Jewish students. Shepard Hall, the campus flagship, was built on the lines of a massive English cathedral. Locally excavated schist metamorphic rock, the bedrock foundation of Manhattan Island, was used in constructing the buildings.

Shepard became the center of gravity in my student life. I registered for class each semester in Shepard and took most of my physics, biology, biochemistry, and geology courses there. I studied in its Great Hall and ate lunch daily in the basement cafeteria. In the 1930s, this cafeteria served as the center of political activity for the student body as they debated the virtues of Trotskyite versus Stalinist

North Campus Quadrangle. Photo from City University of New York archives.

*Another view of North Campus Quadrangle.
Photo from City University of New York archives.*

communism. In the more sedate atmosphere of my time, the tables were territorialized for use by various student organizations and clubs, almost all apolitical.

Although CCNY did not have a traditional campus, it did have a Reserve Officers Training Corps (ROTC) program whereby students could earn a commission as a Reserve Officer in the US Army. ROTC was what made CCNY a viable part of my life strategy. I was determined to test the ROTC program's effectiveness in serving as a vehicle to both develop myself as a warrior and to propel myself into WASP culture. The ROTC program was one of the few things that convinced me I was actually in college. It compensated for the absence of football, dorms, and an expansive campus. My initial plan was to pursue a pre-med course of study and decide later, based on my experience with ROTC and academics, whether to apply to medical school upon graduation or serve in the Army for two years and then go to medical school.

CCNY ROTC patch.

The size of the cadet corps was a function of the prevailing social, cultural, political, and economic influences. At the height of the Korean War (1950-1953), the corps reached its maximum size of fifteen hundred cadets.[22] This probably resulted from the belief that during a war in which the draft was operative and everyone was vulnerable, it was better to serve as an officer than an enlisted man. Additionally, the Rosenberg trial gripped New York City in the same period. Julius and Ethel Rosenberg were American Jews convicted of passing atomic secrets to Russia, enabling them to develop their nuclear bomb. The Rosenbergs were executed in 1953 in response to the grievous damage to America's security they had caused. The American Jewish community anticipated an anti-Semitic backlash, as Americans might conflate Jews with communists. To add a bit of insult to injury, Julius Rosenberg was a 1939 graduate of CCNY. The Rosenberg case may have motivated more students to enroll in ROTC to demonstrate patriotism. When I registered, the Corps of Cadets' strength was around six hundred. The smaller size of the Corps from just a few years earlier may have resulted from a smaller student population than

---

[22] Greg Jaffee, "A Retreat From Big Cities Hurts ROTC Recruiting," *The Wall Street Journal*, February 22, 2007, p.1, col. 2.

in the mid-1950s. Also, perhaps as the Rosenberg trial faded from memory, there was less need to appear patriotic by joining ROTC.

The ROTC program was voluntary and divided into two parts. The first two years provided basic military education and experience, and those enrolled were free to leave without prejudice during this period. The last two years were on a contract basis and led to a commission as a Reserve Officer. About fifty-five to sixty-five cadets were commissioned each year, and of these, about ten to fifteen were competitively selected for the Regular Army, just like West Point graduates.[23] The ROTC curriculum was divided into two tracks: Infantry and Engineer. The basic classes were the same for all, but the advanced courses in our junior and senior years, as were the ROTC Summer Camps, were specialized. Engineering and physics majors were tracked into the Engineer branch, and all others, including me, into the Infantry.

The ROTC program was not easy and added inordinately to my academic labors. As freshmen and sophomores, we had class once a week and drill and ceremonies twice weekly. The total weekly investment was five to six hours, in class and out, which was disproportionately large for the one credit hour earned. By comparison, my mandatory science, math, and language courses met three hours a week for three credits each. I found the drill field to be as stressful as freshman calculus. The uniform inspection was exacting. Our brass insignia had to be precisely positioned and polished, our shoes spit-shined. This preparation, this attention to "chicken shit" detail, added extra hours to already long days.

Our freshman "bible" was Field Manual (FM) 22-5, Drill and Ceremonies, which instructed us how to march, assemble in formation, execute complicated file and column maneuvers, and perform the manual of arms with the M-1 rifle. All this was accomplished while being yelled at by the upperclassmen. Initially, I found it unnerving. It made me sweat in the already heavy woolen uniform as we drilled in the late autumn heat. Our drill instruction

---

[23] I have to estimate the size of the Corps, and the number commissioned because the ROTC records seem to have been lost after numerous warehousing shifts after the college terminated the ROTC program in 1972.

culminated twice a year with a full-scale parade called a Review, where the entire corps was presented to and inspected by the college president, followed by an award ceremony for the highest-achieving cadets. The standard of performance was perfection. We had to be exactly aligned, both side to side and front to rear. Our rifles had to be uniformly sloped, and we had to be in step with the music. We were taught how to help each other maintain this perfection by having the cadet to our rear pass on corrections such as, "Change Step, you're out of beat," or "(Rifle) Butt Left or Right" to get our M-1s in proper alignment. There was no time for daydreaming in these parades. It was exacting work and demanded our total mental concentration.

ROTC squad drill.

ROTC platoon drill.

ROTC Review parade.
Photos courtesy of Dr. Ted Drzewiecki, CCNY '65, Society of American Military Engineers (SAME) fraternity archivist.

At first glance, drill and parades seem trivial, dull pursuits for college men. In actuality, they served an important military and social function. Drill and ceremonies were designed to inculcate in us a habit of both giving and following orders, foster teamwork, and enable the learning and application of tactics based on individuals functioning and moving as units of action. The ultimate aim of drill was to teach the individual to subordinate himself to and function as a member of a larger unit. The ability to become comfortable with the subordination process was a key predictor of the potential for adaptation to the military culture. There is a fine line between the rational and psychotic when conducting drill training, and I think, for the most part, we stayed on the right side of that line.

Classroom subjects included military history, leadership, small unit tactics, map reading, weapons, and marksmanship on an indoor .22 caliber rifle range. I liked the challenge of mastering new skills. I integrated learning new skills as an extension of my Boy Scout experience in earning various skill merit badges. Maybe the Boy Scouts had sufficiently conditioned me to the more demanding military environment. At any rate, military training was a challenge instead of a burden. I did well enough to be promoted to platoon sergeant in my sophomore year.

The Corps presented an interesting sociological amalgam. Politically, the cadets were, for the most part, agnostic or conservative. On average, it was generally representative of the student body in terms of demographics but probably a bit less Jewish than the college as a whole. The Corps was as ethnically diverse as the college population. In addition to the Jewish cadets, there were Greek, Italian, Hispanic, Ukrainian, Baltic, and African American cohorts.

The Corps was also socially ordered. Unit cohesion is the *sine qua non* for military effectiveness. Armies cultivate cohesion in their basic drill, training, and tactical formations, the squads, platoons, and companies. For ROTC purposes, these units existed for two hours a week for drill and three to four hours in the classroom, and their composition changed from one semester to the next based on the cadets' class schedules. They were too transient to serve as venues to produce socially ordered, cohesive units. Instead, ROTC military fraternities, which brought their members together for several hours a day, served this function.

I am going to provide a seemingly distractive elaboration on this ROTC fraternity system for two reasons. First, the ethos they inspired helped produce the right culture for an easy transition to military life and its sometimes-extraordinary demands. Second, because ROTC was banned at CCNY from 1972 to 2013, all known recorded college historical documents on this subject were lost due to records being shifted from place to place and eventually lost altogether. Thus, this memoir serves as a "Cliffs Notes" summary of that history.

CCNY had six platoon-size military fraternities of between thirty to seventy members. Each had a unique ethos and a distinct shoulder cord, and this later accouterment was part of the appeal, as it conferred a degree of dash and élan to the uniform. I would estimate that about three hundred of the six hundred or so cadets belonged to these fraternities.

Two of the fraternities were local. The Webb Patrol, established in 1942, was named in honor of General Alexander Webb, a Civil War hero and the college's second president. They wore a maroon and gold fourragere and were militarily and socially oriented, hosting field training and leadership exercises at nearby military installations and a semi-annual induction dinner at a base officers' club. They had a table in the Shepard Hall cafeteria and impressed me as enjoying each other's company.

The other local fraternity was named The Carolan Guard, in the Bernard Baruch School of Business. It was named in honor of Lieutenant James Carolan, a former cadet colonel at the Baruch School who was killed in action during the Korean conflict. They wore a green and white fourragere and had their own campus downtown. Therefore, we had little interaction with them, and I formed no strong opinion of them or their fraternity, other than they were "other" by physical separation.

The remaining four fraternities were national: The National Honor Society of the Pershing Rifles, the Society of American Military Engineers, the Association of the United States Army, and Scabbard and Blade.

The Pershing Rifles (PR) was formed by then Lieutenant and later General John J. Pershing at the University of Nebraska in 1894. The CCNY contingent was formed in 1937. They emphasized drill and ceremonies and wore a blue and white fourragere.

Their military appearance was exemplary, and they held many ROTC leadership positions, ranging from squad leader to cadet colonel.

The Society of American Military Engineers (SAME) was chartered in 1951. Its members were predominately from the ROTC Engineer track. Their focus was both military and scholarly. They were very cohesive, maintained a table in Shepard Hall, wore a black, red, and white fourragere, and produced more than their share of senior cadet leaders.

The Association of the United States Army (AUSA) was formed in 1950, and its members wore a gold and black fourragere. They, like SAME, were the college minor leagues of the adult professional organizations whose name they bore. AUSA members engaged in a wide range of military, professional, and social activities.

Scabbard and Blade was a national honor society for ROTC, open only to upperclassmen. It was founded at the University of Wisconsin in 1904 and chartered at CCNY in 1953. Some of its more famous members included General John J. Pershing and Presidents Herbert Hoover and Franklin Roosevelt. Its members wore a blue and red shoulder cord. Scabbard and Blade produced its share of cadet senior leaders. Some members held dual membership in SAME, AUSA, and Webb Patrol. However, because it was a two-year fraternity, I do not think Scabbard and Blade fostered the enduring comradeship associated with the four-year fraternities.

Although many fraternity members became leaders, a nuanced cause-and-effect mechanism was in play. The fraternities did not produce leaders as much as attract them. The most military-oriented cadets self-selected into the fraternity system. Cadets who wanted to be tested and verified as the best flocked to these organizations. All the fraternities had rigorous pledge programs. Some were more demanding than others based on both the actual protocols and the personalities of the upperclassmen who implemented them. All were roughly modeled after the West Point plebe system for the initiation of first-year cadets. The CCNY fraternities required the pledges to meet a certain number of members each day to be grilled on fraternity lore and customs and general military knowledge, as well as perform specified rites and rituals, many of which were "secret." Regardless, all the pledge programs were rites of passage and conferred a sense of confidence and exclusiveness upon their members.

The PR pledge program was the most rigorous and demanded the largest portion of a pledge's time budget. Only the most dedicated cadets were prepared to place foremost importance in membership in the PRs. Accordingly, the PRs probably represented the far end of the spectrum of exclusivity, separateness, and self-absorption. At first, I resented that exclusiveness. As a sophomore, I was one of the few platoon sergeants not in a fraternity. I felt all the platoon sergeants should be buddies, bound by their shared responsibilities. That was not the case; comradeship was based on fraternity membership. But, after I was accepted into a military fraternity a year later, I gained an appreciation for the exclusivity dynamic; my chosen friends were my fraternity brothers.

Moreover, my appreciation sharpened once I was in the Army and subjected to more severe rites of passage. After completing Airborne School and serving in combat, I held in low regard those who had not, but could have, shared my exposure to hardship and danger. I avoided friendships with those officers who had not chosen to qualify as paratroopers. The non-Airborne qualified officers were called, dismissively, "Legs." In Vietnam, we referred to those who shared the same uniform but not the same danger as "REMFs"— Rear Echelon Mother Fuckers. It is unfair to judge or characterize men like this because it requires us to make sweeping generalizations about people we do not know. The emotion associated with these terms is universal, and all armies have social processes that separate those who bear hardship from those who do not.

While I do not think the fraternities had a term to differentiate themselves from those who did not pledge, they did seem to act out the associated emotion. Their shared experience produced a sense of exclusivity and engendered long-term bonds of comradeship that lasted long after the cadets had left college.

I need to close the discussion on the ROTC fraternities by fast-forwarding to the future. Six ROTC graduates were killed in Vietnam.[24] Five were members of our college's military fraternities. Three were PRs: Major Allen Pasco, '59, Major Antonio Mavroudis, '60, and Captain John Young, '60. One was from SAME: Captain Kenneth Rosenberg, '65. Second Lieutenant William Lyons III, '68, belonged to AUSA. The sixth, First Lieutenant Peter Bushey, '65, did not belong to a fraternity. The fact that five out of six did says more than I can ever write of the military motivation of the cadets who joined and the ethos these fraternities fostered.

Cadets in the ROTC program reached a major decision point at the end of their sophomore year. They could terminate or go on to the Advanced Course, which entailed contracting to train as a Reserve Officer for a commission. Classroom hours increased to two a week, and the credit hours awarded increased to two. Cadets received a monthly stipend of $27.90, or approximately $300.00 in 2025 dollars, which helped defray college-related expenses. I, and about one-third of my ROTC entering class, elected to continue on to the Advanced Course as contract cadets.

In my junior year, I pledged the Scabbard and Blade Honor Society. The pledge process was difficult enough, but compared with the PRs, it was probably little more than a cakewalk. There was a twenty-mile, all-day hike which left me stiff and sore and a hell-night ordeal deep in the woods of upstate New York. I was dispatched on a "Snipe Hunt," blindfolded, questioned on fraternity history, and made to perform push-ups. The affair was well orchestrated and designed to produce stress within reasonable limits. The members under whom I pledged were top-notch people. They were balanced and mature and mentored as much as they terrified us. Scabbard and Blade also offered the opportunity to meet and interact with the ROTC cadre on a social basis. They were excellent role models.

As a member, I was assigned to the Saber Drill Team. We had to learn highly choreographed routines, using the classical cavalry saber instead of a rifle, and the drills had to be memorized, as the commands were "silent," based solely on timing. My favorite

---

[24] In addition to these six cadets, one of our ROTC instructors, Sergeant First Class Bernard Kelley, was also killed in the Vietnam War.

event was the annual "Dining In," a formal, men-only dinner at Mamma Leone's Restaurant in Manhattan's Theatre District. There, I learned how to eat a multi-course meal, employing a vast array of silverware at the right time, how to make dinner conversation, and how and when to toast. It was a pivotal adjunct to my military education that, along with becoming handy with a saber, gave me the impression that I was a member of an elite gentlemen's club.

Cadet major, 1962-1963.

The defining event in ROTC was Summer Camp, a six-week program between our junior and senior years. It was conducted at active Army bases and was essentially infantry basic training. The cadets were, however, evaluated for leadership skills and military potential. Based on my overall academics and performance in ROTC, I was designated as a "Tentative Distinguished Military Student" (TDMS). As such, I would be eligible for a Regular Army commission. Regular Army officers were considered elite. They were tenured. Reserve Army officers served on active duty for six months to two and a half years. They were labeled, derisively, Christmas Help. If they served beyond their initial obligation, they were subject to dismissal based on staffing and budgetary constraints. The TDMS selection rate was 10 percent and was controlled by the Army based on their Regular Officer accession needs in a given period. As a TDMS, I was subjected to increased scrutiny and evaluation at Summer Camp. If I did well, I would be designated a Distinguished Military Student (DMS) and offered a Regular Army commission upon graduation. If not, I would be Christmas Help.

I reported to Summer Camp at Fort Devens, Massachusetts, with a broken heart. My college soulmate for life had just broken up with me. A few weeks earlier, we could be found dallying behind Klapper Hall, having cut classes to be together. Sometimes a female professor would spy us and through an open window shoo us away while ringing a hand-held bell—the academic equivalent of shouting, "Get a room!" Once, she even summoned the campus police to figuratively throw water on us to cool us down. Now that spark was extinguished. I was driving myself mad with the thought of her engaging in a new summer love tryst, while I languished in a grown-up version of Boy Scout camp with guns.

My new home, my platoon, comprised forty-four cadets from all the major colleges along the East Coast. It was organized according to standard Army doctrine and was almost as large as a CCNY cadet company. There were four platoons in the company, making it one-third of the entire CCNY Corps. The increase in scale and the fact that we would be soldiers twenty-four hours a day, seven days a week, for six weeks impressed upon me that things would be more demanding than the drill field at CCNY.

We lived in old two-level World War II wooden barracks, two squads of eleven men each to a floor. There was a common latrine on the lower level, with hot water generated by a coal-fired heater. Cleaning the latrine and keeping the coal stack neat and looking like a pyramid were major chores. Our M-1s were secured in rifle racks in our living space. I was the only cadet from CCNY and the only Jewish platoon member. This did not matter much, as we were always too busy with assigned duties to waste time on each other's pedigree. Other platoons had time off in the evenings, but not ours.

Our days were long and physically exhausting. We marched or double-timed everywhere, usually under the load of a pack and M-1 rifle, in the humid heat of midsummer. We learned squad and platoon infantry tactics, how to operate and fire the basic infantry weapons—the M-1 Rifle, the Browning Automatic Rifle (BAR), the 106mm recoilless rifle, and the 3.5-inch "Bazooka." We learned how to read a topographic map and to use the lensatic compass, in both daylight and darkness. We did PT every morning, well before breakfast, and cleaned our rifles and equipment deep into the night. Reveille came every morning at 0500. We stood countless inspections and parades. Our barracks and equipment were kept immaculate.

Paradoxically, the most stressful moments were the parades and inspections; the patrols, platoon, and company tactics were easy. Cadet leadership positions were assigned for major training events and our performance and potential were evaluated. I was designated as the company commander for the first of our Saturday morning parades. I couldn't sleep the night before, fretting over whether or not I could remember all the commands and protocols that guided the parade, but thankful that the tough drill standards at CCNY had taken away my parade ground virginity.

However, my near-Waterloo experience came before the parade ever started. While marching my company to the parade field in a column of platoons, I cut through the formation of another company from our battalion, arriving from a different direction, maneuvering toward its pre-parade assembly area. To this day, I have no idea how that happened, but it was a mess. It looked like two blind centipedes had collided at right angles to each other. It was a goat-fuck, and I was in charge. I took an on-the-spot asschewing from our cadre officers as they untangled us. I was sure my military career had come to an early end. I got through both the parade and the march back to our company area in a haze, contemplating with dread the more detailed forensic analysis of my performance that was sure to follow. But the ass-chewing was the end of it. I was given dispensation after it was determined that the other company commander was the "bad driver" and had contributed more to the collision than I.

That experience, and others like it, taught me that I could cope with a strict military regimen. It was reaffirming that Jews could produce good soldiers, or at least good cadets. I felt I had grown stronger and liked the new me. Our platoon tactical officer, Captain Moran, gave us an overall ranking based on periodic quantitative and qualitative assessments at the end of the training period. He ran the toughest platoon in the Summer Camp battalion. His fellow officers called him "Captain Nails." I was afraid of him. He never said much to me, either by way of praise or rebuke. Despite this distance between us, he gave me a good rating. He told me I was going to be designated a DMS and that I would get a Regular Army Commission. Having dispensed with the good news, he enumerated the few dozen ways I could have and should have done better. I would interact with him again four years later in Vietnam. He would be instrumental in placing me at Hill 150.

My life strategy evolved further when I returned for my senior year. I now planned to forgo medical school and see if I had what it took to be a Regular Army career officer. I am sure my friends thought I had taken leave of my senses. Medical school was the preferred and most difficult course of action for them. But not me. Now, more than ever, I viewed the Army as a demanding and honorable test of manhood. For example, I would have to take paratrooper training, and, in my mind, this was ever more challenging and defining than any medical school course, no matter how difficult. My family was somewhat surprised by my career choice but supportive. I think they saw this coming a bit before I did; I had never written home complaining about the rigors of Summer Camp.

Upon returning to the campus, I was promoted to cadet major. There was one colonel who commanded the Corps and two lieutenant colonels who commanded the battalions. These were the plum positions. However, my third-tier majority, of which there were several, was not without distinction.

In my last semester, within weeks of graduation, I made a poor decision that almost derailed my plans for my future. One of the ROTC instructors had arranged for me and four other Regular Army designees to spend Friday through Sunday at West Point. I had done this the previous semester, mirroring the life of a cadet and gaining early socialization with other Regular Army officers-to-be. We slept in the barracks, ate in the mess hall, and attended class and mandatory athletics with an appointed cadet sponsor. It was a wonderful experience, except this time, I had a scheduling conflict that I resolved most unwisely. I had just started karate lessons and threw myself into this new endeavor with unjustified enthusiasm. I did not want to miss a class scheduled for Saturday morning. Early that week, I informed my instructor that my father was in the hospital and that I had to remain at home to assist my mother. It was a lie, but not wholly baseless; my father had been in the hospital the month before. I was excused from going to West Point and took the karate class.

The following week, the instructor inquired how my father was progressing. I saw my original lie would cascade to another and yet another, *ad infinitum*. I confessed to my falsehood. He called for a board of officers to hear my case. He was one of the least popular of our instructors. But he was a West Pointer, and my lie violated the West Point honor code and Army tradition. Officers were expected to always tell the truth in militarily relevant matters. The standard for truth-telling was not as extreme as Kant's Categorical Imperative; it was probably allowable to tell small lies, such as when a future wife might inquire, "Does this dress make me look fat?" But my lie was relevant to my military obligations; it was a serious matter when viewed through the lens of principle.

I knew I was in trouble and that an unwise and unnecessary falsehood could wreck my career goal. However, as if in a preview to my response to the stress of combat, I went into a psychological state of detached neutrality, watching my ongoing ordeal as an observer rather than a participant.

Major John Gilbert, the most popular and respected ROTC instructor, and our Scabbard and Blade advisor, volunteered to serve as my counsel. He worked his magic with the board. I was demoted to cadet second lieutenant. It could have been much worse; they could have blocked my Regular Army commission and ended my chances of entering the Army and the world of the WASPS as a career officer. Furthermore, this experience could have soured me on the military, but Major Gilbert's coming to my defense produced a desire to become as good and well-respected an officer as he.

In June 1963, I graduated from CCNY with a BS in biology and a respectable B average that could have gotten me into a reputable medical school. Instead, I chose the Army. As a Regular Army officer candidate, I was free to select from any of the combat arms. I chose artillery because it impressed me as a bit more gentlemanly and technical than the infantry. Accordingly, I was commissioned a second lieutenant of artillery, poised to enter a new world.

CHAPTER 5

FITTING IN

"Experientia docet"
(Experience teaches)
TACITUS

*"Education is what survives when
what has been learned has been forgotten."*
B.F. SKINNER

Several of my college friends celebrated graduation by treating themselves to a trip to Europe. It was the thing to do. France, in general, and Paris, in particular, held a special allure for my generation. We pictured ourselves in black sweaters, sitting in student cafes along the Seine, reading Sartre, Camus, and Kierkegaard, smoking a pipe, and sipping espresso. It was Bohemian and avant-garde Greenwich Village writ large. I, too, went to Europe, but my route was indirect and highly militarized.

My first stop was Fort Bliss, located in El Paso, Texas. There, I attended the Air Defense Officers' Basic Course. In nine weeks, I would become technically and tactically qualified to serve as a platoon leader in an air defense battery. El Paso is in the westernmost corner of Texas, along the Rio Grande River, bordering its sister city, Juarez, Mexico. In 1963, the population of El Paso was about 275,000, compared with almost eight million for New York City. I arrived on a four-engine, propeller-driven Super Constellation airliner. "Jetways" were not yet invented; we deplaned via a mobile stairway and walked across the taxiway to one of the two airport gates. The sheriff was there to look over the arriving passengers;

his deputies did the same at the train and bus depots. I had traveled thirty years back in time.

There were other surprises. The Irish Catholics ran supreme in the Bronx but not at Fort Bliss. The reigning class of my youth was no more. It was like the extinction of the dinosaurs. The Baptists and the Episcopalians had replaced them as the rulers of the universe. I was finally in the world of the WASPs. In Parkchester, religion was a defining characteristic; it served as a sociological shorthand for all one needed to know about another. At Fort Bliss, we were defined as Army officers; religion was a second or third-order characteristic. I calibrated myself precisely to my new environment. My military records listed my religion as Jewish, and my dog tags were so stamped. Other than that, I did little else to differentiate myself. I tried to dress, talk, and behave like those around me.

We had class eight hours a day and study hall some nights, especially before exams. The courses covered the Nike Hercules and HAWK air defense systems: their radars, interceptors, and computerized fire control equipment. We also learned how the Army was organized, administered, and utilized for combat. But my real education occurred after class and on free weekends. I was in school with members of the West Point class of 1963 who had also selected the Air Defense track of the Artillery branch. I lived with them in the Bachelor Officers' Quarters (BOQ)[25], ate with them in the officers' field ration mess, drank beer, played pinball, sunned and swam at the officers' club pool. In a manner, I was experiencing a delayed "college experience." But, by virtue of their regimented West Point lifestyle and sudden exposure to a higher degree of personal freedom at Fort Bliss, they had a studied casualness with the military that approximates the affected disinterest in money that those born to wealth confidently exhibit. It was important not to be thought of as trying too hard in class or on exams. For example, if one were too attentive in class, raised his hand too often to indicate a question, and rose to pose it, he was labeled "A Spring Butt," and that was not a flattering sobriquet. It

---

[25] Large two-story building comprised of about 30 two-man rooms with a shared bathroom. It included daily maid service and a small laundry service annex for our uniforms.

was the opposite of the CCNY culture, and I had to dial down my impulse to excel.

There was a small group of fellow students in the BOQ with whom I engaged in casual bull sessions and hallway "man-speak." One evening, when I returned from karate class at the post gym, one of them, Ken, engaged me in a more focused and protracted conversation. Eventually, he asked if I was Jewish. After we got over the "isn't that a coincidence, so am I" dance, we entered a new level of comradeship: he was to be my mentor, and I his wingman and protégé. I accepted this social dynamic without reservation: Ken was a West Pointer, tall, muscular, fastidious in dress, "cool," and respected, if not always liked, by our classmates. He seemed to have mastered the art of assimilating into the Gentile world.

Ken and other West Point Jewish officers I encountered followed a discernible pattern of behavior. Their method was not to appear different, ungentlemanly, or unmilitary. The model was to blend in, do as others do, carry your weight while supporting the team, and be "surprisingly" Jewish. In one regard, this method was an extension of the mores of Reform Judaism beyond the synagogue walls into the heart of the military. Assimilationist German Jewish immigrants to America inaugurated the Reform movement in the nineteenth century. They sought to make their Jewish liturgy, and thus themselves, more like their Gentile neighbors. They introduced the use of choirs, organ music, prayer in English, robes, and mixed seating of men and women. I followed Ken in applying this method of self-transformational accommodation into the ranks of the military.

In late October, we graduated from class at Fort Bliss, and Ken drove us to our next stop, Fort Benning, Georgia, to attend Airborne School and qualify as paratroopers. The requirement for Regular Army officers to complete paratroop training was established in 1954, based on the Army's experience in the Korean War and the fact that the upper leadership of the Army was composed of the best of the officers who had served in the Airborne Divisions during World War II. It was reasoned that airborne training would increase the aggressiveness and self-confidence of the officer corps. But there was a subtlety in this assertion. Whoever decided to become a Regular Army officer had pre-volunteered for this course; he was already aggressive and a self-selected risk-taker. Thus, the training operated to refine these pre-existing tendencies and shape them to a military end.

The Army had honed paratrooper training to give the soldier a new understanding of the outer limits of his physical endurance and ability to face danger. The course was three weeks duration. The first week, The Ground Phase was devoted to physical fitness and basic mind-muscle memory drills to inculcate reflexive responses to the nine "jump commands," correct body position to exit the aircraft, controlling the parachute while in the air, and landing.

The second week was the Tower Phase, centered primarily on the thirty-four-foot tower, from which we made practice jumps, suspended on a four-hundred-foot trolley line. The tower was fearsome; you dropped twelve feet in free fall until your parachute harness lines took up the slack. Then you experienced the

34-foot tower. Photo courtesy SFC Robert Contratto, US Army Airborne School Historian.

equivalent of a real "opening shock," mainly where the parachute harness snaked around your groin.

Urban legend claimed that thirty-four feet represented the "knee" of the height-fear graph, which Army psychologists and biomedical engineers diabolically determined. On the other hand, skeptics pointed out that thirty-four feet was merely the useable length of standard forty-foot telephone poles, buried six feet in the ground used in its construction. Regardless, the tower was one of the most challenging aspects of jump school.

The Army had conducted an experiment utilizing thirteen hundred new, untrained candidates' performance on the tower versus their future performance in the full airborne course. It found that those who were "slow" or hesitant to jump from the tower were twice as likely to fail the course as those who went quickly, and those who refused to jump were almost guaranteed to fail. The tower predicted future performance in jump school and, by extension, future performance in the high-stress combat environment.[26] Essentially, the tower predicted a soldier's ability to manage fear. Once a soldier knew he could do so, he was better prepared to do so again, even under more stressful circumstances.

Then there was the 250-foot tower. Students were lifted to its top by a cable and then released with a deployed canopy. The purpose was to practice actual parachute landing falls. Although it was seven times taller than the thirty-four-foot tower, I found it less fearsome. After a certain height, more height does not add appreciably to one's fear. This observation reinforced my belief in the hypothesis that the height of the tower was scientifically determined.

250-foot tower. Official US Army photo.

The first two weeks contained a common core. The training day commenced with a strict uniform and personal inspection; it made my freshman and Summer Camp ROTC inspections seem like a day at the

---

[26] Sebastian Junger, *War* (New York: Hachette Book Group, 2010), 122.

beach. The inspection was designed to be failed. Our hair had to be kept short, very short. Some of us eventually shaved our heads after being failed for "hair not in accordance with standards." Shaved was definitely short; it allowed no room for an errant judgment call on the part of the inspector. Our boots, which had been scuffed raw from a hard day's training, much of it on graveled surfaces, had to be spit-shined. We could either do it ourselves or have it accomplished for a fee by a concessionaire. Most of us bought ourselves an extra hour of downtime by paying to have our boots shined. Our brass belt buckles had to be polished free of scratches. We focused on the obvious, the outside. The instructors, the "Black Hats" (they wore black baseball caps), inspected the inside. Infractions were met with orders for push-ups.

We then double-timed off to Eubanks Field for physical training, aka PT. There, we descended into an olive-drab version of *Dante's Inferno*. PT was like a fraternity pledge process run amok. Our instructors produced an abundance of yelling, sarcasm, hazing, and assignment of demerits, concomitant with delivering excellent instruction on how to be a paratrooper. We were tracked by our roster numbers, which were taped to our helmets and recorded on grade sheets attached to the ever-present instructor's clipboard. We had given up our names and rank. We were now just three-digit numbers to be trained. I had become roster number 464.

PT was centered on the push-up— those which were part of the exercise protocol and those added for not doing the former correctly. Push-ups were followed by a two to five-mile run in formation. There were more push-ups for not keeping in step. Then, there were more push-ups for not being attentive to the technical training. And finally, there were push-ups for collapsing while performing push-ups. I wondered how many push-ups were in me. Just like one could estimate how many heartbeats one had in him until the lifetime limit expired, I wondered how many push-ups I had left until I gave out.

We trained until sunset, followed by "mail call" outside the company orderly room. A slightly perfumed letter from a girlfriend was the bright spot of the day. Next came a short night devoted to a shower, dinner, a trip to the laundry concession to exchange sweated-out fatigues for freshly starched ones, a trip to the boot concession to trade today's scruffy boots for a freshly spit-shined pair, and back to our rooms to re-polish our belt buckles. Sometimes, there was time left for a beer or two, but we mostly cherished the few hours of sleep before the routine started the following day. Fort Benning was a bastion of organized sadism and studied insanity, and we delighted in it. Each day we survived, each day the cadre failed to break us, made us that much more confident in our own toughness and invincibility. There was a method to the Army's madness.

Throughout the long days, I dreamed continually of fulfilling my "European" experience. I had hardly ever left New York City. I was eager to get overseas to my first assignment in Mainz, Germany. I was going to ski in Europe. I was going to climb mountains in Europe. I was going to have girlfriends. I was going to re-invent myself. Looking back, I realize how insular and protected Bronx life had made me. I used the term "Europe" like it was a country. It was like some bumpkin from Germany, about to travel to New York, telling his friends he was going to North America, which would have defined any location between the Arctic Ocean and the Panama Canal.

But, before I could see Europe, I had to execute my fifth and final jump from the twin-engine C-123 "Provider" aircraft in which I was seated. I was in the Jump Phase, the last week, wherein we made five actual jumps from tactical aircraft. It was the easiest phase physically and the most stressful mentally. In the civilian world, they could teach novice skydivers how to jump from an airplane in hours. What would make us different is having gone through the crucible of the two preceding weeks. Ground Week and Tower Week were as much a rite of passage and a "character-building" experience as they were preparatory training.

The last jump was a "mass exit": we would follow the first man out the door without pause. My first jump had been "an individual tap out": each man had to stand in the door, awaiting the jumpmaster (JM), the man responsible for our safety and all aspects of the jump, to "tap" him out. That first jump was mind-bending.

Pre-jump check by Black Hat. Photo courtesy SFC Robert Contratto, US Army Airborne School Historian.

There were sixty of us sitting in nylon web seats arrayed in four rows: two "outboard, against the aircraft fuselage, and two "inboard" along the centerline, facing the "outboard" seats. Each row was known as a "stick."

The JM shouted, "Get Ready," the first of the nine jump commands. Next, he announced, "Outboard Personnel, Stand Up." That was my cue, and I stood up robotically, just like I had been conditioned to do. Then came, "Inboard Personnel, Stand Up." Then, "Hook Up" and "Check Static Lines," as we formed a downward-facing loop in our static lines, snapped them onto the overhead cables running the length of the aircraft, and bent the static line safety pins to the closed position. Next, "Check Equipment," as every man checked his front and the back of the man

Student jumpers in C-123. Photo courtesy SFC Robert Contratto, US Army Airborne School Historian.

in front of him for obvious faults in the parachute harness and ensured that the static line was connected to the overhead cable and locked shut. The JM then signaled, "Sound Off For Equipment Check." Every man slapped the back of the thigh of the man ahead while shouting out his stick number and a loud "OK." Then, we waited for the final signal.

Student jumpers in C-123. Photo courtesy SFC Robert Contratto, US Army Airborne School Historian.

"Stand In The Door," the almost final order was shouted out. The JM supplemented this verbal command with great exaggeration as he thrust his hand to the aircraft's open door. The first man in the stick shuffle-stepped forward. Then he pivoted, made eye contact with the safety person by the door, handed him his static line, and positioned himself in the open door. He then placed his hands on the outside of the fuselage to assist in pulling himself out when he jumped and to make it all the more difficult to grab the inside of the aircraft and brace oneself against leaving, should he ever be overcome with logic. The first man remained poised until the JM yelled, "Go," and tapped him out by slapping his left thigh. The trigger for this tap-out was a green jump light illuminated when we were over the leading-edge drop zone. The first man had too much time to contemplate what he was about to do. I was grateful not to be him.

On the "Go" command, we started our controlled migration to the door. Then I was in the door. There was no tap out. I had time

CHAPTER 5—FITTING IN

to think. All I could see was the doorframe suspended in space over the drop zone. Then I looked down. From 1250 feet altitude, everything seemed small. Only one thing looked larger than life. It was the three-quarter-ton ambulance. My gaze was riveted on the Red Cross emblazoned in the white circle on its roof. It seemed like minutes passed. My mind turned toward the path to reason and self-preservation. I could not imagine why the JM had not tapped me out. I could not imagine what could be wrong.

Suddenly, I felt the sting of the JM's tap out on my left thigh. Out I went. I forced my eyes open. I saw blue sky and puffy clouds over the tips of my spit-shined Corcoran jump boots. I realized that I was slightly inverted, that my head was closer to the ground than my feet. I counted, "One thousand, two thousand, three thousand, four thousand." You had four seconds for the static line to play out. When the slack was gone, the tension between the fixed cable in the aircraft and the parachute caused the chute to deploy. If you did not feel the violent tug of the air inflating the deploying parachute, you would be in trouble. You had only seconds to activate your reserve chute and manually shake it out so it would fill with air.

At the "four thousand" mark, I felt the jerk and looked up to see my canopy filled. There was a fleeting moment of elation, as I floated through the air with a mild, periodic oscillation. Then, I approached the next hurdle, the landing. I would hit the ground at about twenty-one feet per second, which was roughly equivalent to running the hundred-yard dash in fourteen seconds and taking a bad fall midway through. I was prepared, both mentally and physically. In the past two weeks, I had done thousands of push-ups, pull-ups, and sit-ups. I had run between two to five miles a day. I had made hundreds of practice landings from elevated platforms and the thirty-four and 250-foot towers.

My first landing was reflexive and quasi-instinctive, which is the whole purpose of the training that proceeded. Later that night, I asked the men in the stick who were behind me why the JM kept me so long in the door. They looked puzzled. They told me I was gone in a flash, just like everyone else.

I was shaken from the reverie of that first jump as the JM barked, "Get Ready." The final countdown to my last jump had

Jumpers exiting C-123. Photo courtesy SFC Robert Contratto, US Army Airborne School Historian.

begun. The other jump commands went by in a whirl. At "Go," we surged forward. My feet barely touched the floor; I was pulled along by the vacuum created by those ahead of me in the stick and pushed by the momentum of those behind me, eager as I was to get this over with. In sequence, I saw the safety person, the door, the sky, and then the ground. The objects and people on the ground grew bigger and bigger. I hit hard and rolled. Then I stood, recovered my parachute, stuffed it into a gray canvas kit bag, slung it over my shoulder, and ran off the drop zone. I was Airborne qualified.

Jump school taught me much more than just how to parachute from an airplane. It toughened much more than my body. Benning disciplined my mind. And that is why the Army required all Regular officers to take jump training. It prepared them, mentally, for *that day* if and when it ever came.

While I matriculated at the "Benning School for Boys," across the post, in the officers' club powder room, my then seventeen-year-old future wife attended the "Benning School for Girls." Seated at a vanity, looking into the mirror, hiding out from their parents, she and her "Army Brat" friends perfected looking cool. They practiced smoking, the most effective way to flip their hair, and other such moves they had seen beautiful women perform in the movies. They were training for the upcoming "hops" with the Officer Candidate School (OCS) men and West Point cadets. It was a sign of the innocence of the times. They practiced behaving and dressing like adults in the adult world's institutions. They were practicing being like their mothers. When I met her five years later, Carol was an Army nurse. Her "vamp" training was long since completed, though she no longer smoked for effect, and her regulation-length hair was a bit too short to flip.

CHAPTER 6

EUROPE

"To God I speak Spanish, to women Italian, to men French, and to my horse—German."
ATTRIBUTED TO CHARLES V, HOLY ROMAN EMPEROR, 1519-56

Airborne School was a significant, formative life-shaping experience. Initially, however, it was little more than the final gate into Europe. One week after graduating from Fort Benning, I am in my BOQ in Mainz, Germany. Fighting jet lag, I sit in my room sedating myself with bottles of Mainzer Akien beer. American rock and roll plays on Radio Luxemburg. The host announces, "It is midnight in Central Europe."

Mainz, an ancient, picturesque city on the west bank of the Rhine River, dates to Roman times when it was called Mogontiacum. It had long been home to foreign armies. Starting in 13 BC, the First and Fifth Roman Legions were garrisoned there.[27] Mainz was situated at the confluence of the Rhine and Main Rivers and had strategic value. The Romans used the Rhine, flowing south to north, as a barrier between them and the Germanic tribes to the east. They established a series of military bases, of which Mainz was but one, along its length to ensure control over this barrier. Mainz remained a Roman military base and city until the middle of the fourth century AD, when barbarian tribes surpassed Roman influence in Germany, setting the conditions for the Dark Ages.

Napoleon's forces occupied the city from 1797 to 1814. After World War I, the French maintained a garrison there from 1919

---

[27] Peter S. Wells, *The Battle That Stopped Rome*, (New York: W.W. Norton & Company, 2003), 89.

Mainz, February 1945. Photo by Margaret Bourke-White.

to 1930. In World War II, Mainz was taken by the US 90th Infantry Division on 22 March 1945 without much resistance. A month previous, Mainz was bombed and 80 percent destroyed by a raid of 435 British Royal Air Force (RAF) bombers. After the war, Mainz was in the French zone and remained occupied until 1949. In 1951, the French departed the zone entirely,

Mainz, 1945. Photo from the West Virginia and Regional History Center.

and US forces took their place. When I arrive in November 1963, little war damage is evident—a tribute to German fortitude and industriousness.

I live in a life support area named Mainz University Housing Area (MUHA), named after the nearby college some of whose former property and infrastructure are now allocated to US forces. MUHA contains a PX, commissary, grade school, officers' club, auto service station, and family housing. The officers' club is the hub of our social life. The Airborne Brigade of the 8th Infantry Division is stationed just outside Mainz. Many of its bachelor lieutenants live in the BOQ[28] and frequent the club, as do many young helicopter pilots from a nearby aviation company. They are a relatively wild bunch and they, of all those stationed here, know how to have a good time.

The club also has a strong female presence. The US Department of Defense maintains a separate elementary school for the children of married soldiers living in Mainz. Upwards of twenty single female schoolteachers reside in a separate BOQ. They are of all ages and are in Germany to teach, travel, and perhaps marry an officer. I did not come to Germany to seek out an American girlfriend, but there is no denying that they catch my interest. Some are very attractive. Some are "party animals." Some drive Porsche 356s. And some check all three boxes.

Another new milestone is achieved. I am twenty-one years old but have never owned a car and do not even know how to drive. That situation is quickly remedied. One of the senior lieutenants in my battery plans on trading his 1963 Volkswagen Beetle for a TR-4. He offers to teach me to drive and sell me his VW at a reasonable price. It is not a 356, but I master the art of shifting within the week and pass my driver's test. I am, finally, independently mobile.

I am happy to be in Germany, on my own, and ready for adventure. But I am conflicted; I am in the land of the Holocaust. I take perverse pleasure in being a member of the Army that defeated Germany and now stationed there. I am suspicious of any Germans I meet who were at least teenagers during World War II. I try to imagine if they could have been involved with the

---

[28] My BOQ was different than in the United States. It was a one-story building, one to a room, with a shared bathroom between every two rooms. The rooms were relatively spacious and served their purpose with a minor hint of luxury. Still, many officers sought to live off-base in rented rooms for a variety of reasons, not the least of which was to have a greater sense of privacy, especially if one had a German girlfriend who did not have a place of her own.

Holocaust. I wonder what they did and where they were during the war. They invariably supply the answer, even though I never ask the question. Every German veteran of World War II sooner or later proclaims to have served on the Eastern Front. They all fought the Russians. None fought the Americans. None were SS, and none were extermination camp staff. I cannot help wondering where all the bad Germans had gone.

The unanimous "Eastern Front" response was disingenuous, based probably on a combination of motivations. On one level, the evasion represented a polite social lie designed to preserve American sensibilities; there was no sense in angering current allies over past events. On another level, it served as a passport to moral rehabilitation. The "Eastern Front" response was the centerpiece of a German self-cleansing narrative. It was leveraged against the current American resolve to resist further communist hegemony in Europe: the communists are bad; whoever fought them or were fighting them now are good.

As a brand-new second lieutenant, I serve as a platoon leader in Battery A, 5th Battalion, 1st Artillery, located in Wackernheim, Germany, about five miles west of Mainz. Wackernheim was a German caserne (military camp) built in 1936 as part of Germany's rearmament and preparation for war.

German Pre-War postcard showing Wackernheim Barracks, mid 1930s.

Typical NATO Launch Area with Nike Hercules interceptor missiles erected for firing.

Our battalion is equipped with the Nike Hercules weapon system consisting of radar-directed, nuclear-tipped air defense missiles. Our mission is to defend the main US air bases at Ramstein, Bitburg, Hahn, and Spangdahlem, the Rhine River bridges, and the logistical support bases in Kaiserslautern from attack by massed formations of Russian bombers. We are a small part of the larger context of the Cold War in Western Europe. A large Soviet formation, the Group of Soviet Forces, Germany (GSFG), is stationed in East Germany. The West and East Germany border is called the Inner German Border (IGB) and is patrolled by armed US soldiers from the two armored cavalry regiments. The United States forces and those of our NATO allies continually war-game how to counter the GSFG if they pour across the IGB in an anticipated invasion.

Battery Control Central firing console (computer system), my duty postion in wartime.

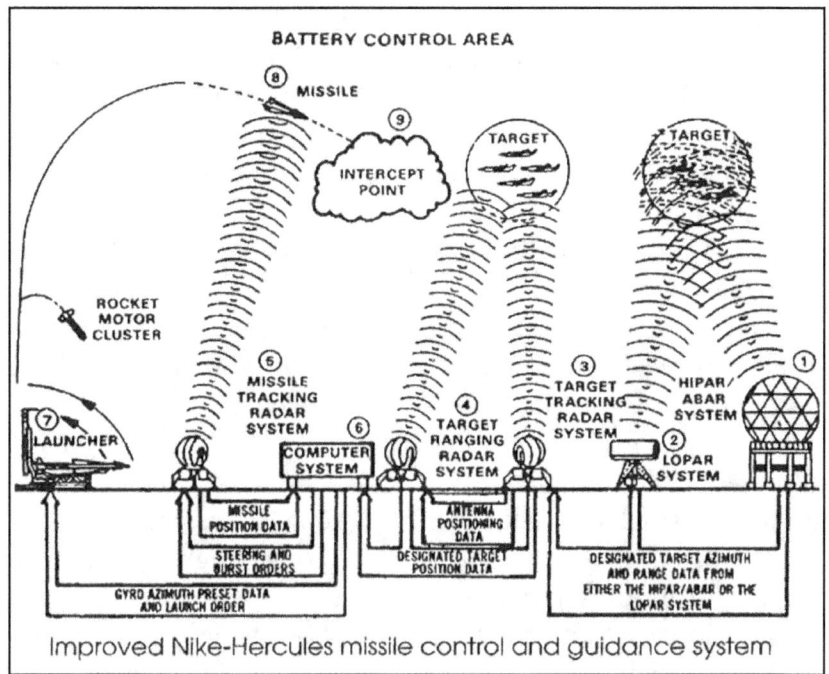

Schematic of Integrated Fire Control Platoon radars and method of operation.

I am the platoon leader of the Integrated Fire Control (IFC) Platoon. Our five radars and computers are designed to detect and track large formations of Russian bombers and guide our interceptor missiles to them. My wartime duty position is at the Battery Control Central, with my thumb on the toggle fire switch. The other platoon in the battery is the Launcher Platoon which contains the interceptor missiles that one of my radars will guide to the target.

The IFC equipment requires constant attention to keep it operational. It is based on vacuum tube technology. In addition to the platoon soldiers who operate the equipment, a large contingent of technicians and maintenance specialists armed with voltmeters and oscilloscopes perform the daily checks and adjustments and repair the fire control system.

One of these men is Chief Warrant Officer Nick Nicosia, a veteran of World War II, having served in an anti-aircraft artillery battalion. He subsequently rose through the NCO ranks[29] and transitioned to a Nike Hercules technician after passing a year-long course in electronics. He is a fellow New Yorker from the Bronx. He takes me under his wing and helps minimize my stupid second-lieutenant mistakes. I spend many off-duty hours with him, his teen-age daughter, Linda, and his wife, Rene, who treats me as her son or younger brother. We form a lifelong friendship. Five years later, I will be married in their El Paso, Texas, living room.

Thus, while at peace, we are on a war footing. We have monthly unannounced alerts, usually shortly after midnight, requiring us to issue weapons, load our vehicles, and sortie from garrison to our "training" (not actual) wartime battle positions. Absent the alerts, we are always on duty guarding against the preliminary airstrikes that would precede the Soviet ground invasion.

The battery workday is a matter of competing priorities. The nuclear warheads, the radars, and the diesel generators that supply the electrical power get the most effort, which consumes almost all available time. We operate within a NATO air defense environment, wherein we are assigned on a weekly basis various "readiness states," ranging from minutes to hours within which we are to be at "Battle Stations" and ready to fire. Mercifully, there is also a "12-hour released" status in which to accomplish deep maintenance and basic soldiering tasks. Naturally, when at the readiness states measured in minutes, I live on the equipment. At night, a battery duty officer, who could be me, runs battle drills against simulated targets, checks the on-duty launcher crews and nuclear weapon guard force in another area, a mile away. Then a few hours' sleep, maybe on a cot, next to the Battery Control Central van. Based on a rigorous practical exam, we have only seven officers qualified to perform this duty, so it comes weekly. The soldiers in my platoon are organized into two shifts, day and night. But, when I am the duty officer, it is a 24-hour duty day—12 hours as platoon leader and another 12 as the duty officer.

---

[29] Non-Commissioned Officer (NCO) is a generic term for the various grades of sergeant. A warrant officer is one with a specialized technical skill and responsibility. They do have the command authority of commissioned officers.

American border patrol. Official US Army photograph.

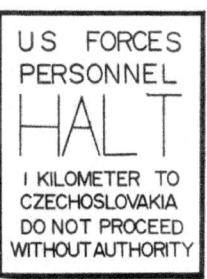
Border warning sign.

Sometimes being the duty officer could be unexpectedly exciting. Once, just as I was finishing my tour and contemplating a trip to the mess hall for a Melamite mug of scalding hot black coffee with scrambled eggs and bacon swimming in grease on a metal tray, I am summoned to the launcher area to address a crisis. It seems that one of the guards in one of the watch towers had just shot a deer emerging from the state forest surrounding the launch complex, wherein our nuclear warheads were also stored. Once there, I ascertain that Specialist Four Milton, a good old boy from Tennessee, using his M-14 rifle and iron sights at a range of about 100 meters, had, out of some combination of boredom and pre-existing hunting skills, shot a stag red deer as it approached the launch area fence line. It briefly crossed my mind that maybe I was involved, because I had previously checked the guards to make sure they were awake and cognizant of their rules of engagement, which did not include the shooting of deer, no matter how close to the fence they approached. Absent my diligence, Milton may have been inclined to doze off and thereby miss his serendipitous hunting opportunity.

But that was just the beginning of the episode. A gaggle of German officials, ranging from the forest manager to the chief of police of the nearby town, arrive clamoring to get onto the site to seek justice. It didn't help matters that I had previously dated the police chief's daughter before that liaison ended abruptly over a failure to agree on when to become intimate—I considered the third date rule as the gold standard, whilst her magic number ran into double digits and included an engagement ring.

When my chain of command arrives, it is decided to hold court outside the fence line, at the scene of the shooting. There is little to investigate. The deer is dead, shot cleanly through the heart. Milton's rifle has been fired, and he is short one round from the 20 he had been issued. The sergeant of the guard has a spent shell casing, retrieved from the guard tower floor, albeit now contaminated with his own fingerprints. Furthermore, Milton needlessly confesses, adding that he first confirmed the deer was a mature-enough male before sending his 7.62 mm NATO standard round down range to slay Bambi's father. End of crime scene investigation; beginning of a political-military bruhaha. The Germans love, really, really love, their forests and all that live therein, especially the deer. Milton gets to see the inside of the Manheim Stockade after being convicted for dereliction of duty by a Summary Court-Martial. Nonetheless, he eventually returns to the unit as a minor Davey Crockett-lite folk hero.

But, aside from rare moments like this, little time is left for the "fun" part of being a soldier. There are no organized unit PT formations; we go on maneuvers less frequently than the nearby infantry and artillery units; parades are infrequent; and we hardly ever fire our pistols, rifles, and machine guns. We are measured by our ability to keep the Nike Hercules system operational and to fulfill our assigned air defense readiness status. When it comes to basic soldiering, corners are cut.

One experience I had running a machine gun range summarizes this situation. Our battery has several M-2, .50 caliber machine guns. They are ring-mounted on key vehicles for air defense or on tripods for ground defense. They are very effective weapons if properly employed. One day in February 1964, I am informed on very short notice that I will run an M-2 machine gun range for the battalion. Someone had sat on the requirement for some time. Maybe it had been assigned initially to a more senior lieutenant who was subsequently diverted for a more important mission. Whatever the reason, I have almost no time to prepare while performing my primary platoon leader duties. If I had training on the M-2 in ROTC, it left little impression. My only crutch is the warrant officer assigned as my assistant. He has the M-2 machine gun field manual, which shows various training methodologies and range preparation tasks. At some time in his career, he had done some of this or at least witnessed it being done. There was much for me to learn and then teach the gun crews.

But I have an even more pressing problem: setting up the range so training could proceed. Here, I receive some institutional help. The battery executive officer (XO) gives me a verbal checklist of what I had to accomplish, who to see, and what to do. The range is in Baumholder, one of the most notoriously austere training areas, especially in winter. I travel to the range in an open jeep two days early to set up the basic infrastructure. I arrange for the pickup of the ammunition, establish communications with Range Control, position an ambulance and medics, ensure the targets are in place, set up traffic control points and roadblocks to prevent errant entry into the impact area, etc. There is no time to learn and logically think through how to effectively conduct the actual training.

When the soldiers arrive, a minor backlog is created as I learn and then instruct them on how to set up the machine gun, headspace and time it, and put its crew into action. The Army calls this "discovery learning," and it is not the preferred method. As if that were not enough, it is freezing, toe-numbing cold. Sometimes, cold is a state of mind; sometimes, you can mentally reduce its effect. But on this occasion, it is meteorologically and certifiably cold.

One of the first lieutenants from another battery usurps control to minimize the backlog and exposure to the cold. He commandeers one of the functional machine guns and has his backlogged crews line up behind it in a single file, much like people lining up to use a payphone. He then literally runs them through the gun on an assembly line basis. Each soldier fires off about ten rounds, dashes off, and is replaced by the next in line. When he relinquishes control to me, the backlog is cleared, and his soldiers are out of the biting wind and into their trucks for the trip home. Their requirement to at least fire the machine gun is fulfilled, albeit in a non-doctrinal and half-assed manner. His men spend more time getting into and out of their trucks than learning about the machine gun. The training benefit is zero. My soldiers remain, and we try to do it right. But I am sure not a few wonder why I could not be as practical as that more senior lieutenant. They attach no virtue to being a good soldier, at least not when they are shivering.

My devotion to duty is not without reward. I attend special training courses in Bavaria, which, in addition to being professionally rewarding, allow me to travel and see a picturesque part of Germany. I especially enjoy the Demolition and Mine Warfare Course, which provides realistic, hands-on experience in using explosives to create barriers and destroy roads, bridges, and equipment. When promoted to first lieutenant, I am brought up to battalion staff and selected to command the headquarters battery. These command positions are coded for captains. My selection for this position is an unusual reward. Commanding a battery presents new challenges and learning experiences. I go through a similar set of bumps and grinds, akin to those experienced learning to be a platoon leader. The days are long, but I have the stamina of youth. And I make time to see Europe. I play Baccarat in Baden Baden, ski in Kitzbuhel, bar-hop in Madrid, and watch the world go by from an outdoor café on the Champs Elysees.

Daily garrison life, while demanding, is not all work and no play. Weekend fun there was, albeit somewhat regimented, as one would expect in a military environment. Friday nights are happy hour at the club, which is scandalously profitable from its slot machines, so much so that it practically gives away burgers and beer for free. The evening comes in two waves. The first ends at about 6 PM when the more senior and married officers depart for home. Then the lieutenants get things rolling with loud music from the juke box, howls from payoffs and near misses at the slots, and new romances forged, and old ones shattered. This goes on till closing

Off duty, 1965.

time at midnight. Saturdays are devoted to washing and waxing our cars, hitting the PX, picking up laundry and fresh uniforms and resting up for the upcoming night operation. If it is a payday weekend, we dress up and go to the casino in Wiesbaden to play roulette and Baccarat till our chips run out and then go girl chasing and clubbing on Taunusstraße. Sundays are devoted to sleeping in, dosing on Alka-Seltzer and Visine, and if able, a trip to the gym to weightlift and sauna. After all this, reporting back to work at 6 AM Monday is a blessing in disguise—a chance to recover and get ready for the next Friday.

And I learn something about attitudes toward Jews in my newly chosen profession. At the officers' club one Friday night, during happy hour, I am at the bar chatting up one of the more attractive schoolteachers. She is slightly older than I and Boston-Irish, in fact South-Boston-Irish, which adds to my finding her mysteriously appealing. She is like the forbidden fruit of my youth in Parkchester. Things proceed swimmingly. We have lots of laughs and deliberate physical contact—shoulders, elbows, knees.

Off in a corner, several lieutenants from the Honest John artillery unit are getting soused, and boisterously so. They are ribbing a fellow lieutenant about his being African American. I overhear occasional snippets, and it all sounds good-natured.

However, the lieutenant does not share my analysis. Suddenly, out of context, as if to shock and deflect his drinking buddies, he shouts out, "Hey, it's cold in here; throw another Jew on the fire." My hackles go up, my muscles tense, and I anticipate having to do something about that. But, my South Boston "hottie" takes no notice of the outburst, and the guy's tablemates go on as if he had said nothing. I am not wearing my religion on my sleeve, so nothing is expected or required of me. I choose to act like a cat in the grass and observe before moving. I treat the situation like a lab experiment—I will watch and measure the anti-Jewish atmospherics in my carefully selected career field.

The other lieutenants are not seduced by the suggestion that they turn their attention to the Jews. They stay on topic and continue to verbally jab away at the African American. So, like a kid in school who had called out the wrong answer once already to no avail, he again shouts out, this time more loudly and desperately, "Hey, it's cold in here; throw another Jew on the fire." But his friends stay on topic, which is him.

The lieutenant then jumps up, way out of balance due to excessive drink, and tries to punch the officer to his right. His intended target easily blocks the loping right overhand punch, and a minor melee ensues as others try to break it up or punish him for disturbing the bull session. In short order the bartender restores the peace and sends the lieutenants back to the BOQ—an adult "time out." In the momentary confusion, the teacher fled, probably on her "Southie" instincts that a full-scale barroom donnybrook might develop.

I mused on the event with mixed feelings. I was glad the lieutenants did not take the twice-offered bait to divert to an anti-Semitic thrust. I was delighted the Boston Irish object of my attention did not see fit to acknowledge the "Throw another Jew" suggestion. I was angry that an educated African American officer would stoop to generate an antisemitic "escape hatch" at a time when Jews were prominent in the Civil Rights movement. Likewise, I was a bit ashamed, as a Jewish man, to take satisfaction in the lieutenants' refusal to take the antisemitic offering and persist in their racially oriented line of dark humor. I was also relieved that the situation ended without my having to test myself by going over to the table and calling the African American to account. Lastly, the teacher was a good looker, and everything was going in the right direction for me until it all blew up because of him.

By late 1965, it becomes clear that we are no longer a peacetime Army. There is a war in Vietnam. I want to know, need to know if I am a real soldier, or just a dress-up one, a neat-looking Ken doll in uniform. It is time to discover if I have what it takes to be a Jewish fighting man. All my thoughts on Jewish passivity have to be put to the test. Standing up to Irish toughs in a fistfight in Parkchester was one thing; fighting in a war was another.

Accordingly, I submit my paperwork to volunteer for duty in Vietnam. My battalion commander, a decorated and wounded veteran of the Korean War, rejects my request. He counsels me to wait. He tells me there will be plenty of war to go around; he implores me not to seek it out. His wisdom is wasted on me. After a short interval, I resubmit my application. This time, the Army, desperately needing officers in Vietnam, overrides my commander's disapproval and grants me my wish.

Almost immediately thereafter, I am struck with a depressing sense of foreboding. The immediate trigger is the 1965 movie *The War Lord* with Charlton Heston and Richard Boone, which I had gone to see in the base theater. Besides the main plot of Charlton Heston taking the bride of a young Norman villager, there were bloody scenes of combat between raiding Frisians and the villagers led by their feudal overlords. Normally, I would have enjoyed the vivid depictions of men being beheaded and disemboweled, but now, on orders to Vietnam, I feel that I could be part of that formerly entertaining scene. I walk out of the theater on wobbly knees and do not sleep particularly well until I am actually in Vietnam, at which time it is pointless to worry anymore.

To assuage my discomfort, I apply to attend the Army's Jungle Warfare School in Panama en route to Vietnam. This school was originally created to provide unique training for soldiers assigned to defend the Panama Canal. But now, with a war raging in Southeast Asia, the school serves to prepare selected junior leaders for warfare in a jungle many time zones removed from the Canal. My request is denied, stating that as a senior lieutenant, I will not be assigned duties requiring combat expertise in the jungle environment. I am disappointed at the prospect of not serving at the cutting edge but also relieved to learn that I would probably be somewhat removed from the perils of the jungle. My disappointment and relief are to be short-lived.

CHAPTER 7

FOR TIN AND TUNGSTEN

"...If Indochina goes, several things happen right away. The Malayan peninsula...would be scarcely defensible— and tin and tungsten that we so greatly value from that area would cease coming..."
PRESIDENT DWIGHT EISENHOWER, 4 AUGUST 1953 SPEECH TO GOVERNORS' CONFERENCE IN SEATTLE, EXPLAINING WHY THE US IS HELPING FINANCE THE FRENCH WAR EFFORT IN INDOCHINA DURING THE FIRST INDOCHINA WAR, 1946-54

Tin hardly seems worthy of justification for supporting a faraway war. It is an unimpressive word and an unimpressive metal. It sounds cheap. It is used to make solder, toy soldiers, and line soda cans. But tungsten has gravitas. The word invokes the intersection of technology with geopolitical strategy. In Swedish, tungsten means heavy stone, as contrasted with the lightness of tin. Tungsten is used to produce hard metal alloys and electronic vacuum tubes. The President's speechwriters combined tungsten's aural appeal with an image of endangered natural resources to rationalize our financial aid for France, which was engaged in war in a place most Americans could not locate on a map.

Notwithstanding speechwriting skills and financial aid, the French lost the First Indochina War in 1954, yet the free world retained access to Southeast Asian tin and tungsten ore. But what did happen is that, in 1966, large numbers of American soldiers had replaced the French as the policemen of Southeast Asia, and the Second Indochina War was in full bloom.

CHAPTER 7—FOR TIN AND TUNGSTEN

I arrive in Vietnam in mid-May 1966, one of nine thousand new soldiers who join the war that month.[30] I enter a part of the world I knew only by empty pages representing hard-to-pronounce countries in my boyhood stamp collection album. I am in the land of broken empires. I have transited from Europe, the realm of the empire builders, to the lands of the formerly colonized. The British had once possessed India, Burma, Malaya, and Singapore, which are now free. The Dutch colonized Borneo, Sumatra, Celebes, and Java, which are currently free and renamed Indonesia. The French had colonized and then lost Indochina.

My unit of assignment is the 1st Infantry Division. The division shoulder patch is a red "1" on an olive drab background shaped like a medieval shield. Thus, the division is nicknamed "The Big Red One." Created in the First World War, it fought at Cantigny, Soissons, St. Michiel, and the Meuse-Argonne Forest. In World War II, it made amphibious assaults into North Africa, Sicily, and Normandy. It fought its way into Germany and then to the Czechoslovakian border. Its demanding military culture is summed up by its motto, "No mission too difficult. No sacrifice too great—Duty first." The division is nicknamed "The Bloody Red One" due to its casualty rates in World War II. Nothing happens in my year with the Division to detract from that.

The chain of events that brought the 1st Infantry Division to Vietnam had originated over 100 years earlier. Commencing in 1859, the French conducted a forty-eight-year campaign to colonize Vietnam. In 1897, the first rubber plantation was established. By 1907, the French formed the Vietnamese states of Tonkin, Annam, and Cochin-China, joined by Cambodia and Laos, into a political unit known as the Indochinese Union. The term "Indochina" was coined by the Danish geographer Konrad Malte-Brun (1755-1826) to describe this large peninsula between the key trade areas of India and China.

---

[30] Troop strength on 1 May was 252,000. On 1 June it rose to 261,000. Source: Military Assistance Command, Vietnam (MACV) Daily Staff Journals, 1966.

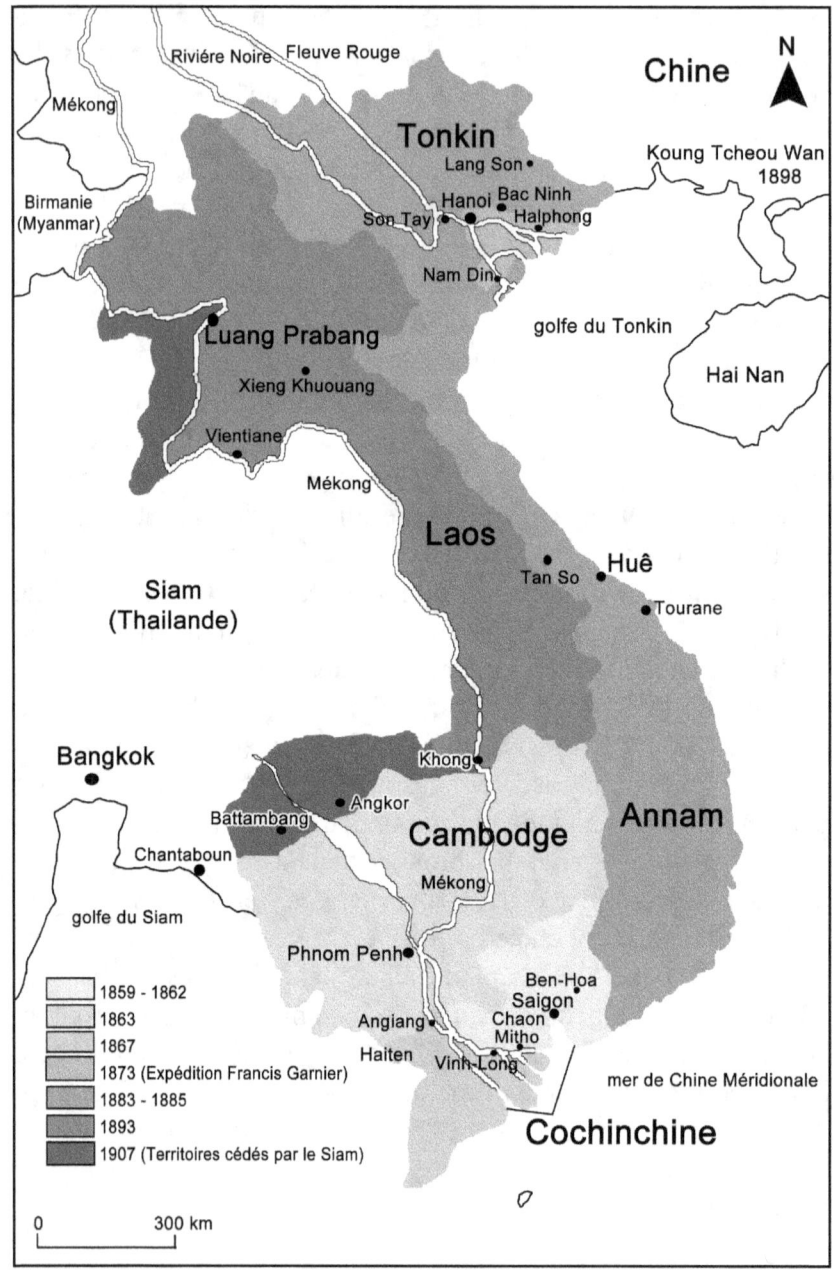

Map depicting French colonization of Indochina, 1859-1907.

French rule was harsh and economically exploitative, with the indentured workers on the Michelin rubber plantations suffering the worst. In the early 1920s, a communist-led Vietnamese resistance movement was born. In 1940, the Germans overran France, directly occupied the northern part of the country, and installed a collaborationist Vichy Government in the South. The Japanese, allied to Germany, were permitted by the Vichy Government to station troops in Vietnam to enable their ongoing invasion of China. In 1940-41, Thailand (Siam), with Japanese collusion, went to war against France and regained territories forcibly ceded to French Indochina in 1907. It was forced to return these lands to Cambodia at the end of the war. In 1945, the last year of World War II, the Japanese openly occupied Vietnam and interned all French soldiers. These events accumulated to shatter the aura of Caucasian invincibility.

France's perceived weakness galvanized Vietnamese nationalistic aspirations. Under the leadership of Ho Chi Minh, a communist, they fought the Japanese occupation, with the long view of gaining freedom from France. The United States supported the Vietnamese resistance movement with teams of American guerillas from the Office of Strategic Services, the OSS, which was the forerunner of our CIA.

After Japan was defeated, France was keen to re-establish its colonial status. As a quid pro quo for its support of NATO and containment of communism in Europe, the United States acceded to French desires in Indochina. The Vietnamese did not. War ensued. The United States supported France under both Democratic and Republican presidencies. We financed 80 percent of the French war effort, guided by President Truman's containment doctrine and President Eisenhower's "domino theory." In a 7 April 1954 press conference, Eisenhower was asked to comment on the importance of Indochina to the free world. He stated that we had both economic and political interests in Indochina and that if one country fell to communism, others would quickly follow, like falling dominoes.

The war went badly for France; in 1954, they lost Vietnam as a colony. A communist government was established in the northern part of the country. Its ultimate goal was to reunify the non-communist southern half by force. In 1956, the last of the French Expeditionary Army exited Vietnam, and the United States inherited the task of supporting the Republic of Vietnam (South Vietnam) in resisting the war of unification waged by the communist North.[31]

By 1960, it became clear that the Republic of Vietnam was incapable of dealing with the growing threat presented by North Vietnam. The VC overran a South Vietnamese Army regimental headquarters in Tay Ninh Province. In response to the increased effectiveness of the VC, US advisors were assigned down to infantry regiment and artillery, armored, and separate marine battalion levels in the South Vietnamese Army.[32]

Despite the US presence, the communist insurgency increased its dominance. By late 1961, a larger and more powerful advisory effort, the Military Assistance Command Vietnam (MACV), was established to oversee an expanded aid and training program. By the end of 1964, it became apparent that MACV had been too optimistic regarding the expected outcomes of its materiel support and increased placement of US advisory teams. In early 1965, the VC launched a division-size attack against the village of Binh Gia, close to Saigon, where they destroyed two South Vietnamese battalions and held the battlefield for four days. On 7 February 1965, the VC attacked the US advisory team compound at Pleiku in the Central Highlands region. American forces suffered 136 casualties, and twenty-two aircraft were damaged or destroyed. On 10 February, the VC destroyed a US barracks at Qui Nhon, causing forty-four American losses.[33]

The United States responded to this challenge with the decision to introduce US combat forces into South Vietnam (as opposed to the advisory teams and support troops already in place). By the end of 1965, US troop strength rose from 23,300 to 184,300

---

[31] BG James Lawton Collins Jr., *The Development and Training of the South Vietnamese Army, 1950-1972*, (Department of the Army: Washington, D.C. 1975), Chapter I.

[32] Collins, Chapter II.

[33] Collins, Chapter II.

personnel in-country.[34] The 1st Infantry Division was a part of this exponential increase, arriving in Vietnam from July to October 1965. And through it all, Frenchmen continued to live in manor houses and harvest rubber. The French, who are much better with language than war, have an appropriate expression that summarizes the whole thrust of this history: *Plus ça change, plus c'est la même chose*—the more things change, the more they remain the same.

---

[34] Collins, Chapter III.

CHAPTER 8

THE FO AND THE ARTILLERY KILL CHAIN

"The Guns, Thank God the Guns."
RUDYARD KIPLING

"For the want of a nail, the shoe was lost. For the want of a shoe, the horse was lost. For want of a horse, the knight was lost; for want of a knight, the battle was lost. For want of a battle, the kingdom was lost. All for the want of a nail."
PROVERB

My assignment to this division is little more than a foot in the door. I must sell myself to be assigned to a combat unit. I am a senior first lieutenant trained in air defense. But the VC have no air force, and we, therefore, have no air defense forces in-country to protect us from a threat that does not exist. Besides, even if we did, it is not what I would want. I want to be assigned to a field artillery unit supporting the infantry. I hope to have the opportunity to become a battery commander when I am promoted to captain. I am a shameless, self-serving, career-mongering ladder-climber.

And I am a lucky one. The Division Assignment Officer is Captain "Nails" (Moran), my ROTC Summer Camp tactical officer from 1962. He is now a major, just promoted to staff from an infantry battalion. He looks like a wreck. His face is drawn and there are dark circles under his eyes. I wonder why he hasn't taken better care of himself, though, in a few weeks, I will look no better and understand why. He remembers me. I tell him, politely, I do not want a desk job. I tell him I want to "see action." He is equally polite in suppressing an urge to laugh. But Moran must still have a soft spot in his heart for me. Logically, I should be assigned to staff or a non-combat unit. Instead, he obliges me. He assigns me as a forward observer (FO), the penultimate combat task available to any artilleryman.

Artillery, infantry, and cavalry were always the key components of modern warfare. The march of twentieth-century technology propelled artillery to the forefront. The advent of portable battery-powered field radios, light observation aircraft, radar-directed proximity fuses, and advancements in meteorology, cartography, and metallurgy all combined to enable the rapid and accurate concentration of fires. In World War II, artillery was the greatest producer of enemy casualties. Artillery thus earned the title "The King of Battle," whereas infantry had previously reigned supreme as "The Queen of Battle." This is iconized in our drinking ditty, "Balls, cried the Queen; if I had some, I'd be the King"—the "balls" being a double entendre on gonads and cannon balls.

The FO is a crucial member of the "Artillery Kill Chain." But the extended concept of this kill chain involves many, many more people than just the FO—civilians and soldiers alike. They all must function according to plan, or the process will fail "for the want of a nail."

Thus, the kill chain begins far from the battlefield, in factories in the United States, where the cannon and the associated repair parts and projectiles are manufactured and shipped to the warzone. Also, in the United States, the artillery soldiers and officers are trained for their roles in this kill chain. The men, cannon, and projectiles must then be transported to the warzone by sea-lift vessels and distributed to the units engaged in combat. In the 1st Infantry Division, air-mobile operations are the norm. Men and equipment are moved about the battle zone by helicopter. Thus, the movement and transport links of the chain involve a whole other, separate, and complex aviation chain.

At the more lethal end of the kill chain, soldiers emplace the cannon, load the projectiles into the breech blocks, set the sights

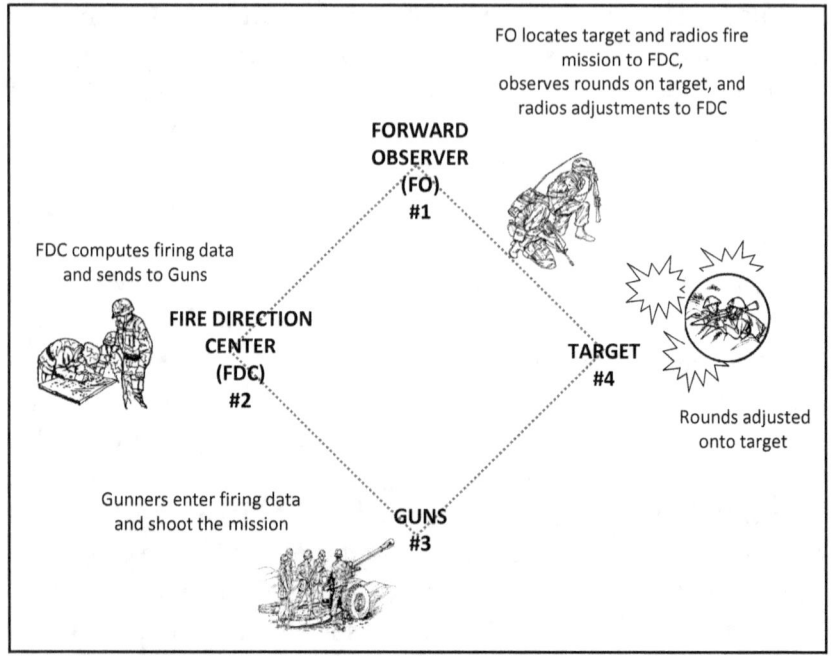

The artillery team, showing the role of the FO, the FDC, and the howitzers. Diagram by the author.

for the correct deflection and elevation, and pull the firing lanyards. This is the "muscle" part of the chain. In a Fire Direction Center (FDC), other soldiers compute these settings and transmit them to the gunners. They are the "brains." Neither muscle nor brain is sufficient in and of itself. Both must function together, in harmony, to produce the desired effect.

Finally, at the most lethal link in the chain, the FO, with the infantry unit, locates the enemy, calls for artillery fire, and adjusts the effects onto the enemy.

In Vietnam, the Army is organized for combat by the rule of "threes." Each infantry division has three brigades. Each brigade has three infantry battalions. Each battalion has three rifle companies. A "habitually associated" 105mm howitzer battalion supports the brigade with artillery fires. These 105mm artillery battalions have three firing batteries. Each artillery battery supports one of the infantry battalions and has three FOs, in the grade of lieutenant, in support of each rifle company.

Paradoxically, despite subsequent technological improvements, the Vietnam War represented a technical step backward from what the Army had experienced during World War II and the Korean Wars. In those wars, the FO was usually located in an observation post (OP), offering a commanding view of the surrounding terrain. He utilized binoculars to locate and adjust the massed fires of several artillery battalions onto distant targets. This OP might be in a church steeple or a fortified bunker on a high hill mass or mountain, affording an unobstructed view of the surrounding area. The flat terrain of the jungle and rubber plantation country offers no such opportunity for long-range observation. Except in the larger cities, there are no church steeples. Commanding hill masses are equally nonexistent. Binoculars are useless; I never use the pair issued to me.

Almost all fire missions involve using the sense of sound rather than sight. The enemy is elusive, and the terrain restricts observation beyond several meters. The FO has to deduce the enemy's location by the sound of its weapons' fire. Likewise, his adjustment of the artillery rounds is done by sound. An FO can have nonfunctional eyes, but he best have two good ears, and the ability to correlate the loudness of the artillery impacts to direction and distance from himself and the assumed enemy location.

The terrain's limited visibility dictates that combat occurs at close range. The closer the range, the greater the danger posed by the inherent accuracy limitations of the artillery. Problems in adhering to a strict standard in the large-scale manufacture of artillery propellants, tube wear on howitzer barrels, weather conditions, and non-controlled ammunition storage conditions combine to produce an unavoidable dispersion of artillery fire that is statistically described as the "range probable error." For the 105mm howitzer, the range probable error is on the order of twenty-five meters. Translated into practical terms, this means that 95 percent of the artillery rounds would fall plus or minus twenty-five meters from where they were intended to impact. The 105mm howitzer artillery round has a weapons' effects radius of twenty-five meters. The conflation of the range probable error and the shells' bursting radius can combine to cause artillery effects to be felt approximately fifty meters closer to the friendly forces than intended. If human error is introduced, the results can be even worse.

Requesting and adjusting artillery support is not terribly complicated, but there is ample room for human error. The FO can make a mistake in estimating his or the enemy's location on the ground and translating this to the corresponding map coordinates. He, or the FDC, can make a mistake in transposing some of the digits of the enemy location on the map, the FDC can erroneously compute or transmit the firing data to hit the target, or the howitzer gunners can erroneously apply the data to their cannon. Finally, the FO can fail to properly visualize how his adjustment orders, e.g., "Left 100, Drop 100" translate into the actual movement of the impact points on the ground before him. In my time, more than one FO killed himself and those around him when they "accidentally" adjusted artillery fire onto their positions.

Suppose the enemy is about one hundred meters away. In that case, the inherent errors induced by technology can combine with the whole menu of possible human error, resulting in the unintended infliction of friendly casualties. We are cautioned to use the minimum caliber of artillery and number of howitzers consistent with the nature of the target and its proximity to our force. Thus, most of our close-fire missions are conducted with no more than one battery of six howitzers firing for effect. By comparison, in World War II, more distantly situated targets would have been "serviced" by at least three times as many guns.

The FO also provides close air support. He can radio to an airborne Forward Air Controller (FAC) a request for support from F-105 Thunder Chiefs, AC-47 Gun Ships, or A-7 Sky Raiders aircraft, much like the request radioed to the FDC. Again, determining location is everything. A pilot flying above the jungle or rubber tree canopy can see nothing of the underlying ground. The FO typically sets off a colored smoke grenade. When the smoke rises above the tree canopy, and the FAC or supporting pilots see it and correctly identify its color, the FO vectors the pilots to the target by relating the enemy's position by direction and range from his smoke. The pilot(s) then proceed to drop napalm, cluster bombs, or strafe the presumed enemy location. Here again, the potential for error is not insignificant. An aircraft traveling at a relatively slow speed of four hundred miles per hour will cover a distance of two hundred meters in a little more than one second. A bomb dropped by this same aircraft will initially move laterally at the same velocity while falling under the influence of gravity. A pilot error in judgment of just one second could result in either the bomb falling well beyond the target if the pilot released his ordnance a second late or hitting the friendly troops if he released a second early.

A study of artillery accidents and incidents during the Vietnam War attributed 47 percent of the errors to the FDC-firing battery combination. However, if the FO did not radio in a correct request, everybody else in the fire support chain could do no better than to efficiently propagate his error. The FO had to be skilled in map reading and visualizing how to properly adjust onto the target the initial spotting rounds fired in immediate response to his request for fires. If he could not do this, he was, at best, a burden to the infantry he was charged to support; at worst, he was a danger.

CHAPTER 9

COMPANY TOWN

*"Sure, the lion is king of the jungle, but airdrop him into the
Antarctic, and he's just a penguin's bitch."*
DENNIS MILLER, AMERICAN COMEDIAN

Moran assigns me to Charlie Battery, 2d Battalion, 33d Artillery, which supports the 2d Battalion, 28th Infantry, one of the three infantry battalions of the 3d Brigade. I will be the FO for Alpha Company of this battalion. We are based at Lai Khe, a rubber plantation twenty miles north of Saigon and astride Route 13, a major highway, by primitive standards, running from Saigon to the Cambodian border. It is not a working plantation but a small experimental station of the more extensive Michelin plantation system. Foreign soldiers have trod here before; our base was a staging area for a Senegalese regiment of the French Expeditionary Army preparing to return home after the armistice ending the Indochina War was signed in 1954.[35]

When I join the Division, we are fighting five inter-related campaigns. The first is the diplomatic dimension: the effort to garner allies and minimize the influence of Russia and China. The second is the strategic bombing effort over North Vietnam by the US Air Force and Naval Aviation to destroy selected components of the North Vietnamese war-related infrastructure. The third is the interdiction campaign being waged along the Ho Chi Minh

---

[35] Native units from Tunisia, Algeria, Morocco, and Senegal, which were French colonies in Africa, along with native colonial units from Laos, Cambodia, and Vietnam, made up a major portion of the French Forces that fought the First Indochina War, 1946-54.

Trail, running almost the length of the Indochina peninsula, from North Vietnam, through Laos and Cambodia to South Vietnam, by US Special Operations units and the Air Force, to decrease the flow of soldiers and war materiel from North to South Vietnam. The fourth is the fight conducted by US Advisory Teams and the South Vietnamese forces for "the hearts and minds" of the South Vietnamese civilian population living in villages throughout the countryside to wean them from their pro-VC sympathies or preclude them from falling under VC sway. Then, there is the fifth, the one that involves me and other US Army and Marine Corps units' efforts to find and destroy the mobile Viet Cong and North Vietnamese combat formations.[36]

Within this framework, the 3d Brigade has two objectives. One is to secure the northern approaches of Saigon from attack. The second is to conduct offensive operations against VC base areas located east of us in War Zone C, northwest of us in War Zone D, and south of us in The Iron Triangle region. To accomplish the dual defensive-offensive mission, three infantry battalions, one towed 105mm artillery battalion, plus several company-size units from the Division and II Field Forces, the corps-like headquarters, garrison the base.

All of Vietnam is in the tropics, north of the equator. In the summer, the Northern Hemisphere, mostly a landmass, is tilted toward the sun. The land heats up more rapidly than the oceans, which have a higher heat capacity. The hot air over the landmass rises and is replaced by cooler air rushing in from the sea, which is further cooled and condenses as rain over Vietnam. This part of the weather cycle is known as the summer monsoon.

When I arrive, this rain cycle is at its finest. It will rain daily for five months, producing almost twelve inches monthly. The built-up areas rest on a red clay substrate known as laterite. It is the devil's mix. It derives its red tint from its iron content. When wet, it exerts a greater suction than plain mud, and when dry, it raises fine, choking dust. The unpaved roads within the camp are alternately slurpy quagmires during the monsoon season and

---

[36] Paddy Griffith, *Forward Into Battle* (Novato, California: Presidio Press, 1992), 137-39.

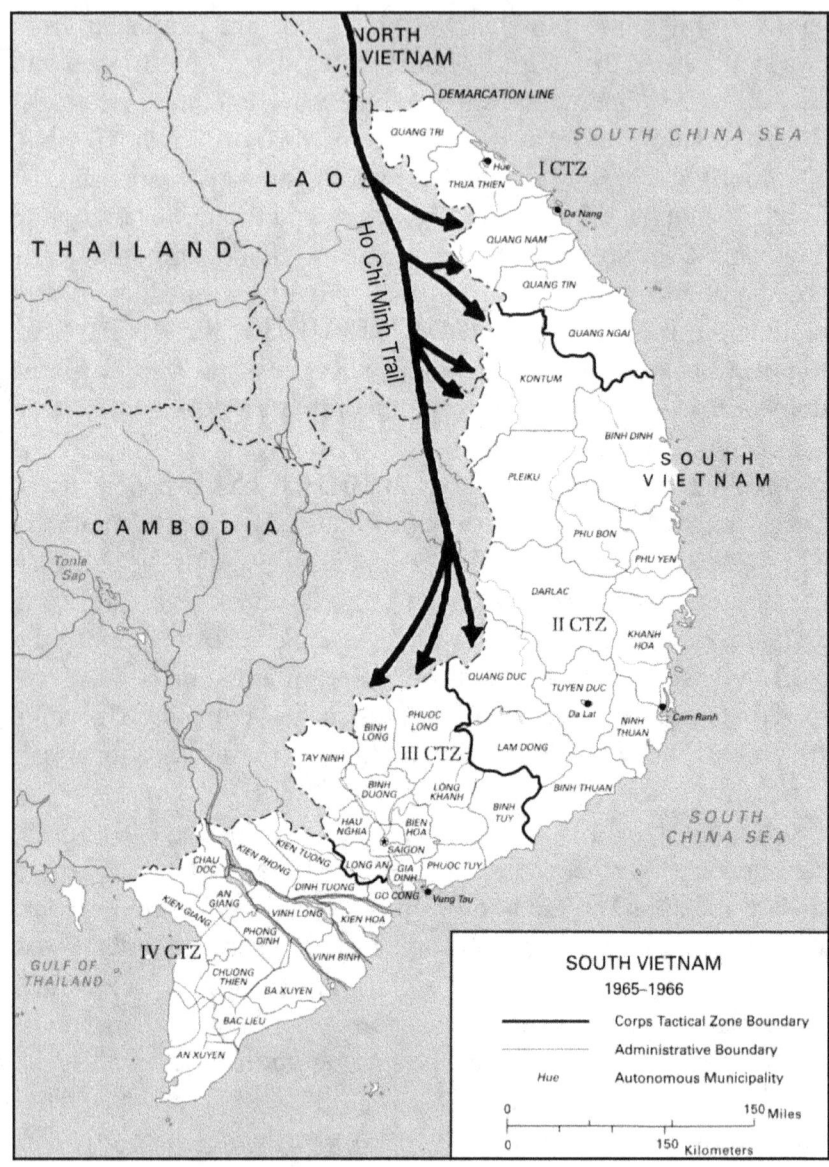

Infiltration routes into South Vietnam. Adapted from Stemming the Tide, *Center of Military History, United States Army.*

linear dustbowls for the next half of the year. The temperature and humidity are in the nineties. It is hot enough to be uncomfortable just doing nothing. It can be physically debilitating when performing manual labor on the perimeter or fitted out in full battle

Lai Khe and surrounding III Corps Tactical Zone (CTZ), showing War Zones C and D, and The Iron Triangle. Adapted from Stemming the Tide, *Center of Military History, United States Army.*

dress and marching under the load of extra ammunition, rations, and water.

The base is about one mile in diameter, bisected on a north-south axis by Highway 13. Running parallel to and just east of Highway 13 is an all-weather airstrip that is the *sine qua non* for the brigade's airmobile capability. Our assault helicopter company, which carries us into combat, is stationed here, and the strip can also support CH-47 Chinook Helicopters, C-7 Caribou, and C-130 Hercules aircraft to deploy us to more distant battle areas. The village of Lai Khe is nestled in the southwest quadrant of the base. In the year since the brigade first arrived, it adapted its economy to the demands of about four thousand young, feral US warriors. There are "mom and pop" laundry services, shops selling metal footlockers fabricated from beer can sheet metal, which we use to store and somewhat secure our worldly possessions, and a plethora of shanties offering a massage, steam bath, and sex, depending on one's legal or emotional attachment to the woman left behind on the home front.

Alpha Company is billeted on the northwest quadrant of the base perimeter. The company headquarters is located in one of the lesser villas on the plantation. The rest of us live in tents. My GP Medium tent houses the company's two FO teams: my three-man artillery party containing my RTO and our reconnaissance sergeant and the 4.2-inch mortar party comprising a sergeant and his RTO. Our living conditions are relatively spacious. We sleep five in a tent designed to hold upwards of twelve. We have a plywood floor and canvas folding cots. This arrangement keeps us relatively clean and dry. We wash and shave each morning in metal pans procured in the village. Our running water system is based on our RTOs filling our five-gallon water cans. Our abode doubles as a fighting position. It is sandbagged waist-high to protect us from mortar attacks while sleeping, and there is a sandbagged bunker attached to the rear entrance. We are on the local high ground overlooking our company's defense sector. In case of an attack on our portion of the perimeter, we are to call in preplanned artillery and mortar barrages, adjust them as necessary, and hold our position against ground assault.

The surrounding terrain between us and the Cambodian border is primarily flat. It contains a mixture of pockets of rice paddy, marsh, savannah, working rubber plantation, and single, double, or triple canopy jungle. The jungle "canopies" consist of an underlayer of heavy vegetation, vines, "air plants," roots, and thick brush rising to about twelve feet. Above this are interwoven, overlapping treetop layers at about eighty and 130 feet. This type of jungle is especially nightmarish and miserable. Movement is difficult. It is a world of shadows; little sunlight filters down to the ground, and the dense vegetation limits visibility. Surprise is routine; a bad situation can be on you in the blink of an eye. Absent combat, the jungle is still host to torturers of human flesh, ranging from fire ants to mosquitoes, leeches, scorpions, giant spiders, snakes, and, reportedly, tigers. In all seasons, it is hot. But, as our veteran NCOs from Korean War winters tell us, "Cold kills. Hot just makes you wish you were dead."

CHAPTER 10

COMPANY MEN

"The mission of the infantry rifle company is to close with the enemy by means of fire and maneuver in order to destroy or capture him…"
FM 7-10, THE INFANTRY RIFLE COMPANY

The infantry rifle company is the Army's combat workhorse. It is the primary unit of action. It is organized into fire teams, squads, and platoons, from the smallest sub-unit to the largest. Each sub-unit is thoughtfully structured and equipped, informed by the Army's cumulative combat experience since World War I, to produce maximum effect on the battlefield. However, the functioning of the rifle company depends ultimately on its soldiers.

The 1st Infantry Division did not arrive in Vietnam all at once. Its 2d Brigade deployed three months ahead of the main body. Before it departed Fort Riley, Kansas, it was brought to full strength at the expense of the non-deploying units. Thus, Alpha Company, a 3d Brigade unit, comprises those who were surplus to the "pick of the litter" process in rounding out the 2d Brigade.

We are authorized 184 soldiers and have about 145 present for duty, of which about 110 are available and involved in direct combat daily.[37] The 110 men routinely present for patrol operations away from our base area include a small company headquarters and the three rifle platoons, each with about 33 of its 44 authorized soldiers. About 27 soldiers are in the weapons platoon, manning the three 81mm mortars and two 106mm recoilless rifles.

---

[37] Email exchange, June 2007, with our Company Commander (CO) Captain Ray Blanford, on our average daily personnel strength.

Finally, one wounded platoon leader who is recuperating, the company XO, and about six logistical support-type soldiers tend our housekeeping chores. The difference between 184 authorized and 145 present for duty is accounted for by soldiers on emergency leave, away for a week of rest and recuperation (R&R) leave, sick or wounded in hospital, killed in action and not yet replaced, or in "administrative" positions outside the company. Our personnel strength is about average for all rifle companies in Vietnam. We lose soldiers faster than they can be replaced. There is no dispensation for the shortfall. The attitude is "just get it done."

Who are these soldiers, and how do they come to the rifle company? Some are high school graduates; others are dropouts and victims of all the poor life strategy choices that condition connotes. It is inaccurate to generalize, but I knew these types of men in high school, and I am ashamed to admit that I snobbishly avoided them. They were not academically gifted, and few were college-bound. The men of Alpha Company descend from the boys in the vocational trades, the boys who married their childhood sweethearts, and the boys who could also have become policemen, firemen, tradesmen, and mechanics were it not for a wartime draft.

Ten years earlier, I looked down my nose at boys like these. Now, I am one of them. We have in common the only important thing—we need each other to survive. War brings one of their best facets into focus. They face danger with quiet grace, and they do so repeatedly. Anyone can face danger once, out of ignorance. To do so repeatedly, with full knowledge of the liabilities, is a different matter. The racial strife, drug abuse, and anti-war sentiment that were to rack the Army in the late 1960s and early 1970s are still well below the horizon in mid-1966. The men of Alpha are different, but not apart. Alpha is innocently obedient, unified, and well-motivated.

About half of Alpha's soldiers are draftees; the other half are volunteers. However, this statistical stratification reflects a peacetime dynamic. Men who volunteered for the infantry in 1964, a year before the buildup in Vietnam, had no forewarning that their three-year active service obligation could include combat in Vietnam. Those considering volunteering after the 1965 buildup could factor this possibility into their decision-making process. With the television networks transmitting the horrors of the Vietnam War into American living rooms, it is certain that after 1965, young men were reluctant to volunteer for the infantry. By 1969, draftees comprised 88 percent of the infantry force in Vietnam, versus about 50 percent in 1966.[38]

The drafted soldiers did not arrive in Alpha Company by accident. In July 1965, the Johnson administration allegedly issued, and eventually withdrew, the "Channeling Memo," instructing some four thousand local draft boards to give deferments to college undergraduate and postgraduate students pursuing selected courses of study. The stated purpose of this policy was to "deliver manpower to the armed services in such a manner as to reduce to a minimum any adverse effect upon the national health, safety, and interest in progress."

Unstated was the administration's belief that the death of the sons of the elites would inspire objection to the war and that draft deferments for the elites would serve to contain such complaint.[39]

A partial listing of those prominent in government and the media who were granted deferments is eye-opening. Dick Cheney, a two-term vice president, received five student deferments. The list also includes past President Bill Clinton, two other past vice presidents, three Supreme Court justices, one attorney general, two Republican mayors of New York City, eighteen members of Congress, an Assistant Secretary of Defense, and several columnists and talk show hosts. This listing supports that the Channeling Memorandum's intent was met: the nation's elites were not made to serve.

Others avoided serving in Vietnam by entering the National Guard and Reserve Components. Traditionally, the National Guard had provided a large portion of American combat power. Notwithstanding, no major Guard or Reserve forces were mobilized for Vietnam, and service in the Guard and Reserves became

---

[38] William F. Abbott Jr, "Names on the Wall: A Closer Look," *Historynet*, 06/12/2006, http://www.americanwarlibrary.com/vietnam/vwc20.htm.

[39] Edward Hasbrouck, "Channeling Memo," Draft Resistance News, Jan 1967, https://hasbrouck.org/draft/channeling.html.

a socially accepted way to avoid combat while appearing to fulfill one's obligations of citizenship.[40]

Finally, even after allowing for the social dynamics of who gets drafted, some men end up in Alpha Company the same way Fresca does. A PX supply convoy full of soft drinks leaves Saigon for a forward base camp far from civilization. Before the convoy even clears Saigon, the rear echelon troops get first pick—Coke, 7-Up, and Dr. Pepper. Every intervening headquarters takes in its preferences at each stop along the way. By the time the convoy reaches the rifle companies, all that is left is pallet upon pallet of the much-hated Fresca, some of which are so old that the cans are rusted. Now, picture a functionally similar process for a stream of infantry replacements. Anyone who looks good in uniform, can type, can write, can add and subtract rapidly and infallibly, gets picked off en route for a less dangerous staff-type job. The remainder, the human equivalent of the rusty cans of Fresca, make it to the end of the trail—the infantry rifle companies.

Despite their low perch on society's totem pole, the men of Alpha constitute a perverse exclusivity. From 1964 to 1975, three and a half million men and about eight thousand women served in the Vietnam area of operations. The men represent only 13 percent of the 27 million male Americans who (based on age alone) were eligible to serve during that period.[41] Of these, even a much smaller percentage actually served in direct combat. Again, think about a "kill chain," explained in Chapter 8—many soldiers are involved in producing the desired lethal effect. Most are "enablers," and very few are actual fighters. It has been estimated that no more than 15 percent of our strength in Vietnam were combat troops.[42] If you run the numbers, the average infantryman in Vietnam came from a cohort representing less than 2 percent of all

---

[40] David R. and Mady Wechsler Segal, "US Military's Reliance on Reserves," 2005, https://www.prb.org/wp-content/uploads/2005/12/59.4AmericanMilitary.pdf. Only about 1 percent of US Army deaths in Vietnam were suffered by the Guard/Reserve.

[41] Veterans Affairs data.

[42] Victor Davis Hanson, *Why The West Has Won* (New York: Doubleday, 2001), 416.

male Americans of military age. Contrast this with a 10 to 15 percent admittance rate to the "Ivy League" colleges, and you have a new definition of exclusivity.

Alpha Company is racially mixed, but I am unsure of the actual statistic that defines this composition. The two groups most evident to me are white and African American. My sensing is that Alpha is predominately white, certainly at least to the 85 percent mark. African Americans constituted about 12 percent of the US population during the Vietnam War era. It has been alleged that African American soldiers were statistically overrepresented in the infantry and, therefore, suffered disproportionately high casualty rates. The real question is whether or not second or third-order social or economic effects directed African Americans disproportionately into the infantry. The answer is yes, especially given the aforementioned "Channeling Memo" and the college deferment dynamic. It would seem that on a per capita basis, African American youths were less likely to be college-bound than their white counterparts. It is possible that African American families had less access to political and social influence and thus were less able to circumvent or seek relief from the draft.

Regardless of any racial inequity in Alpha's composition, discipline is purposeful and strict, especially when it comes to following orders and doing one's share. The company commander, Captain Ray Blanford, is also singularly diligent in suppressing carnal knowledge. He will have no truck with prostitution. Unfortunately, in Lai Khe, prostitution, along with laundry service, is the main industry. When I join the company at Lai Khe, I am informed that Blanford had personally applied a canoe paddle to the fanny of a prostitute found in the company area. Her "client" was consigned to toil in the company water well. One day, I see him shoveling dirt from a hole in the ground, the rim several feet above his head. In fact, I see the dirt flying up from the ground long before I ascertain the source.

Even within a rifle company, some, by virtue of the particular jobs they hold, are more likely to be killed than others. All the jobs are dangerous; some are just much more dangerous. The men who man the mortars in the weapons platoon are safe as bugs in the rug compared with the man walking point in one of the rifle platoons. The men pray for the "safer" jobs in an inherently unsafe combat formation. And they also pray for the safety of the men in the dangerous jobs, partly out of comradeship and partly out of the knowledge that if one of those men is killed or wounded, they might be selected to take his place.

The men in the infantry companies develop their own internal, unofficial "rotation" system to enhance their chances of survival. The standard tour of duty in Vietnam is twelve months. In a non-combat unit, this time drags on with a mind-numbing monotony. The men in these units probably measure their time by months to go. In the infantry, where danger is never far away, the men measure their time to go in days, maybe even hours. Typically, soldiers in our company describe their remaining time in-country as "So many days, and a wake up"—the wake up being the morning on which the journey home commences.

Thus, each infantry company creates "safe" slots that selected men rotate into after six months of combat—relatively safe jobs that promise to ensure their survival. It is not a fair system since only a few men benefit. But still, it is a necessary, symbiotic system designed to give a few men hope, providing for the increased comfort of all the others. For example, each company has a Club NCO. His job is to build, maintain, stock, and run the company club, where the soldiers drink beer and listen to country and soul music when back from patrol. These clubs begin as tents with dirt floors and often evolve into wooden, air-conditioned structures with the latest tape deck and speaker systems straight from the PX. These clubs are built, stocked, and nurtured by the wile and audacity of the Club NCO, who, in return for his newfound safety, devotes his life to the club.

Another common position is "Scrounge NCO." This man's mission in life is to procure, by hook or crook, better rations, beer, soft drinks, and building material for the company than is provided by the "official" supply system. The Scrounge and Club NCOs work together to dominate a barter-based micro-economy. The unit of exchange in this marketplace is "trading material." The small change is pallets of paint, sheets of plywood, cases of frozen lobster tails, and bottles of Johnny Walker Red and Jack Daniels Black Label. The large-denomination currency is jeeps and electrical generators declared a "combat loss" by the giving unit and "found on post" by the gaining unit. All the barter goods leak, if not hemorrhage, from the official supply system in all manner of ways, to which the adult leadership wisely looks the other way. This barter market becomes so efficient that it soon eclipses the official supply system as the means to obtain anything except substantial quantities of howitzer ammunition.

Part of who we are is what we call ourselves. By tradition, all units in the division have radio call signs beginning with the letter "D." The division is, appropriately, "Danger;" infantry battalions have names like "Defiant," "Daring," "Devour," "Dauntless," and "Dobol." Some of these call signs seem presumptuous, and others a trifle silly. At least one is sentimental; Dobol is the last name of the sergeant major of the 26th Infantry, Ted Dobol, who spent most of his adult life in that regiment. One of the artillery battalions is called "Dynamite," another, "Detonate." These seem to fit; they make sense. My parent artillery battalion is "Dungeon." That does not make sense. Our company radio call sign is "Dauntless Alpha," Dauntless signifying the 2d Battalion, 28th Infantry, and

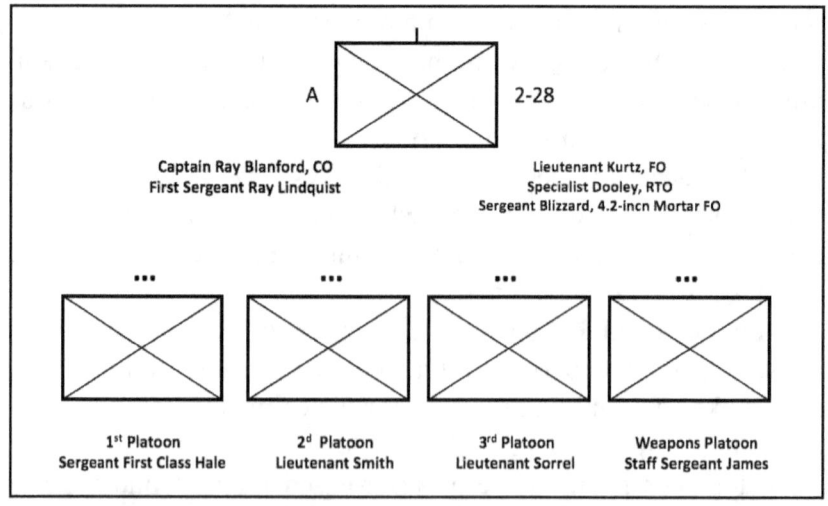

Organization of Alpha Company, 2d Battalion, 28th Infantry, early June 1966.

Alpha signifying Company A thereof. To me, dauntless indicates not the absence of fear but rather the absence of inaction due to fear. I take dauntless to stand for the ability to accomplish the mission no matter how extreme the danger. Dauntless is a good name; it balances bombast with inspiration nicely. It is something to live up to.

The culture of Alpha is distinctly non-elite, unpretentious, and working class. There are no West Pointers in its officer ranks. Blanford is a Catholic, self-made up from poverty, National Guard OCS graduate. The other two lieutenants who lead platoons are products of Army OCS at Fort Benning. Al Sorrel is an economic dropout from college: he just ran out of tuition. Elvin Smith is a previous career Army staff sergeant. The acting weapons platoon leader is a staff sergeant, and the remaining rifle platoon leader, Sergeant First Class Loyal Hale, is an American Indian, acting as the operational stand-in for his ROTC lieutenant recovering from a friendly fire wound and not available for combat duties.

One incident exemplifies the fundamental charter of the company's officers: Sorrel, Smith, and I are having a beer one night at the battalion officers' club, located in one of the plantation's former homes. A West Point platoon leader from Bravo Company stops by to say hello, telling us, officiously and dramatically, that he has to rush off to take out a night patrol. After he departs, Sorrel and Smith break out laughing derisively. They tell me that they had heard his actual "patrol" was no more than a sweep of Lai Khe village for soldiers breaking curfew. His mission is totally within the base perimeter. I understand instantly what he did to earn their rebuke and what I must be sure never to do in Alpha. I, indeed, had lied in my lifetime. Some were whoppers, and some were deceitful, but I had not lied about combat. The lieutenant could have claimed that one of the Red Cross "Donut Dollies" had just fucked his eyes out in the back room, and we would have laughed skeptically. But to Alpha's combat veteran lieutenants, his "night patrol" statement was not a fib but a breach of honor.

The incident serves as a cautionary moment for me. In Alpha, authenticity is paramount. Your pedigree and past credentials count for little. Alpha is a meritocracy. You will be known for what you do and judged by how well you do it and how you behave. Alpha is the CCNY of combat. I am comfortable here. If I pay attention, Alpha will make me a good soldier.

While I drink with the officers, I am an unknown quantity to the enlisted men, but they make me welcome. Artillery is a lifesaver in a tough fight. The enemy knows the jungle better than we do. He can surprise us. Artillery is our equalizer. The soldiers expect me to produce it when needed, no matter what. All I exist for is to produce artillery support. I am an instrument of the company's survival in combat. They get that point across without ever saying as much. The soldiers give me that look that says, "You are going to take care of us, aren't you?" It is not so much a question as it is an imperative.

My religion comes up only once, in an almost comical fashion. I am stacking sandbags around our tent, wearing my tee shirt as my outer garment. I receive word that I am wanted at the company command post (CP). I put on my helmet, grab my M-16, and run up the trail. En route, I encounter the company XO, the senior lieutenant and second in command. I had known him briefly in Germany; we attended a training course together. We talk a bit about old times. All the while, he stares at my dog tag chain, from which my mezuzah[43] also hangs. Finally, he blurts it out, "I didn't know you were a Jew." "Jewish," I say, "I am Jewish." He looks perplexed. He must be thinking, What? He is a *Jewish* Jew? What is that? I explain to him that the word Jew is too strident, too edgy. It could be interpreted as derogatory. I tell him that Jewish is the more appropriate term. In a matter-of-fact tone, he replies, "OK, nobody ever told me that before."

On 2 June, I am told to pack in preparation for a long mission. We will not be returning to Lai Khe for quite a while. Initially,

---

[43] Mezuzah is Hebrew for "door post." Religious Jews affix a small cylindrical container, called a mezuzah, to the door posts of their homes. The mezuzah contains a roll of parchment on which is inscribed the prayer, "Shema Yisrael," which begins: "Hear O Israel the Lord our God, The Lord is One." The mezuzah brings good luck and happiness to those who dwell within the door posts to which it is affixed. Smaller, silver metallic versions of the mezuzah are also worn around the neck, both for good luck and to exhibit a sense of Jewish identity.

I have no idea why, and do not care. I focus on the immediate packing problems that confront me. I sift through my possessions, deciding what is to be left behind in storage in the company supply room. More pressingly, I have to fit several changes of underwear and socks into a small "butt pack" and leave room for my shaving kit.

Having accomplished all this, the FO parties and I move by truck to the Lai Khe airstrip. There Blanford briefs us on the mission—*Division intelligence indicates that Viet Cong and North Vietnamese forces are poised to resume their "Monsoon Campaign" by attacking Government of Vietnam and US Special Forces compounds along Route 13. The Commanding General, II Field Force, has directed that one infantry and one artillery battalion of the 1st Infantry Division, be sent to Loc Ninh to strengthen its defenses. The mission is named Operation El Paso II.*

Alpha Company is part of that "one infantry battalion." We then load onto C-130 transport aircraft and fly to Loc Ninh. I am childishly excited. I feel like I am embarking on a great adventure, a combat version of the college "Road Trip." Some men seated near me in the aircraft have a more neutral countenance. This is not the first time they have been told to pack.

CHAPTER 11

LOC NINH

"You are not going to die in the fucking jungle…"
APOCRYPHAL WAR STORY

Loc Ninh and its namesake rubber plantation are located seventy miles north of Saigon and seven miles, by winding road, south of the Cambodian border. Loc Ninh is the District capital, a function similar to a United States county seat. Size-wise, its population of ten thousand places it somewhere between a large town and a small city. It has inherent political value as the local seat of government and strategic value as a transportation hub. It sits astride Highway 13 and an unused rail line linking Binh Long Province, in which it is located, to Saigon. It contains a large, all-weather airfield that can accommodate four-engine C-130 aircraft. During World War II, it served as a Japanese fighter base. The plantation covers about thirty square miles and is a subdivision of the extensive *Societe des Caoutchoucs d'Extreme-Orient* rubber plantation complex. Loc Ninh is at its southern end, and the plantation runs northward within four miles of the Cambodian border. Its green rubber trees contrast sharply with the red laterite earth, *la terre rouge*, as the French describe it. The plantation buildings, with their red tile roofs and swimming pools, hark back to a genteel, 1920-ish French colonial lifestyle. Dispersed around the periphery of the tracts of rubber are several villages in which the resident workers reside. Absent war, the plantation looks like it could be provincially peaceful.

Our living conditions at Loc Ninh are more rustic than at Lai Khe. We sleep on the ground on air mattresses and use a light

CHAPTER 11—LOC NINH

A C-130 aircraft landing at Loc Ninh airfield. The Special Forces and CIDG camp are at the southwest end of the airfield. The elevated terrain mass in the background is the Hill 150 area. Photo from the Texas Tech University Vietnam Archives.

nylon comforter, called a poncho liner, for warmth. My protective (gas) mask serves as my pillow. We sleep with our boots on and weapons by our sides. To keep ourselves dry, we use our theoretically waterproof ponchos to rig lean-to-type shelters, which almost protect us from light rain. When not on night patrol or ambush duty, I am down for the night by 2100. If we have a patrol out that night, I keep the radio on, headset by my ear, in case they call for artillery support. Regardless, I have preplanned artillery fires, known as Harassing and Interdiction (H&I), going on most of the night at places where the enemy might pass or congregate. Sleep is accomplished in spurts, but I get used to it.

It is hot and humid. We patrol the woods heavily loaded down with gear. We are pack mules on two legs. Most of the load is weapons and ammunition; then, in descending order, come water, radios, extra batteries for the radios, canned C-rations, and finally, our "personal" items—razor, toothbrush, dry socks, a change of underwear, poncho, air mattress, and poncho liner. Newly joined soldiers are continually passing out from heat exertion. I drop twenty pounds in less than a month.

Then, there are the scorpions, giant spiders, and leeches. It is hard to keep clean. I shave and bathe out of my helmet. I have a lingering fungus infection in my groin. Sometimes, I think that being wounded wouldn't be so bad. It would get me a few days' rest in a hospital, hot meals, and a shower. It is, in retrospect, a bad idea. However, it had momentary merit.

Bathroom facilities are spartan but hygienically correct. We have one latrine, consisting of a large wooden box with two places cut into the hinged top—a "two-holer." Inside the box, under the holes, are cut down fifty-five-gallon drums to contain the waste. These are periodically "flushed" by incineration with diesel fuel.

Our weapons platoon's 81mm mortar section functions as the general contractor for latrine construction. Perhaps it is because most available wood comes from their ammunition boxes. In the combat units, wood, especially plywood, is one of the more valuable coins of the realm. In return for their labor, they use the latrine drums to hold the unused mortar propellant bags, which are eventually destroyed when the drums are burned. The propellant bags contain a kind of black powder—it will detonate if hit by a shock wave from a primer, but only flash burn, like a flare or sparkler, when lit. Naturally, one must be careful not to throw lit cigarettes down the holes when *reading*. Crude, hand-painted signs are strategically placed in the latrines to remind us of that. Not having yet fully outgrown our childhood ways, we pray for the fool who cannot read or will not heed, but no one's rear end is ever set aflame.

The urinals are empty fiberglass tubes that formerly held 81mm mortar rounds. The ends are cut off; the tubes are then dug into the ground at a forty-five-degree angle and topped off with a mesh screen to keep out the flies. A makeshift, waist-high canvas privacy screen surrounds the whole facility. Despite all this effort, most of us go in the woods and cover our "tracks" with an entrenching tool. We hardly ever shower. When we do, it is like this: you stand on a wood shipping pallet and pour water from a five-gallon can over your head, if you are strong enough to lift it yourself. If not, someone has to do that for you. You soap up and rinse off. You could stay clean for an hour or so. Then you might tumble in the mud, get splashed by a passing jeep, pelted by a hovering helicopter, or get a bad case of the "runs," especially after downing the monthly anti-malarial prophylactic pill.

One day we encounter indoor plumbing. Our patrol mission takes us to the home of the Frenchman who nominally manages the rubber plantation. He is gone. As I will relate later, he is not our friend. We do not like him. We encourage his house staff to take the day off and make his mini-mansion our CP. There is a swimming pool in the backyard. The water is slightly turbid; he has not had many pool parties since we arrived at Loc Ninh. Our more rambunctious soldiers toss in a few fragmentation grenades to kill snakes or other life forms that may be in residence. Then we all take turns jumping in, soaping up, cleaning off, and concurrently doing our laundry. Later, we discover the bidet. Having just come from Germany, I am proud to explain its intended use. Then I suggest how we males might avail ourselves as well. We pretty much trash the rest of the house. We punch a hole in the tile roof to accommodate an RC 292 radio antenna. Our M-60 machine gun crew hacks out some of the wooden balusters from the porch of the master bedroom to give them a clear field of fire. The CO and I sleep on his oversized bed with our boots on. The manager later submits a property damage claim to our battalion commander. It arrives just after the fight for Hill 150. Nobody is in the mood for trivialities; the paperwork keeps getting lost.

First Sergeant Lindquist wakes us at 0430 each morning to prepare for the 0500 "Stand-To," when all soldiers have to be in their positions, weapons and radios manned, in case of a dawn enemy attack. Then we shave and have a C-ration breakfast. I usually have canned fruit and cheese and crackers. If there is time, I boil water for powdered cocoa. Then, we depart on patrol. We eat lunch on the march. I usually have a can or two of fruit cocktail or applesauce. A fair amount of our lives revolves around the C-ration, most of which were manufactured (and I think I am using that word precisely) during World War II. It's all pretty bad; some are not as bad as the rest. Spiced Beef with Potatoes is OK, if doused with enough Tabasco sauce; Ham and Lima Beans is not—nothing can be done to make it palatable. Beans and Franks are OK; Tuna and Noodles are not—the name says all there is to know about this little item. Chopped Eggs and Ham are the best of all the meat items, hot or cold. All the canned fruit is good; the syrup has enough sugar to double as an amphetamine. The square crackers are hard, but the cheese spread tastes just fine. The peanut butter and grape jelly are OK; the chocolate disks are not—they could double for hockey pucks. No one smokes the unfiltered Chesterfields and Camels. They are relics from World War II; we give them to our South Vietnamese auxiliaries.

The meals come in a cardboard box, twelve to a container. Each of the twelve "menus" is a fixed apportionment of a meat item, fruit, cake, cheese, crackers, etc. We are free to trade back and forth with each other, like a Chinese menu, one of this from that box, and one of those from another. This process is democratic and utilitarian, since we have to carry what we eat, and no one wants to carry what he will not eat. We usually have the meat item cold. Occasionally, we heat them by punching a hole in the top of the can, placing it in the cardboard carrying box, and setting it afire. If you are lucky, the can will vent from the hole in its top cover and not explode, and a portion of the contents will be somewhat warm.

Every soldier has their way of carrying their gear and ammunition. Some use the standard-issue butt packs and web gear; some use all the pockets on their uniforms. The more senior soldiers carry their own private arms or whatever suits them. Blanford has an Army-issue Remington pump-action shotgun. He is the only company commander in the battalion thusly armed. Accordingly, his unofficial radio call sign is "Shotgun 6"— "6" being the universal radio designator for a unit commander. I have an Army-issue M-16 and a pre-World War I 9mm Parabellum Lugar that I brought with me from Germany. It is old, and the bluing is worn off. It rusts quickly, and the intricate toggle mechanism seems too prone to failure. I eventually trade it in for the standard-issue Colt 45. No two soldiers in the company look exactly the same; we are in uniform, but we are not uniform. No one of authority has the heart to hassle the men who do the real dirty work of war. The soldiers appreciate this. It is part of "the deal." They fight, and "higher" doesn't screw with them over the small stuff. Going from Lai Khe to Loc Ninh is like backsliding on the timescale of civilization from the Bronze Age to the Stone Age.

We conduct almost daily company-size patrols. These patrols aim to gain an appreciation for the surrounding terrain, provide security by the early detection and engagement of enemy forces in our vicinity, and locate and engage local and main force VC units. An additional, non-doctrinal purpose is to keep the soldiers on their toes, enable them to hone their martial skills, and prevent boredom. In my case, these patrols are the only school I get to prepare me for combat.

As the company FO, I become an instrument for measuring the war's strategic progress. The Vietnam War is peculiar. It defies an easy understanding of the big picture. We are not fighting to take and hold land or to liberate an area by ejecting an oppressive occupying power. Progress is not visualized or measured on a map, as it was in World War II, where we could map our progress as we liberated North Africa, Sicily, Italy, and France, and fought our way across the Pacific to gain and hold island bases and liberate the Philippines. The Korean War was not as clear-cut. Neither our own security nor Western civilization was directly threatened. Regardless, any schoolboy could look at a news map of the peninsula and tell who was winning by virtue of where our forces were located relative to the 38th parallel, which divided Korea in two. Indochina is also peninsula-like and divided in the middle by the 17th parallel. But there, the similarity ends. This war is fluid. We try to destroy the enemy whenever and wherever we find him— or he finds us. The only territories we hold permanently are the larger cities and the small parcels in the country upon which we build our bases and keep house. In combat, we take a hill one day and usually give it up shortly thereafter. Absent ground permanently gained and posted to a map, "the body count," dead VC, becomes the war's central metric of progress.

Sometimes this all-important count is based on actual inventory, deliberate fabrication, or innocent stupidity. I am adjusting artillery fire on suspected enemy locations on one of my early training patrols. This technique is known as "reconnaissance by fire." The last element of the call for fire protocol, the fire mission, is for the FO to "send surveillance," an assessment of the results. Since all we can see for results are smoking holes in the ground and blasted treetops, I have no meaningful "surveillance" to send. Dooley informs me that it is usual practice to send positive feedback to the FDC in the form of "estimated" casualties in the absence of hard evidence. This estimate can be based on judgment and nebulous forensic evidence, such as blood spots or drag marks, indicating that the surviving enemy had dragged off the dead ones. This estimated surveillance aims to make the artillerymen feel important to the success of our mission and encourage their continued support.

That idea seems childish, presaging the "self-esteem" movement that will invade our school systems two or three decades hence. Nonetheless, I throw the dog a bone. After that, I send reports estimating two to three VC killed each time the artillery fires for us. We never find a single body or supporting forensics, but I keep sending surveillance "treats" to the hard-working gunners. I figure if a bit of praise is good, more is better. I am not trying to deceive the American public by deceitfully inflating the enemy casualty count. I am telling little white lies to keep up the artillerymen's morale. I am happy making people happy.

I spread happiness all morning. Finally, the artillery fire direction officer (FDO), who runs the FDC, radios me to summarize that thus far, I have cumulatively reported over fifty VC killed and inquires if I see any end in sight to my future *estimates*. Immediately, I realize that I have reported more VC killed than there were ever alive anywhere in our vicinity. Presumably, I have killed some of this enemy overabundance more than once. I am embarrassed but must give the FDO credit for tact. His slightly inflected sentence serves to convey, politely enough, the fundamental question that must be poised on the lips of all personnel in the FDC, "Hey, fucking new lieutenant, have you totally lost your fucking mind?"

We usually arrive back from our daily patrols in the late afternoon. Blanford and I then repair to battalion headquarters and debrief the operations officer on what we did or did not find and receive the order for the following day. We then get a hot supper from the battalion mess section to which our company cooks are assigned. The challenge is to get the meal down before the resupply helicopters arrive. The downwash from their blades blows dust and grit all over the only decent meal of the day. The grit does not show up on the gray-brown "Salisbury steak," but there is no ignoring it when it "peppers" the powdered instant mashed potatoes. Our nightly resupply helicopter, shepherded by the company XO, brings our mail, clean uniforms, new boots, and whatever new replacements might be assigned to us. When the helicopter departs, it takes our outgoing mail and soldiers who are to rotate home or depart for leave.

Within Loc Ninh base, the rifle companies are dug in to form a perimeter around the airstrip. I spend my "spare" time walking our portion of the perimeter so I can associate our defensive positions on the ground and mark them on my map. I need to be sure of our locations and where we tie in with our adjacent rifle companies so I can safely call for close-in artillery fire if we are attacked. The soldiers have two-man fighting positions spaced about ten meters apart. Each platoon also sends out a "listening post" at night—usually two to three soldiers fifty to 100 meters in front of our main defensive positions to listen for approaching enemy and engage them early with fire. I need to know *exactly* where these listening posts are located each night. If we are attacked, they will need artillery cover to help them return safely to our main line of defense. The company CP is in the center and to the rear of the platoon fighting positions. It is a big hole in the ground with a log and sandbag roof. There are chest-high vision and firing ports on three sides and a chicken wire screen in front to deflect or cause the early detonation of incoming hand and rocket-propelled grenades (RPG). We have extra grenades, ammunition, radio batteries, and a small switchboard connecting us

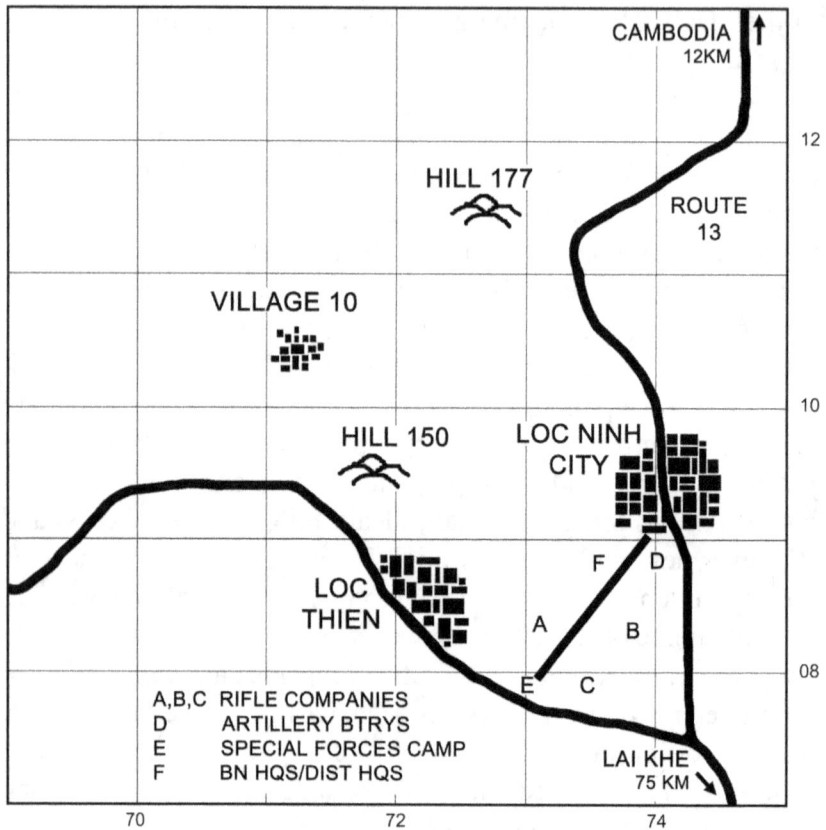

Location of units and facilities at Loc Ninh. By Amy Moore.

by field phone to our platoons and battalion headquarters. This bunker is home to Blanford, First Sergeant Lindquist, me, the battalion heavy mortar (4.2-inch) FO, and our RTOs. From here, we will conduct the last stand if the outer perimeter is penetrated. It is our Alamo.

The second night at Loc Ninh, the VC welcome us with an 82mm mortar attack. I awaken to the sound of mortar rounds going off in the treetops, just northeast of our positions, in the direction of battalion headquarters. It takes a second for my brain to integrate these acoustic inputs, and by then my RTO and I are at the CP bunker, which is still under construction. Blanford and First Sergeant Lindquist are not there. The radio guard informs us that they were bored and, taking the mortar platoon sergeant

CHAPTER 11—LOC NINH

along, went on a "boys' night out" patrol, about an hour before the mortar attack commenced. They eventually return, breathless, having run back through our lines, obviously no longer bored. While out, they heard the VC crews setting up their mortars. They knew where the enemy was located. Unfortunately, their radio had a dead battery and carried no spares. They knew but could not report. Thus, they could do nothing until they returned to our lines. Luckily, our outposts did not kill them as they worked their way back in, screaming at the tops of their lungs that they are friends and not to shoot.

I listen to the sounds of the attack. I can actually hear the VC mortar rounds going down the tube, the dull "thunk" as they compress the air in the tube and strike bottom, the "woof" type sound as the igniter charges and propellant bags detonate and the round leaves the tube, and finally the loud "crack" as they detonate in the treetops, showering the ground with fragmentation.

Blanford sets our own mortars to work on the suspected VC position. Now I hear everything in surround sound: our rounds and theirs going down the tubes, thunking out, and crumping and cracking when they strike at the terminus of their trajectories. I radio in a fire mission to the FDC, telling them it is a confirmed, 100 percent accurate, VC mortar location. The FDO tells me the target location is too close, under the howitzers' minimum range. If I could have seen the future, I would have recognized this as the prologue to the fight for Hill 150. Instead, our artillery and the battalion heavy mortars fire at probable enemy routes of egress, further out from our perimeter, while our own 81mm mortar section fires on the VC position as reported by Blanford.

The whole affair goes on for less than forty-five minutes. In the morning we run a patrol and find the VC firing position. We can see where they had broken through a wooden fence to reach a small clear area, less than 200 meters from our perimeter. We can see the indentations in the ground resulting from settling the base plates of their 82mm mortars. We find fifteen unused mortar rounds that they were not able to fire. Best of all, we find tail fins from our own 81mm mortars stuck in the ground. We were right on target. It is comforting for me to realize that Blanford is competent. He knows how to conduct war. A short distance away, we find empty antibiotic packets and injector vials in the front yard of the French plantation manager's residence. The VC mortar crews treated their wounded there as they withdrew. The Frenchman tells us it is medicine for his dogs. We all know he is lying. We know he has cut a "live and let live" deal with the VC.

There is an ironic coda to this tale. The "buzz" in the company is that the battalion reconnaissance platoon was wiped out in the mortar attack. The story is that they were all killed asleep, above ground. They had returned late from patrol and opted not to dig slit trenches before lying down to rest. The tree-burst mortar fragmentation wreaked havoc on their exposed bodies. This incident makes a big impression on me. A few months later, as a battery commander, I insist on digging in, no matter how tired the soldiers are or how late the hour. One night, one of my senior sergeants asks me for an exception; he says the men are too tired to dig. He begs my indulgence. I tell him the story of the recon platoon dead at Loc Ninh. Later that night, while making the rounds of our perimeter, I hear him telling his soldiers, "Shut the fuck up and dig; better tired than dead." In the ensuing years of my army career, I tell that story over and over, to good effect, playing a militarized "Mr. Wizard," explaining to Jimmy how bad things happen to people who yield to fatigue. The story portrays two valuable teaching points: there are no tired soldiers, just tired leaders, and no matter how tired you are now, you can sleep when the ordeal is over.

The trouble with the story is that it did not happen. It was a rumor, a combat urban legend, right up there with a colony of alligators living in the Manhattan sewer system as the offspring of a pet flushed down a toilet in the Bronx. While gathering background for this book, I talk and e-mail with a former member of the recon platoon. I ask him about that night. He replies that he doesn't know what I am talking about.

Notwithstanding the hardships and occasional danger, the rubber plantation country is relatively more pleasant than the surrounding jungle. This otherwise meaningless distinction brings to mind the apocryphal tale of a young soldier who, cracking under the pressure of relentless patrols, screams out that he doesn't want to die in some fucking jungle, far, far from home. His squad leader grabs him by his lapels and shouts back into his face, "Look around you, you fucking idiot. You are not going to die in the fucking *jungle*; we're in a fucking *rubber plantation.*"

CHAPTER 12

THE CAPTAIN

"A brave captain is as a root out of which, as branches, the courage of his soldiers doth spring."
SIR PHILIP SIDNEY, ELIZABETHAN POET COURTIER, AND SOLDIER (1554-86)

I am by nature not inclined to charity when describing other men, especially those who exercise authority over me. Furthermore, I judge others with the acerbic skills of the skeptic armed with the full catalog of human shortcomings. I knew Captain Blanford relatively briefly, under very narrowly defined conditions. But those conditions existed in the crucible of combat and danger, and I liked what I saw.

Blanford was the captain of 184 soldiers. He was responsible for their lives, safety, and combat performance. Blanford was good at these things. As the artillery FO, I was technically an outsider, not in the infantry chain of command. Soldiers spoke freely in my presence. They grumbled and complained about all manner of issues, save one: they never expressed a complaint about the company leadership. No one worries about being needlessly killed or injured in Alpha due to the leadership's stupidity or incompetence.

Captain Raymond Blanford. Official US Army photo.

CHAPTER 12—THE CAPTAIN

Raymond Blanford began the journey to Hill 150 from Mishawaka, Indiana. He was born there on 5 August 1934, the fourth child of five. The population of Mishawaka is today under 50,000. It is a small town along the Saint Joseph River in north-central Indiana, between South Bend and Elkhart, just south of Michigan. By today's standards, Blanford was not born to privilege. He struggled through Catholic grade school at the mercy of the Sisters, who did not spare the rod. Due to academics, he did not graduate. Along the way, his father succumbed to a heart attack. At sixteen, he followed an older brother into the Indiana National Guard. Blanford went to work cutting rubber for car seats while pondering whether or not to attend summer school to earn his high school diploma. He did not say as much, but for him to have decided to enlist in the Army during the Korean War and to volunteer for paratroop training speaks volumes of the comparative opportunities life offered in Mishawaka. His thought process is summarized as follows:

My friend had gotten into a fight with his father and was going to run off and join the Army. I told him to wait a few weeks, and I would go with him. Even though the Korean War was going full blast, it did not cross our minds. My father had died three or four years before, and my mother did not need an 18-year-old around to worry about. My friend and I were sent to Indianapolis for our induction physicals. It was there that we saw our first burlesque show.

Blanford acquired his relaxed but no-nonsense leadership style by coming up and down through the ranks. He enlisted in 1952 as a private and was discharged three years later in the same grade. This was not a trivial accomplishment. He had to work hard at it. He served as a paratrooper in airborne units in the United States and Japan, learning from the best how to misbehave with panache and pay for it dearly. Here is but one example, again in his own words:

I was assigned to the 187th Regimental Combat Team at Camp Chickamauga, Kyushu, Japan. I was in the weapons platoon, in the 57mm recoilless rifle section. I was promoted to buck sergeant and took over the section. When we were in the field, training, one of my guys came up to me and asked to borrow five dollars so he could sneak into town with his buddies. I looked in my wallet. I had nothing smaller than a ten-dollar bill, so I went with them. A month later, I was a private again after being busted for three hours AWOL.

Serving as a paratrooper overseas in the exotic Far East, enjoying the nightlife in postwar Tokyo had to be a major event for a small-town boy. More importantly, his service as an enlisted man taught Blanford how soldiers think or, more accurately, how they do not. He knew from personal experience all of their tricks, excuses, needs, fears, and aspirations. I think this made him exceptionally well-qualified to lead men in combat. Living in open bay barracks with junior sergeants in residence, he knew an army life akin to the character-shaping pre-World War II barracks' life that James Jones portrays in *From Here to Eternity*. Whatever his childhood struggles with academics, in this formative environment, Blanford developed and honed what we today call social intelligence. He learned to read people and how to influence them. He could make people like him and, at the same time, respect him.

Blanford, left, as an enlisted paratrooper in Japan, off duty at a local club. From Ray Blanford personal collection.

After his discharge in 1955, he followed his brother into officer candidate school in the National Guard and was commissioned a second lieutenant of infantry. After completing officer training, Blanford settled into civilian life, married, and worked with the Bendix Corporation, attending to punch cards and their reading machines. He soon realized he would shuffle those punch cards for the rest of his life unless he went to college. At Fort Benning, Georgia, Blanford had earned his high school diploma equivalency. With this hurdle cleared, he used his GI Bill to earn a BS in Business Administration at Indiana University in Bloomington. It was not easy. In addition to the meager GI Bill benefits, he held two part-time jobs, became the father of his first two children, and, in his typical, no-nonsense manner, earned his degree in two years and nine months.

Blanford then applied to return to the Army in active-duty status. The Berlin Wall and the Cuban Missile Crisis of 1961 and 1962 placed increased demands on the military. In 1963, Lieutenant Blanford was accepted for active duty and assigned to the 1st Infantry Division at Fort Riley, Kansas. His wife, with three children all younger than five years, joined him. But the Army had its own plans. He was sent with his battle group to Germany on temporary duty to show the flag in a generalized response to heightened tensions due to the Berlin Wall Crisis. His family was allowed to accompany him.

His battle group was supposed to spend three months training at the notoriously austere and cold Wildflecken Training Area and then three months of comparatively plush duty in Berlin. Wildflecken is located in the center of the Fulda Gap, close to the Cold-War Inner German Border, separating West and East Germany, along one of the fabled Warsaw Pact invasion routes. It served as a training base for the German Army from 1936 to 1945. It was then a displaced persons (DP) camp for Polish refugees until 1951, when it reverted to US Army control as a training area. There is nothing particularly nice about Wildflecken. The name suggests as much: *wild* means wild in German, and *flecken* means place or small town. Soldiers stationed permanently in Germany might spend two to three weeks a year there or at the other two training areas, Grafenwoer and Hohenfels. A standard two- or three-year tour would amount to nine weeks at one of these training areas. As luck would have it, his unit spent eight months at Wildflecken and no time in Berlin.

Upon promotion to captain, Blanford returned to Fort Riley and commanded a special processing company. In 1965 he was transferred to the 2d Battalion 28th Infantry preparing for deployment to Vietnam. Blanford joined the battalion late in the game. He was thus an "outsider." The serving battalion commander did not make it easy for him. Blanford was neither fish nor fowl. He was not West Point, ROTC, or traditional Army OCS. There must have been some snobbery. But maybe this is all my baggage. Blanford told me that none of this bothered him; it is one of his strengths.

He was assigned to the only vacancy in the unit as the battalion intelligence officer, the S-2, a low-visibility, no-glory position. It was, at best, a holding pattern for eventual assignment to higher prestige positions within the battalion. Blanford made the best of it and applied himself to the difficult and often thankless job of obtaining information on the elusive enemy. As he tells it, his efforts went either unnoticed or unappreciated. He nonetheless persevered. Eventually, a new battalion commander gave him Alpha Company.

The previous company commander had been a bit of a glory hound, wont to further his own career and curry favor with the ever-present press. He played favorites with his officers. The whole company knew who was in and who was out. Blanford made changes. All platoon leaders were treated the same. All platoons had to rise to an acceptable level of performance. There were no more laggards, and there were no more star performers. Everyone carried the load. Blanford turned the company into a meritocracy.

I believe one reason I thrived in Alpha was because of this atmosphere. There were no insiders and outsiders; there were only performers and non-performers. The soldiers may have lacked the benefits of higher education, but they were not stupid. I am sure they noticed from the outset that Captain Blanford was all about hard work and making them as good as they could be for the intended purpose of the rifle company—to fight well and survive.

CHAPTER 12—THE CAPTAIN

The S-3, Major Jim Rabdau, the battalion operations officer, initially rated Blanford as a solid, laid-back, but competent commander. When the battalion deployed on an operation, it usually moved through the jungle in a column of companies. The order of march was Bravo Company in the lead, followed by Alpha and then Charlie. This is reflected in how Rabdau rated the companies and their commanders: the best upfront, closest to the expected danger point, and the lesser commanders to the rear, where it would presumably be less dangerous. The companies also moved in a column of three rifle platoons. Again, Rabdau rated the company commanders based on where they positioned themselves. The Bravo commander was way up front. Blanford was behind his lead platoon. The Charlie commander was in front of his third platoon. This was an overly simplistic rating scheme. Being too far upfront could limit a commander's ability to see the fight clearly and issue meaningful orders to his platoons. A company commander in the thick of the opening moments of a developing firefight, using his nose as a shovel to keep himself as close to the ground and as small a target as possible, might be unable to think clearly, analyze the fight, and make appropriate decisions. I think Blanford had it right: up with the lead platoon, close to the action, but not so close as to become no more intellectually effective than a PFC rifleman fighting for his life.

When we arrived in Loc Ninh, Rabdau had "promoted" Blanford to his best company commander. The Bravo commander had been killed in a friendly fire incident, leaving Ray Blanford the most seasoned and combat-reliable of the three rifle company COs. Rabdau later confirms this by stating, years later, "I assigned Alpha Company to cover the west side of the airstrip since it was the most vulnerable (portion of the battalion perimeter)."

My first impressions of Blanford as a company commander were good. He knew what he was doing and exuded a sense of calm. He was older than the average company commander and probably a lot wiser. On one of our first patrols, we were searching a nearby village, and several of us gorged ourselves with bananas from the village grove. As we marched past the village, Blanford noticed us snacking away. He asked if we had paid for our bananas. Our

Blanford (middle) as Alpha Company Commander, Zeedyk (left) as Company XO, Vietnam, 1966. From Ray Blanford personal collection.

mouths stuffed, we shook our heads, "No." Blanford took some money from his wallet and sent a soldier back to reimburse whomever for the produce. We all got the message—Thou shall not steal from the villagers, no matter how inconsequential it might seem. The incident left me with a favorable impression of Blanford as a good man, as well as a good soldier.

In retrospect, I think one of the reasons I liked Blanford was because I saw myself in him. We both had traded our lives to the Army in return for the opportunity to advance ourselves through hard work and service to our nation. I saw an older, wiser, braver, Catholic version of myself in Blanford. He was good at war, and I was trying to be.

CHAPTER 13

AND GOD LAUGHS

Man plans—and God laughs.
GERMAN IDIOM

It is Saturday morning, 11 June 1966. "Back in the world," the soldiers' term for the United States, "Paint it Black" by the Rolling Stones is in the top position on the pop charts. "Monday, Monday" by The Mamas & The Papas has slipped to number seven, and "I am a Rock" by Simon & Garfunkel, peaks at number three. In Loc Ninh, unpredicted fog covers the airstrip. The men of Alpha Company are waiting. They smoke, joke, banter, and try not to worry. The only radios in play are the tactical PRC-25s. What comes out is not music. Instead, we hear the first reports of casualties and continued delay in the air assault phase of the operation. It is not yet 0800, but already our day is not going well.

The night before, Blanford and I had walked to the battalion CP to debrief Rabdau and receive our orders for the following day. I was slightly uncomfortable at the prospect. Rabdau is aggressive, cold, and sarcastic. He is not a man to be trifled with. A few days previous, before we were due to turn in for a few hours' sleep, he called Blanford on the radio to inform him that there was a break in our field phone connection to the battalion CP. He wanted Blanford to send out a wire team immediately to find and repair the break. Blanford demurred, citing the late hour. He said he would do it "First thing in the morning." Rabdau replied. "Fine. Send me a runner (a soldier from our company to sit by the battalion CP and "run" verbal or written messages back and forth) in the meantime." Blanford got the break repaired since this would have been a bigger imposition than sending out a wire team.

When we arrived, Rabdau stood before a large map mounted on an easel. I did my utmost not to bring myself to his attention. This was mostly a waste of effort. He talked past me as if I were not there. He explained our next mission. We were to search Village Number 10 and clear it of local VC. He briefed the concept for two of our platoons to proceed by foot from our perimeter at the airstrip and establish blocking positions east and south of the village complex. Our remaining platoon, plus a platoon of Vietnamese mercenaries, would be moved by helicopter to a landing zone (LZ) northwest of the village, move southeast, and search and clear the village of VC. He estimated that the complex should have no more than ten local VC or VC sympathizers. The operation would commence at 0600 and should conclude by the early afternoon. Charlie Company is designated to be prepared to reinforce us on five minutes' notice. Bravo Company is on twenty minutes' notice.

He handed Blanford a copy of the plan in the form of a tracing paper "overlay order" that depicts our routes, objective, and map reference points for reporting purposes. Rabdau asked if we had any questions and then sent us on our way.

I smiled to myself as we walked back to the company area. We were returning to where I had so ineffectively flirted with the village schoolteacher a week or so earlier. This would be an opportunity to redeem myself. I made a mental note to act more adult-like when I saw her again. Maybe then she would see me in a better light if I did not appear so eager to be noticed.

Now, the heavy fog has us off schedule. Due to poor ground visibility, the foot platoons, led by Smith and Hale, do not depart the perimeter until 0715, one hour and fifteen minutes past the time specified in the order. The helicopter assault, which was scheduled to commence at 0630, is postponed until minimum visibility standards are met to support aviation operations.

I pass the time by talking with the interpreter for the Vietnamese mercenary platoon based at the Special Forces camp at the south end of the airstrip. They are known as the Civilian Irregular Defense

CHAPTER 13—AND GOD LAUGHS

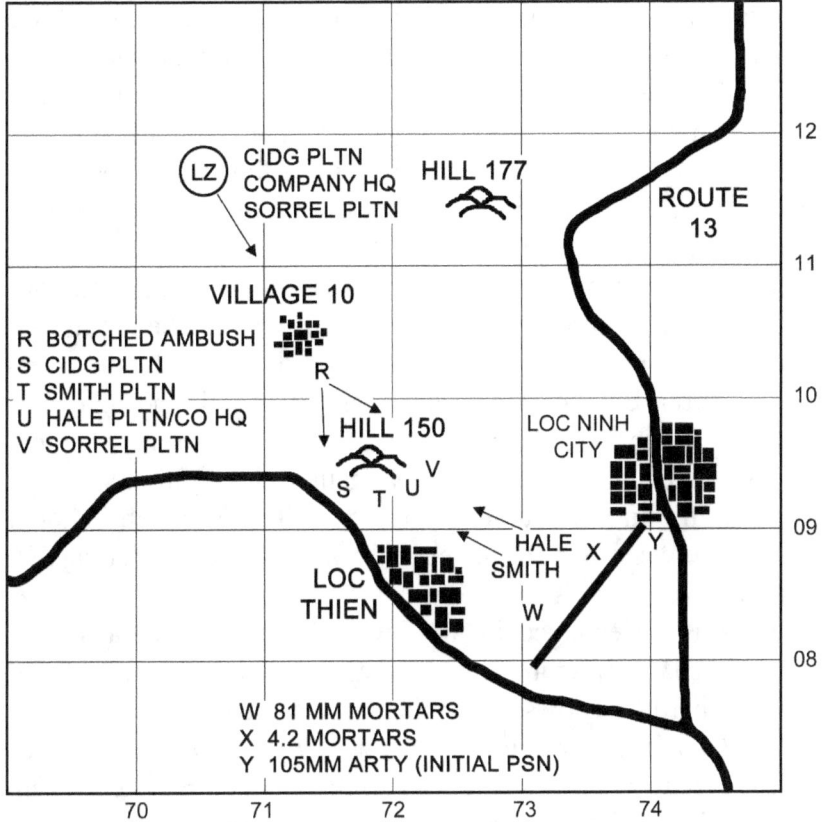

Group (CIDG). The CIA initially employed them to watch over key border areas for North Vietnamese infiltration. Later, our Special Forces became their paymasters. They are an exotic curiosity. The rumor is that they are part ethnic Chinese, known as Nungs, descended from the remnants of Chiang Kai-Shek's Kuomintang forces that crossed the border into Vietnam in 1949 to escape integration into the Chinese Communist Army. They are alleged to incline to banditry, smuggling, and the drug trade, when not otherwise hired out as fighters. They look like characters straight out of *Terry and the Pirates*. They smoke strong Vietnamese cigarettes or unfiltered Chesterfields and Camels from our C-ration packets. They are armed with an odd assortment of World War II vintage weapons: Thompson submachine guns, BARs, and M-1 carbines. They have a Special Forces sergeant first class as their leader, but we attach First Sergeant Lindquist to be with them. We want one of our men with them to forestall their acting too independently.

At 0735, Sergeant Hale reports that his ambush squad, in place from the night before to protect our perimeter, has made contact and is engaged in a small firefight with a few VC. Subsequent reports indicate both his and Smith's platoons are engaging unknown-size VC elements. By 0810, we have reports of three wounded. Smith calls for 81mm mortar fire from our weapons platoon to help neutralize the VC force with which he is engaged in a moving firefight. It is difficult to visualize the situation from these reports. Both platoon leaders are seasoned, and neither is prone to exaggerate or panic. The reports are, therefore, probably slightly understated. From what we gather, the fighting seems to be centering on the southern slope of Hill 150, which is about midway between our perimeter at the airstrip and the Village 10 complex.

Even those engaged in the developing fight have a narrow view of the larger picture. Here is what one soldier, Specialist Four (E-4) Richard Meadows, remembers of those early minutes:

On the morning of June 11, we were told by our squad leaders to prepare to move out. I was an M-60 machine gunner with 1st Squad, 1st Platoon. Our platoon was commanded by Platoon Sergeant Loyal Hale, a very competent leader that the whole platoon had confidence in. We were told that we were going on a patrol. As a specialist four, I wasn't privy to the details of the operation. I simply followed the man ahead of me.

In a short while, we heard small arms fire coming from the front. I heard later that day that our point squad had made light contact with the Viet Cong. Soon, the firing intensified. We all faced to the right, forming a skirmish line. Immediately, we started taking heavy small arms and automatic weapons fire from a hill to our front. The noise was deafening.

We took cover behind the rubber trees which were only about twelve inches in diameter. I was never able to learn the art of firing the M-60 from the prone position, so I was kneeling behind a tree. I watched as the leaves on the ground all around me were jumping up and down. It took a second or so for me to understand that it

CHAPTER 13—AND GOD LAUGHS

was enemy fire hitting all around. I remember getting mad as hell that someone was intentionally trying to kill me.

At 0800, the fog is still not lifted. Blanford formulates an alternate plan. We will go on foot, meet with the blocking platoons, engage the VC, and push to the village complex. We just about get the "ground option audible" set when the fog begins to lift, and the air assault is back in play.

At 0815, we lift off with the third platoon, led by Lieutenant Sorrel. The Nungs will follow in the next lift. I sit at the right door of the UH-1D helicopter, known in military slang as a "Huey," with my legs dangling in the slipstream. The brown-red roads and cleared areas contrast nicely with the geometrically arrayed green canopies of the rubber trees. The terrain is gently rolling; deceptively, it looks idyllic. Just as we begin our descent, the Huey door gunners place M-60 machine gunfire into the wood line where the LZ meets the jungle. When we land, the M-60 door gunners lift

Typical FO party awaiting pickup at an LZ.
Photo from the Texas Tech University Vietnam Archives.

*Flight of UH-1Ds en route to an LZ.
Photo from the Texas Tech University Vietnam Archives.*

their fires, and we rush the southeast wood line, firing our weapons from the hip to further suppress any VC who might be there. There are none; the LZ is ours alone. It takes two round trips for the "Hueys" to complete our movement. By 0847, we are all on the ground and begin a cautious movement toward the northern edge of the village complex. Sorrel's platoon is in the lead. Blanford and the two FO parties are next in line, and the CIDG platoon, with First Sergeant Lindquist, brings up the rear.

We find the village uncharacteristically still. The streets and houses are empty of people. We are so preoccupied with overcoming the fog and hurrying to reinforce our two platoons in contact that we fail to appreciate the full significance of the deserted village. It is more than likely that the villagers had already seen their teacher and others marched off for execution by elements of a large VC force. They knew before we did that there would be a big fight, and they had probably fled to the safety of the far ends of the plantation to avoid being caught in the middle.

At about 0950, as we clear the southern end of the village complex, the point element from Sorrel's platoon reports a VC platoon of some thirty troops moving northeast, at forty-five degrees to

*UH-1D helicopters coming into an LZ.
Photo from the Texas Tech University Vietnam Archives.*

our direction of movement (south). Blanford and I rapidly move forward. We join the point element positioned on a slight rise. I see ten or twelve VC moving quickly, about 100 meters distant. Along with the three-man point element, the CO, me, our RTOs, Sorrel and his RTO, and an M-60 machine gun team, we have about twelve soldiers on the rise. The geometric pattern of the rubber trees provides a checkerboard view of the VC force; one moment, they are in view, the next, they are not. They will remain in our kill zone for only a few seconds more.

Blanford decides to engage them now. I drop down to a kneeling position, put my M-16 to my shoulder, and take aim. I see nothing. My rear sight is obscuring the scene. I look over my front sight instead. It is bobbing up and down. I am breathing heavily. My throat is so dry that it burns. In training, on the rifle range, I always qualified as "Expert," the highest category of marksmanship. But this is not training. The targets are humans, and they can shoot back. I am afraid of both killing and being hurt in the process. But I am also conscious of my responsibility to be an effective member of the unit. Accordingly, I concentrate on the fundamental work of the soldier—shooting the bad guys. The moral issues of killing are deferred.

The VC are moving across my front, from my right to my left, at a combat trot; they move like they are pulling rickshaws. I aim for the center of mass of the leftmost VC and plan to work rightward. This will maximize the exposure time of the VC in my little slice of the killing zone. I fire off single shots, at a rapid rate, swinging my aim point from left to right along the column. I have three red tracers at the top of my twenty-round magazine.[44] Their angry red tails stream over the running figures' heads. I lower my aim point to their feet and fire off the remaining seventeen rounds of ball ammunition, hoping for the best. By then, the VC have moved out of the kill zone. I am oblivious to the others firing around me, but when I pause to change magazines, I see that everyone else is reloading, too.

The aftermath astounds me; we have made a hash of the ambush. There are no VC bodies in front of us. It was a very non-lethal event. I estimate that each of the nine soldiers armed with an M-16 fired off a full magazine of twenty 5.56mm rounds, and the M-60 gunner finished off a belt of one hundred 7.62mm rounds. Blanford, armed with a 12-gauge shotgun, did not shoot, nor did the assistant M-60 gunner, armed with a .45 caliber pistol. All told, we probably put out close to three hundred bullets. That would equate to twenty-five bullets, on average, per each of the twelve VC. And it was fast; it was all over in about fifteen seconds. Maybe I missed, but everyone else, too?

As I contemplate this marksmanship debacle, we hear M-16 and AK-47 fire coming from the south. From the radio reports, a plausible tactical picture emerges. Our blocking platoons (Smith and Hale) have been moving north, toward us, engaged in a moving gunfight of increasing intensity with a sizeable VC force. Eventually, the situation solidifies with the VC occupying Hill 150, about 1000 meters southeast of us. Our two blocking platoons

---

[44] The Division later published a Standing Operating Procedure (SOP) specifying that M-16 magazines would be loaded with only eighteen rounds, vice the maximum capacity of twenty, in order to minimize possible failure of the magazine feeder spring.

are positioned on the southern slope. From the size of the hill and the volume of fire they are receiving, they estimate that up to a company-size element of about 100 VC are entrenched. We radio battalion our intent to move toward Hill 150 and develop the situation. Battalion notifies Charlie Company, located at the airstrip, to move out by foot and reinforce us, per the order.

Blanford formulates a plan of action. At approximately 1000, he orders the Nung platoon to proceed through the village and move south-southwest. Sorrel's platoon will move south-southeast. Blanford plans to form a shallow horseshoe around the VC on Hill 150, oriented to the northwest. The CIDG platoon will form the horseshoe's left (west) leg. Smith and Hale's platoons form the base, and Sorrel's platoon will be the right leg. Blanford deliberately chooses the open "U" shaped horseshoe so we can "walk in" artillery fire onto Hill 150 from the northwest with minimal risk to our men.

When the CIDG platoon reaches the rear northern slope of Hill 150, they attempt on their own volition to penetrate the VC from behind. They are repulsed by heavy fire and take their first casualties. After this, they recoil off the hill and take up their assigned position as the left leg of the horseshoe.

Blanford, our RTOs, and I move through the rubber trees with Sorrel's platoon. I am too preoccupied with constantly scanning the terrain for signs of VC to take the time to check my map. As long as the firing is in front of me, I can place myself on the map, moving south from the botched ambush site to Hill 150. In a matter of minutes, the sounds of the battle become more stereophonic. They are no longer just to my front and seem to be getting louder. Then, I am hyper-aware that we are alone. We are in a small clearing, a transition zone between the rubber trees and the non-cultivated native vegetation. We are separated from Sorrel's platoon, and I am now somewhat disoriented. I am not sure where we are located and am too embarrassed to ask. I curse myself for not having checked my map and compass while we were moving.

Blanford forms us into a small defensive coil. It is a precaution, but it reminds me of a circled wagon train waiting for the Indians to attack. I look at Blanford. He is calm. I force myself to appear so. Dooley announces that his hemorrhoids are killing him and ambles off into some tall grass with a roll of toilet paper and his M-16. I briefly flash back to my elderly uncles and cousins who used to complain about their "piles" at family social gatherings. I could not imagine how grown men could discuss the inner workings of their rear ends in public and who would care to listen. And now, my young RTO is doing likewise. I didn't think Dooley was even old enough for this affliction, but I couldn't see why he would lie about something that personal. At any rate, one would never see anything like that in a war movie, not in a million years. It is a moment of reality that artificially calms the situation.

The calm does not last. The sounds of the once distant AK-47 fire come closer. We seem to be in the middle of small, moving VC forces, unaware of us and preoccupied with whatever they are doing. I find it highly disconcerting to contemplate being surrounded. If we are, a dramatic shift has just occurred. We have gone from being hunters to the hunted. I am not particularly afraid of dying so long as it is over quickly. Selfishly, I do not want to die right now, not before I am promoted to captain and not before I reach my twenty-fourth birthday.

Around 1030, the firing around us slacks off. Then Charlie Company arrives. Their approach forced the VC in our immediate vicinity to move northeast, or the fight around Hill 150 is in a momentary lull. We are free to move again, and we join Sorrel's platoon in short order. Blanford positions the command group at the left rear of the Hale platoon at the base of the horseshoe.

The Charlie Company commander confers with Blanford. Based on our radio reports of VC moving northeast (the botched ambush), battalion orders Charlie Company to move in that direction and develop the situation. I get a good look at the Charlie Company commander before he departs. He is wearing civilian prescription sunglasses. He looks incongruous, like he is out for a day at the beach. In actuality, his day will turn out to be anything but that.

Our immediate problem, the portion of Hill 150 occupied by the VC, is covered with rubber trees and is slightly elliptical in shape, with an average diameter of about 300 meters. As its map name implies, it is 150 meters above sea level. To our senior sergeants who had fought desperate battles in rugged terrain during the Korean War, Hill 150 is a topographic joke. It can only be categorized as a hill because everything else is so flat. A soldier, fully loaded with his combat kit, could sprint to the top without breathing too hard.

A drainage ditch, typical of the variety found throughout the plantation, about one meter wide and deep, runs around its circumference about two-thirds of the way to its crest. The length of this ditch-cum-trench line is about 900 meters and allows the VC to shift their men from sector to sector in response to their appreciation of the threat we present. By US Army standards, using one and two-man fighting positions, situated about ten meters apart, the trench could accommodate between 100 and 200 men. This confirms our earlier estimate that a VC company opposes us. Number-wise, we appear evenly matched. However, US doctrine calls for a three-to-one advantage when attacking a dug-in enemy. But the reality is that the attack has already begun, regardless of the relative force ratios. If we use our artillery and other fire support properly, the absence of a three-to-one force ratio will be mooted. In this regard, Blanford's foresight in leaving a path for mortar and artillery fires to be walked into the open end of the horseshoe from the northwest is fortuitous.

All this time, the fight has been continuing. Again, here is the view from Meadows' position:

I was in a gun duel with an enemy machine gun. I carried 600 rounds of ammo for my gun. I went through that pretty quick, so I started yelling for more. My ammo bearer, PFC Arthur Strickland, left the cover of the tree he was behind and ran over to me. He dumped all the machine gun ammo he had, then returned to his original position. He did this while he was under extreme heavy fire. Next, he ran from position to position, collecting the M-60 ammo that was carried as dispersed loads by the rest of the platoon. As he was doing this, my Assistant Gunner, Specialist Four Raymond Rasmussen, was resupplying me with his M-60 ammo. Strickland was gathering ammo from the positions on my right, while Rasmussen handled everything to my left. These two men left the relative safety of their positions and exposed themselves to extremely heavy fire to keep me supplied. Heroism at its finest.

Blanford orders me to bring artillery fire on Hill 150. I radio the fire mission to the FDC. The FDO radios back and asks me to verify the distance between us and the enemy. I tell him we are no more than 100 meters apart. He responds that he cannot safely fire the mission for several reasons. First, the morning fog prevented the helicopter-borne FO from observing the daily registration, which would have allowed the FDC to adjust its firing tables to compensate for normal firing errors. Second, we are located on the margin of the guns' minimum range. He is afraid that the artillery fire will be too erratic for the small distance separating us from the target and that it would cause friendly casualties. Third, they have not yet dug pits under the guns, so they cannot use high-angle fire to overcome the minimum range problem.[45] Last, he is concerned that Charlie Company is out somewhere, maybe not exactly where we think they are. I so inform Blanford. He is not happy. He tells me instead to use the battalion's 4.2-inch (heavy) mortars. The 4.2s aren't as accurate as the 105mm howitzers. Many reasons account for this. Some are materiel related; the mortar sights and leveling bubbles are in poor repair or missing altogether. But it is primarily a people problem that results from the "Fresca" phenomenon. Even in the infantry, there is a quality pecking order. The not-so-best and brightest end up in the heavy mortar section. We joke that the acceptance criterion for a mortar crewman is the ability to see lightning and hear thunder.

The mortar crewmen's capacity for error is boundless. There is a universal narrative that is nearly legendary. It occurs on every firebase in every corner of Vietnam. I have seen it. It goes like this: the mortar crew inadvertently pulls all the propellant bags (the "cheese") from the projectile before dropping it down the tube. The round comes out, propelled only by the shotgun shell primer.

---

[45] The M101A1 105mm howitzer had a minimum range of 2500 meters. Hill 150 was just about 2500 meters distance from the howitzers on the northeast side of the airstrip. Under these conditions, and without the benefit of a daily registration, there is no way to safely predict the impact of the rounds. Errors on the order of the distance separating us and the VC would be quite probable.

It tumbles tip over tail, and falls short, somewhere within the firebase perimeter. The only thing that precludes mass slaughter is that the projectile is not exposed to sufficient centripetal force to arm its fuse. Unless you are unlucky and the tumbling round falls directly on your head, you will ultimately be safe. Meanwhile, the mortar crew stands there gawking, pointing at the tumbling round, like five-year-olds playing with matches, pointing to a friend's home they just set ablaze. They have "sorry about that" grins etched into their faces. They are the grown-up version of "runs with scissors." Knowing all this, we decide, nevertheless, to give them a try—hope springs eternal.

The 4.2 FO, Sergeant Blizzard, confers with Blanford and me. In the interest of safety and self-preservation, we decide to use just two of the four mortar tubes in adjustment and have the initial spotting rounds impact two hundred meters west-northwest of Hill 150. The 4.2 FO sets up the call for fire. When the rounds arrive, the result is, predictably, not good. One round falls 200 meters behind and west-northwest of Hill 150. The second lands one hundred meters behind us, east-southeast of Hill 150. There is about a seven hundred meter spread between the two rounds. Serious work is required to produce an error of this magnitude. Back at Loc Ninh, the four mortars are located within five meters of each other, and the firing data is computed for a common impact point. Technically, both mortars firing in adjustment should have the same elevation and deflection settings, and the same quantity of propellant bags. There should be no more than twice the 40-meter nominal range probable error of the 4.2 weapon system between the two impacts, assuming one goes 40 meters long and the other 40 meters short.

There is no way to adjust the fire. We do not know which round to adjust from and which, if any, represents the correct firing data. Further, given our appreciation of the platoon's IQ, we must consider the possibility of further errors while addressing the original one. Blanford radiates a look of studied resignation. He runs his hand across his throat—the "kill it" signal. Instead, he radios our weapons platoon to provide 81mm mortar fire support. The 81s are relatively small in caliber and might not be effective in getting at the VC in the covered drainage ditch, but we are down to zero options at this point. The 81s come in on target, but many burst in the trees above the drainage ditch, leaving the VC relatively unscathed.[46]

Blanford reasons that the longer we wait, the deeper the VC will dig and thus be harder to dislodge. He decides to assault Hill 150 immediately. He orders all four platoons to conduct a stand-up assault. There will be no base of fire left behind. We will provide the suppressive fires while moving forward. He tells the 81s to make the next volley the last and to use white phosphorus (WP, pronounced as "Willie-Peter") instead of high explosive. He then radios the platoon leaders that the assault will commence when they see white smoke on the objective. Then it will be time to go to work.

---

[46] The 81mm HE round weighed 9 pounds and had 2 pounds of high explosives in its warhead. The 4.2-inch mortar round weighed 25 pounds, and the 105mm round weighed 35 pounds, both with about 7 pounds of high explosive in their warheads. A rough rule of thumb is that heavier warheads are more effective than lighter ones by the cube root of their high explosive weight multiple. Thus, we can approximate the 105mm howitzer round as being 1.5 times as effective as the 81mm mortar round in explosive effects. The 105mm round would also produce larger fragments.

CHAPTER 14

RUNNING INTO BURNING BUILDINGS

The attack must be violent and rapid to shock the enemy and to prevent his recovery until the defense has been destroyed. The attacker must minimize his exposure to enemy fires by using maneuver and counter-fire, avoiding obstacles, maintaining security, ensuring command and control, and remaining organized for the fight on the objective.
FM 100-5, OPERATIONS

The two sentences from FM 100-5 are a masterpiece in brevity. They describe the conduct of a proper attack in crisp, action-packed language. They are the military equivalent of Hemingway—economical, clear, and descriptive. We intend to adhere to the above prescription, but it does not work out that way. The situation goes bad, quickly.

At the airstrip, the 81mm mortar section prepares Blanford's invitation to a gunfight, attendance mandatory, no regrets. In the FDC, they double-check the deflection and elevation settings for the tubes and compute the number of bags of powder required to propel the WP rounds to Hill 150. On the mortar tubes, the gunners set the elevation and deflection, break open the WP rounds from their fiber tubes, screw in the nose fuses, cut the charges, and "hang" the rounds in the muzzles of the three tubes, awaiting the section chief's command to fire.

When it comes, the rounds drop in the tubes, their primers and ignition charges are set off, which in turn ignite the propellant bags, and the "invite rounds" begin their trajectory to Hill 150. The straight-line distance is nineteen hundred meters. Fighting gravity, the rounds climb to a peak elevation of about six hundred meters and then, yielding to gravity, begin their plunging descent toward Hill 150. We can almost hear the thunk as the rounds hit the bottom of the tubes. We have twenty- seconds until they arrive and set us into our assault. It is a long twenty seconds.

The rounds impact. When the dense, blue-white smoke billows up from Hill 150, the line platoons begin their assault. To get the company command group moving, Captain Blanford, without drama, intones, "Move out." We are conducting a classic, by-the-book, stand-up infantry assault. It is the final "F," in the infantry doctrinal ditty of "Find them, Fix them, Fight them, Finish them." I studied company assault tactics in the classroom at CCNY and executed them in ROTC Summer Camp at Fort Devens. The theory is being put into practice, but this time under enemy fire.

Notwithstanding, I have difficulty comprehending the reality of my situation. I feel like I am watching a war movie from inside the screen. I am no longer me. I adopt the persona of my functionality. I have transformed myself into the third person singular. If the FO is killed, it will not be my death; it will be his. That is the trick my mind devises to get me moving, in autopilot mode, into the cadence of the assault. I take a step. I take a deep breath and swallow to wet my parched throat. Then, another step, and the cycle repeats itself. I am surviving the assault one step at a time.

Violently, reality intrudes and terminates my little mind game. Standing upright, we make much better targets than when we were prone or crouched behind the rubber trees. As our platoons close to within hand grenade range of the VC, they are halted and driven to ground by thick fire from the trench line. Our 81mm mortars were not effective. The VC are too well dug in. They are not suppressed; they are ready to take our assault.

The command group is in back of the lead assault elements and unaware that they have been halted. We keep moving forward, like cars, unavoidably heading to a pileup just down the road. Suddenly, Blanford and his RTO are shot. Now we, too, go

CHAPTER 14—RUNNING INTO BURNING BUILDINGS

to ground. The attack is stalled. We have lost all forward momentum. We are worse off than we were when we started. All of this occurs in less than ten seconds.

The initial moments of the assault represent a key threshold in differentiating combat's dimensions. This is active combat; we are moving, consciously, into the danger zone, and it is our intent to close with and kill the enemy. This is not the same as just passively facing danger. Being caught in an ambush or taking mortar fire are life-threatening, but largely passive activities. A soldier has little choice about his participation; he is in danger not of his own doing but of the actions of others and has little opportunity to absent himself from the scene. But to be engaged in an assault on an enemy position is another matter. Here, a soldier must consciously move forward and overcome all survival instincts to remain behind. It is the equivalent of a fireman on the street, at risk of falling debris from a burning building, versus that fireman running into the burning building.

And it matters little that this is not combat on the epic scale of Normandy. The physiology and psychology of war are universal, regardless of historical context. Put any combat action under a microscope, be it retroactively monumental or just a minor ambush at an unnamed crossroad, at the soldier level, the emotions and effects are the same. The soldier must deal with his fear and function as an effective member of his team. And the consequences, the missing limbs and giving up of life are the same; there is no mitigation that the loss occurred in a battle subsequently declared as great. As they move forward, the men of Alpha Company radiate a rare dignity that is only evident in times of peril, when men, acting as a team, face danger with quiet resignation.

These few seconds also take a toll on the Nungs. Some of their most aggressive fighters, including the English-speaking translator, are killed or wounded. Without their translator, meaningful two-way communication with the Americans is impossible. This unfortunate combination of casualties causes them to lose their composure. They quit the battlefield. Doing so, they leave our left flank exposed and deprive us of valuable firepower. First Sergeant Lindquist and the Special Forces NCO remedy the situation. They arm themselves with two M-60 machine guns the departing Nungs have "donated" to them, and cover the gap created by the unseemly exit of our surviving allies.

The VC, on the other hand, are not going away. They are aggressive, highly motivated fighters. At any moment, the VC can swarm off the hill and attempt to roll up the exposed flank created by the Nung's departure. All that prevents this is that the VC may not fully appreciate our predicament.[47]

With our three PRC-25 radios, their long "whip" antennae affixed, the company command group stands out from the common soldiers. Our radios signify that we are the "brains" and leadership of the unit; we are a high-value target. Thus, when Captain Blanford is hit, I assume, from having read of similar circumstances in recent fights, it was by a sniper choosing his shots carefully and seeking a good "return on investment." Accordingly, I yell, "Sniper," rise momentarily to kneeling, aim into the trees immediately to our front, and order Dooley and the 4.2-inch mortar FO party to fire into the treetops. Instead, they stare at me like I have gone mad in the midday sun. They are not buying the "snipers in the treetops" story. Apparently, a novice lieutenant's authority and credibility are not unlimited. Embarrassed, I lower the M-16 from my shoulder.

As I learned in ROTC Summer Camp, I crawl over to Blanford, take the field dressing from the first aid pouch on his web harness, and bandage him. The first aid kits we carry are not for our use on others but for others to use on us. It is a sobering concept. As I work, Blanford tells me a sniper did not hit him; he is sure he was hit straight on from Hill 150. He has not scolded or inflected his tone, but in so many words, he has just told me to calm down and get my act together. I feel even sillier for having ordered, without effect, the troops to fire into the treetops. Second lieutenants are expected to make fools of themselves every now and then. But I am a senior first lieutenant. Allegedly, such sophomoric behavior is behind me.

Initially, I am conscious only of the damage to his right eye. I tell myself that he isn't hit so bad after all. But, as I cradle his head,

---

[47] At Hill 177, just 1500 meters northeast of us, the VC did recognize an exposed flank, and maneuvered a machine gun section to it, decimating the Battalion Reconnaissance Platoon.

CHAPTER 14—RUNNING INTO BURNING BUILDINGS 139

I feel a moist and sticky warmth sensation on my left palm. I rotate my hand away from his skull to see what that is all about. I wonder if I had been shot in the hand and was just now feeling it. My palm is full of blood and hair. Only then do I become aware of the more serious wound behind his ear. This is not good, I say to myself, amazed that my emotions, a complex brew of fear and relief that it is not me who was shot, can be reduced to such a trivial thought.

I take my dressing from my first aid pouch and wrap it around the back of his head. Now we are playing musical chairs with our first aid packets. Someone will have to use his on me if I am shot, and so on down the line until the last man is shot, and he will be shit out of luck.

As I hold Blanford, I imagine that he must have been shot just as he turned to his left rear, apparently to block out some of the direct sound of gunfire from the radio handset he was holding to his left ear. The bullet hit him first behind his right ear. It then ricocheted between his helmet and skull, penetrating his right eye as it exited the front of his helmet. That very same bullet, defying logic and operating under a life of its own, then hit his RTO in the right forearm. That bullet is one of those mysteries of war; one of a class of "things that go bump in the night."

While I am helping Blanford, Dooley tends to his RTO. Blanford is in pain but maintains his composure. He tells me to inform the platoon leaders and battalion headquarters of our situation. When I report to battalion, I pray they will give me a magic solution to get us out of this mess. The battalion S-3 NCO radios back not a magical solution, but only a succinct, "Roger; Out."

Smith, the senior platoon leader, makes his way over to our location to assess the situation and confer with Blanford. Based on radio reports from the other platoons, we tally our casualties. Specialist 4 Henry Burch, of Smith's platoon, is shot in the lower body and ultimately bleeds out before he can be safely evacuated. Sergeant John Miller is shot dead while rising to throw a hand grenade. PFC Roy Pitt is seriously wounded (he dies of his wound after being medically evacuated). We have nine wounded, including Blanford and his RTO, David Nelson. Our casualties amount to about 12 percent of our strength. But one of them is our captain, and this fact, along with the retreat of the Nungs and the ineffectiveness of our 81mm mortar fire, combine to produce the perception of a situation that is a bit worse than it is. Until now, I do not think we realized how much we had come to rely on Blanford as a man who could get us through any danger.

I again radio in a call for fire. Again, it is denied. I doubt that the FDC fully appreciates our situation, yet I am sure there have been other battles like this and that competent operational judgments are being made. I assume that the FDC is reasoning that we are in an "artillery dead zone," and that fact cannot be (easily) changed. They probably are thinking that we are not going to have artillery support, and in today's idiom, we should "get over it." It is not their fault that we do not trust our 4.2-inch mortars for close-in support.[48]

Immediately after this last denial of close-in fires, a new, authoritative voice makes a premiere appearance on my radio. The voice is warbling, like the sound a man would make if he pounded his chest rapidly with his fist while speaking. I can almost feel the vibrations. It is the classical sound of a man speaking on the radio from a vibrating helicopter. He announces himself as "Drumfire 6," and asks, incongruously, as if he were a motorist coming upon a fellow traveler with a flat tire, "Can I be of assistance?"

I tell him I need artillery but can't get it due to technical and safety concerns. I sense he understands. He tells me to have our platoons use smoke grenades to mark their locations so he can locate them on the ground and be sure we get them correctly posted on our maps. His composure and presence re-energize me. I put on my game face and place myself back in the fight. I relay the need for our platoons to mark their locations. While that is being done, he asks me to describe the location of the enemy on Hill 150 in relationship to my platoons; he wants to know just how close we are to the enemy. His voice thus far has been monotonic and matter of

---

[48] According to the Battalion After Action Review, artillery was employed, further out, to seal the battlefield and preclude VC escape or reinforcement. Additionally, the Review states that the Air Force flew several sorties to further seal the areas around Hills 150 and 177. We were being supported. We just had this little problem with obtaining close-in artillery support.

fact. When I tell him the smoke from our platoons rising above the treetops is about one hundred to two hundred meters from the VC, I swear I can detect a note of concern in his voice. I wonder if the promise of assistance will turn into another negative response to my request for artillery support, only this time more politely and understandingly phrased. But he is true to his promise. He tells me that if we pull back slightly, he will arrange for artillery fire support.

I radio these instructions to Smith. Then I ask Dooley to look up the call sign, "Drumfire 6," in our CEOI (Communications and Electronics Operating Instructions), a little book we carry on a lanyard, listing the radio call signs and frequencies in use that day. Dooley, somewhat surprised, informs me "Drumfire 6" is the division artillery commander, Colonel Marlin Camp—a full bird colonel. This person is in command of all the artillery in the 1st Infantry Division.

Many subordinate commanders would complain over the years that the senior leadership of the 1st Infantry over-supervised and micromanaged the war while bypassing their subordinate commanders. The twin technologies of the helicopter and radio allowed our senior commanders to be anywhere they wanted to be and reach out and directly advise or give orders to troops on the ground. Conceptually, micromanagement and bypassing subordinate commanders are not desirable, but I am thankful, actually grateful, for Drumfire 6 bypassing my artillery battalion and directly advising and helping me. To this day, I am unclear exactly what changes he directed, but close-in artillery support was forthcoming.[49]

While we wait for Drumfire 6 to have a more distant artillery battery fire our mission, Smith pulls our forward elements back

---

[49] The Staff Journal of the 2d Battalion 33rd Artillery is frustratingly silent on this phase of the battle. It mentions that an attached battery (C Battery, 2d Battalion 13th Artillery), was ordered to orient its howitzers on azimuth 5700 and 6200 mils to support us. There are 6400 mils in a circle with north being 0 mils. This would have placed the battery south-southeast of us. Loc Ninh was almost due east. Ostensibly, they were thus relocated and diverted from a previously assigned mission, but as the overall artillery commander, Drumfire 6 had the authority to effect that change.

and gets them under what little cover is available—primarily little folds in the ground and whatever drainage ditches are tactically advantageous. At about 1500, the battalion command group and Bravo Company join us. They bring water and ammunition. The medics carry Blanford and our other wounded to the reverse slope of the rise on which we are situated. There, using chain saws, they clear a small LZ to enable the helicopter evacuation of our wounded and dead. Rabdau later told me that he heard a VC squad wandered into this LZ, stared at the equally startled US soldiers, and went on its way, with neither side exchanging a shot.

Smith arrives at our location and coordinates with the battalion commander. Now my life is that much simpler. All I have to do is get the artillery onto the target. Drumfire 6 comes back and tells me to call in my fire mission. I look at my watch; it is now 1630 hours. I call in the mission, asking for the first rounds to land 400 meters to the rear (northwest) of Hill 150. The artillery is located "behind" me. The rounds will be coming over my right shoulder. I plan to "walk" the rounds onto Hill 150. It will be safer for our men if I do it that way.

The first two rounds thud deep behind Hill 150. I can hear them but cannot see them. Being aloft, Drumfire 6 can see them. If he wanted, he could finish the job for me. He is an expert. But he tells me to carry on. It is a tribute to his leadership. He does not need more experience adjusting artillery, and he does not seek the notoriety of being the one who saved the day. He needs seasoned FOs; he is training me. It is like the old proverb, "Give a man a fish and feed him for a day. Teach him to fish and feed him forever."

I bring in the adjusting rounds by hundred-meter increments, judging their location by the sound of the explosions. When the rounds finally burst visibly on the horizon, I am perplexed. They are to the right rear of Hill 150, instead of directly behind it. I order a "Left 100" to bring them back on-line. The subsequent rounds are on-line, but land much closer to our position than I intended. In doing so, one of the rounds goes off in the treetops above the Hale platoon, just forward of my location. Falling tree limbs hit some of our men. I sense a moment of confusion. One or two soldiers "pull back" on their own. This could be the prelude to a minor panic. Platoon Sergeant Hale stops them. I am startled. I am unsure how the rounds came in so close and quickly. I am learning the hard way, by discovery, how to adjust artillery close in.

I was using the horizon as my reference frame. I expected my lateral adjustments to move parallel to the horizon, and my range adjustments to move perpendicular. At the FDC, they are using my line of observation, the "Observer to Target (OT) Line," which, in this case, is about forty-five degrees left of an imaginary line between me and the horizon that I had erroneously assumed as my reference. In the FDC, the adjustments I order are moved perpendicular and parallel to the OT Line, not the horizon. Thus, when I was walking the rounds in, they were "drifting" to the right, parallel to my OT Line. In fact, the original rounds may have impacted 100 meters right of where I called for them, or maybe I was off in reading my map or a combination of both. When I tried to correct this by ordering "Left 100," the rounds moved perpendicular to the OT line and dropped in range, moving them closer in.

This acceleration of coming on target, and the effect of the tall trees on the artillery trajectory, is accentuated because the target is close in. If the target were several hundred meters away, subtle range "surprises" or the height of treetops would not be life-threatening. But these surprises can be disastrous when the target and the "friendlies" are separated by less than one hundred meters. They say that wisdom comes from making mistakes and surviving them. At the moment, I think to myself, You fucking idiot. You will wipe out the entire company and finish off all the survivors while you learn the trade by trial and error.[50]

Smith reports that all is OK; that no one is seriously hurt, and that we need the fires that close. The "I'm going to get us all killed" pit in my stomach resolves, and I rededicate myself to adjusting the artillery. I look to Dooley, my combat-experienced RTO, for help. In a matter of seconds, he goes through several mood changes.

---

[50] Almost every month I was in Vietnam, I learned of an FO who had accidentally called close-in fires on his own location, killing himself and a good many others in the process.

First, he stares straight ahead. He ignores and disavows me, like a teenager out with a parent might upon meeting some friends. Then he looks at me with a mild pity that connotes, "Come on; don't blow your combat debut and embarrass me." Officially, his job is only to carry the radio; adjusting the artillery is my responsibility. He is a draftee; I am an officer and a volunteer. There is a clear division of labor and accountability. It is not as if I have been volunteering to carry his radio or lighten his load. To his credit, he decides to involve himself in a highly problematic situation. He instructs me to switch to "fuse delay." This fuse will not go off in the treetops but will bury itself in the ground before detonating. That will also help dig out the VC. We make that change. I also ask for a "sheaf," a linear lay down of fire, to ensure the maximum number of rounds hit in the trench line, rather than around it. I then say into the PRC-25 handset, "Fire for effect."

The rounds come whistling in, low over our heads. We can feel the pressure wave as they pass over. They slam into the trench line. The effect is immediate. All VC fire from Hill 150 ceases. We have regained the initiative. We are back in the game. I keep up the artillery fire, working it down the trench line to my left. I am now cognizant of the correct reference line to use while moving the rounds left, so as I shift the fires, I add in range to keep them from coming in on us. The effect on our men is electrifying. They hoot and cheer like schoolboys miraculously reprieved from a test. There will not be another ten seconds.

I join them in yipping it up. In today's parlance, I was performing a verbal rendition of the football touchdown dance. In reality, I was probably releasing my pent-up fear. No matter what the reality, Dooley looks at me disapprovingly. I then realize that to him, it looks like I am cheering my own work. This would be especially bad taste on my part because others were figuratively holding my hand as they walked me through the basics of my job. I begin to think that while I will probably survive the battle, my reputation and combat debut will be in tatters.

A future incident serves to place my behavior in context. Months later, I am promoted to captain and placed in charge of three FO parties. A replacement FO joins us in the field. Some of the battalion officers and I are going over the plan for the next day. The new lieutenant saunters up, reports to me for his in-brief, and announces, "I am here to kill (Viet) Cong and fuck." I look at him in disbelief. I have a flashback of me at Hill 150. I am furious. There is no saint like a reformed sinner. I tell him to stand at attention. That sobers him. Then I blast away, screaming, "Kill? Fuck? Fucking grow up. Get out of my sight until you are fucking drained of your fucking bullshit." Dooley was probably thinking something like that at the moment.

My unease is broken by a long rip of M-60 machinegun fire. First Sergeant Lindquist radios in that the VC are breaking out on our left flank. They are quitting Hill 150. Due to the artillery fire, they cannot retreat via the reverse slope, so they are taking their chances with a frontal breakout. Dooley tells me to keep shifting the fires left to keep up with them. I do so, now, almost reflexively and without extra effort.

Meadows' view of this aspect of fight from within the Hale Platoon is a bit different. It is not a Rashomon scale difference. The basic facts are congruent; what is different is what he emphasizes:

The company command post was directly behind me, two or three trees back. At one point, I looked back to see that the Company Commander, Captain Blanford, and his RTO, had been wounded. From that point on, I had no idea who was running the show.

The battle was moving very fast, and time was flying by. Sometime later, there was a loud explosion over my head. A 105mm artillery shell had hit the tree above me. Although not wounded, I was temporarily knocked unconscious. When I regained my senses, I looked around. About 20 feet to my right rear, I saw a large tree branch had fallen. It came down on the head of a soldier (name unknown) and had crushed his helmet.

As I said, time was flying. The battle felt like it was just a short fight, but in reality, it lasted the whole day. I was totally surprised that it was starting to get dark.

Bravo Company is ordered to move through our platoons to secure Hill 150. This means they will check the trench line and clear it of any VC left behind, round up any wounded VC, and search for documents or other items on the enemy that might have value as "intelligence." At the same time, we are ordered to reorganize and then pursue the VC unit that has just bolted from Hill 150.

Almost with resentment, I watch the Bravo soldiers climb Hill 150 in tactical formation. They are taking the prize that was enabled by our toil; it seems unfair that we are not allowed to sweep Hill 150. But my anger passes as the Bravo soldiers disappear from view when they enter the trench lines or cross over to the other side of the hill. As we prepare for our new mission, we hear several single M-16 rifle shots coming from the hilltop. One of the command group RTOs remarks, matter-of-factly, that "Bravo is taking care of business." I nod, agreeing with the assessment but not necessarily with the purported act. The inference is that they are finishing off the VC wounded. But the facts of the matter are not knowable; we cannot see what is happening. Maybe the RTO and I are just indulging in wishful thinking, giving expression to our anger for the pain these VC have caused us.

Our pursuit of the retreating VC unit is cautious and uneventful. We move slowly, anticipating a VC rear guard ambush. We find discarded first aid kits and bloody bandages, indicating that the VC are carrying wounded with them. When we report being within one thousand meters of the Cambodian border, we are ordered to return to Hill 150.

I walk the trench line and inspect the VC positions. They had deepened the existing drainage ditches and added overhead cover using small logs covered with the spoil from the aforementioned excavation. Such positions were proof against our 81mm mortars but not the 105mm howitzer fire. Our medics are treating one badly wounded VC. In my immediate vicinity, I see six to ten dead VC. It is difficult to tell exactly; the howitzers have done their work—not all the bodies are whole. My estimate is based on a quick, haphazard visual correlation of anatomical parts into whole corpses. Their wounds are large and extensive. I do not think any VC wounded were finished off with rifle fire.

The battalion S-2 (Intelligence) staff is bagging up a collection of papers the Bravo soldiers have taken from the shirts, wallets, and backpacks of the dead VC for later analysis. This scene slams

CHAPTER 14—RUNNING INTO BURNING BUILDINGS

home the realization, in the personal dimension, that combat is a zero-sum game—one side's gain is the other's loss.

I picture myself as one of the dead. My most personal effects and dignity are forfeited. Some unnamed enemy soldier will know I will not be coming home long before my mother is notified. He will take my wristwatch and parts of my uniform as trophies. Then he will go through my wallet and mentally appraise the photos of my ex-girlfriends that my vanity had caused me to retain long after they had erased me from their picture collections.

As I survey the battleground, I am unashamedly happy that the VC are dead. They caused us much grief, and it was a "them or us" situation. I am glad it is them. Otherwise, I am emotionally neutral. Were I inclined to brag, I would be hard put to claim the VC dead as my trophies. It is not as if I had killed them by myself, with my rifle. I killed indirectly, as one link, albeit the key link, in a long "kill chain" I called for and adjusted the artillery fire; at least six personnel in the FDC processed that call into firing data that was radioed to the howitzers. There, a crew of ten cannoneers on each of six guns turned cranks to bring the howitzers to the correct elevation and azimuth, prepared and loaded the ammunition and pulled the firing lanyards that sent the 105mm projectiles onto the target. If I were inclined to wrap myself in a hair shirt over the killing, I would be sharing my guilt with too many others for it to amount to much. Thus, neutrality is a prudent posture: I aspire to be neither a braggart nor a penitent. I am the emotional equivalent of the grammatical passive voice— "necessary killing was done."

First Sergeant Lindquist and the Special Forces NCO rejoin us. The first sergeant is carrying a World War II German MG-34 machine gun. He says it is highly accurate, with a long barrel and has a "single shot" selector switch on the trigger group. It fires a relatively large, powerful 7.92 x 57mm round compared to the smaller and shorter 7.62mm round and shorter barrel of the AK-47. The 7.92mm bullet would have a lot of kinetic energy, and it may well be the weapon that shot Captain Blanford and his RTO. I ask what the VC were doing with a German machine gun from World War II. The Special Forces NCO explains that the French probably captured it from the Germans at the close of World War

II and issued it to their Foreign Legion who fought in Vietnam in the late forties and early fifties. He continues to speculate that it was taken from the French when they quit the country and is now being employed against the Americans.

The gun ends up in our war museum at the 3d Brigade Headquarters in Lai Khe. Later in the year, I visit that museum and stare at it. Even today, I can still see the typed inscription on the little 3x5 index card hanging from its muzzle, "Captured by Alpha Company, 2d Battalion, 28th Infantry during the Battle of Hill 150, Loc Ninh Rubber Plantation, Operation El Paso II, 11 June 1966."

CHAPTER 15

RESPITE

"Sleep is sweet to the laboring man."
JOHN BUNYAN, PILGRIM'S PROGRESS

The fight for Hill 150 does not end there. We march back in tactical formation through the rubber trees to our base around the airstrip. As I come down from the adrenaline high of the fight, my mind turns to whether or not I did well and if I passed my initiation into Alpha Company. The rifle company is like a street gang. The members must earn the right to membership and be known as one who can be counted on in a tough situation. In the time it takes to transit the nineteen hundred meters back to the airstrip, I conclude that while I was guilty of some silliness and embarrassing moments, I had acquitted myself favorably, and merited acceptance. The veteran soldiers around me seem to agree—they joke with me with the familiarity of brothers in arms.

Another battalion is manning our perimeter. They have guides out to meet us and take us into our lines. It is past 2100 hours when I reach the spot on the ground that I call home. A few feet away, Dooley lies down with the PRC-25 radio handset by his ear. I am too keyed up to sleep just yet. I clean my M-16; the tracer rounds I fired leave a corrosive residue in the breech and barrel. I check my hand grenades for loose pins and "spoons," take off my helmet, roll down my sleeves for warmth, and sit down. Leaning back against a tree, I let my mind go in neutral. Hours pass. When the moon rises, its glow filters through the branches above, casting un-warlike, bas-relief shadows on the leaf-covered ground. The shifting patterns eventually lull me to sleep.

There I experience the strangest dream of my life. It is about a girl in Parkchester I had known since grade school. I have not seen or thought of her since we both went to college. She was timid, sensitive, and certifiably nice. Although a young teen, she reminded me of my mother, who was also sensitive and caring. I can still picture her in the playground, in the summer after the sixth grade. Some of our classmates were making fun of the clothes she was wearing. Her voice cracked with emotion as she tried to explain that her "good" clothes were packed up for summer camp. Then she ran home, crying. I could easily imagine my mother doing exactly the same under similar circumstances. Another time, in the same playground, she parted her hair and showed her girlfriends small growths on her scalp. It was eerie; my mother had done the same thing for me several days earlier.

Our high school class had some socially aggressive girls who always arranged weekend parties. These were relatively benign affairs—Johnny Mathis records, soft drinks, and adolescent kissing games. This girl was not invited, thus, we had almost no interaction outside of class. But on the dream night of 11 June, none of the girls I had known, kissed, and dated seemed to matter. It was she who held and comforted me. I felt safe and very calm. I was hesitant until recently to acknowledge, much less discuss, the dream in any detail. It was a matter both of image and sensation. Everything was intensely bright and white. She was wearing a white gown; she was angelic. I was bathed in an overwhelming sense of light and well-being, bordering on euphoria. That dream, probably no more than a few seconds in duration, and one that could be safely viewed by a pre-teen Sunday school class, gave me unimaginable rest and solace.

Psychiatrists can make an industry of a dream's interpretation. My immediate reaction to Hill 150 was probably a form of denial. I think it was like escaping serious injury in an accident. You walk away and do not initially give it much thought. Only later does your mind allow you to acknowledge how close to death you might have come. In my case, there was a forty-five-year interval between surviving the event and fully recognizing the danger it posed. Perhaps that dream was meant to help me accept but not dwell on the fact that I had come close to death. That dream may have served to co-opt a looming nightmare of 11 June, transforming it into a more palatable memory that I could safely file away for later analysis. Perhaps it was a mental survival trick, an emotional parlor game. I had to continue functioning as a soldier; there was no way out. Twenty-four hours after the fight, we were back in the woods, on patrol.

The white, bright light is listed in medical literature as a hallmark common denominator in near-death experiences. One of my ROTC instructors told me that during the Korean War, he had cried for his mother when he was under unrelenting artillery fire. At the time, I did not believe him; I thought he was being overly dramatic. Since then, I have heard seriously wounded men cry out for their mothers. My dream might have varied on these themes: near-death and mothering comfort. I am sure that the dream was a gift beyond quantifiable value at the time.

From a practical, logical point of view, it was my dream, not hers; she did not send it to me. But still, I am grateful to her for being who she was and for allowing me that dream. My fight for Hill 150 ended with that dream. It ended sweetly and quietly.

CHAPTER 16

MEANING MAKING

"Is he lucky? I want lucky generals."
NAPOLEON BONAPARTE

Unfortunately, war is the most defining moment and the hardest test for a man as he measures himself against his comrades, the enemy, and what he would like to be. The fight for Hill 150 became part of my life. It changed me. I was one person before the battle and another afterward. I am unsure I can define the difference, though I have felt and lived that difference. It was more than just surviving a dangerous situation. It was knowing that I had, no matter how indirectly, killed in the service of our nation.

After that fight, I became more secure in my place in society, more aware of my rights and freedoms, less tolerant of insults, and more ready to stand up for myself. I felt I had earned, paradoxically, in a plebian, working-class rifle company, full entrance into the world of the WASPs, with or without their blessing.

At Hill 150, I also learned to be more at ease with myself. I realized that I was Everyman, Jewish or otherwise. What scared me scared others. What motivated me motivated others. So, what is true for me must be true for all the participants. This analysis of the battle is my attempt to make meaning of what happened to us there and why. It is meant to be both tactically informative and psychologically calming. It is my attempt to dissect and understand the day in which any of us could have died, and all of us were changed.

The division's historical report of the action at Hill 150 is economically terse and sterile. It focuses on the ninety-eight VC reported as killed as a documented indicator of success. But that indicator is questionable, and it is not the only indicator. I saw between six and ten dead VC on Hill 150. It is hard to be sure, as all the bodies were not whole. Perhaps the other VC dead were located at Hill 177. Another indicator is that our battalion suffered sixty-six killed and wounded. We had about 350 soldiers in the field that day, so our losses were almost one man in five. The Roman practice of mass punishment, the slaying of every tenth man, gives us the word decimation, which we now use to describe a serious combat loss. On 11 June, our battalion was decimated twice over. These are not statistics that invite introspection by the battle's senior leadership, sensitive to how their performance will be perceived from written documentation. Thus, the report focused on the VC dead instead of what we could and should have done better.

Accordingly, the A Company ordeal is reduced to three key sentences: "Due to the intensity of the fighting, C Company was alerted…to assist A Company"; "…in the A Company area, consecutive assaults from the north, south, and west failed to dislodge the VC from their entrenched positions"; "Following a sixteen volley artillery bombardment, B Company assaulted Hill 150…completely overrunning the VC positions." These statements bound the battle; they do not describe it. Like an epitaph on a headstone that states a man was born on this date and died on that date, the story of the man is in the dash that separates the dates.

In military jargon, Hill 150 is classified as a "meeting engagement." In plain English, that translates into the unintended collision of two opposing forces. The unexpected early morning fog delayed our helicopter assault. This delay and an imperfect appreciation of the enemy combined to bring us to Hill 150, which was the wrong place at the wrong time, according to our original plan. A parallel set of unforeseen conditions on the VC side had to mesh with ours to produce a blueprint for combat—the bringing together hundreds of well-armed, aggressive men at a random place at the wrong moment.

It later became clear that we interrupted the 1st Battalion of the 273d Regiment, 9th VC Division, based in Cambodia, which was preparing to attack Loc Ninh. We were looking for about ten local insurgents reported to be located in a small village complex. The VC 1st Battalion was probably deploying to prepare for a night assault on our base. Neither of us found what we expected. Each side "discovered" the true size and disposition of the other incrementally, by trial and error. Everyone was "off" his original plan. The whole battle was based on mutual surprise.

The Loc Ninh rubber plantation was extensive. If either of our forces had been just a few hundred meters from where they were that morning or had gotten there just a few minutes earlier or later, we might have passed each other by. What or who guides these time and place decisions? This is an eternal question. It is a recurring theme in literature. It is the basis for *The Bridge of San Luis Rey,* wherein the reader is led through an examination of how and why five disparate people came together to die when a rope bridge fails in eighteenth-century Peru.

But Thornton Wilder is not required reading for teenage infantrymen. Instead, they mentally massage, "what if." Replacements who had just joined our rifle company must have wondered what if they had missed the resupply helicopter to Loc Ninh, they had caught with only seconds to spare the night before? In fact, with little effort, every soldier in that fight could conjure up at least one plausible "what if."

The events leading up to the fight must be viewed in context. In the summer of 1966, the US Army was conducting the "Counter Offense I and II" campaigns. By comparison, the previous campaigns were designated "Advisory" and "Defense." In the 1st Infantry Division, the commanding general, Major General William DePuy, was an ardent believer in the aggressive pursuit of decisive combat with the VC. General DePuy had served previously as J-3 (Operations) for the Military Assistance Command Vietnam (MACV), the overall headquarters during the war, where he studied operations across a broad spectrum of strategies. He was inclined to analysis with a mathematical bent. He was convinced that to win the war, we just had to do the arithmetic: kill the enemy faster than he could replace himself. This was the strategy of attrition.

A competing strategy was pacification, which focused on protecting major population centers. General DePuy practiced both, but clearly, the division's emphasis and resource allocation were on combat operations designed to seek out and engage the mainline VC forces.

Mechanics tend to see problems in terms of their tools. Blanford is convinced, as an infantryman, that he should have done a better job teaching his company how to shoot and distribute their fires to better effect. He thinks better "musketry" would have been the key to success. There is no argument that some individual and unit skills could have been more perfected, particularly marksmanship under pressure and coordination of organic fires against a fortified position. Blanford recognized this deficiency during the battle and reported it to the battalion commander before he (Blanford) was medically evacuated. As an artilleryman, I say no amount of small arms fire, no matter how expertly applied, would have been sufficient. The VC were too well dug in to be "winkled" out or suppressed by the company's organic weaponry. They had to be blasted out by artillery.

And our artillery support was problematic. The order's fire support graphics reflect anticipated VC action in the LZ area, and the artillery was primed to deal with this expected event. That the actual problem occurred other than where logically forecast was unfortunate.

Fire support from the artillery battalion was based on everything going right and everything working right. Our artillery was prepared to cover the planned objective areas, the LZ and the Village 10 complex. But it was not prepared to support us closer to our perimeter, nor was it anticipated that our 4.2-inch mortars, which should have covered the near ground around the perimeter, would exhibit the appalling inaccuracy that they did.

The artillery battalion planners should have allowed for the contingency of close-in fire support. Recoil pits should have been constructed to permit the application of high angle fire to cover the ground close to the Loc Ninh perimeter. The battalion senior leadership seemed to place a priority on a "zero defects" mentality. They were overly concerned with precluding a *possible* safety incident by shooting close-in fires to support us without having previously conducted the doctrinal registration. They were not responsive to the unique and pressing nature of our situation, especially after the 4.2-inch mortars demonstrated their blatant inaccuracy and our first assault was repulsed.

There were inherent limitations on the ability of the artillery at Loc Ninh to reposition itself in order to better cover our battle area. The artillery had arrived at Loc Ninh by CH-47 helicopter lift; most of the artillery prime mover trucks were left at Lai Khe. Without these trucks being readily available, more heroic efforts would have been required to assemble from within Loc Ninh base the requisite transportation means to relocate the artillery and associated ammunition. Nonetheless, it was not impossible to redeploy the artillery. The decision not to do so can only be explained by a "business as usual" attitude. By mid-August, most of the senior officers were replaced by others who could more responsively balance the trades between not making mistakes and providing viable support to the infantry.

The fire support lesson eventually led to artillery positioning guidelines and force structure changes. Artillery batteries were subsequently positioned to ensure that infantry units always had mutually supporting fires to eliminate "dead zones" around our temporary firebases. Additionally, the Division transferred some of the 4.2-inch mortar units from the infantry battalions to the 105mm artillery battalions, to place them under more professional supervision.

With regard to the actual battle and tactics, I think it is clear, in *retrospect*, that if we could have fought that battle over, we would have made some changes. The dullest student of tactics could easily conclude that we should have massed the battalion and focused our effort against one hill at a time, 150 or 177, while fixing the other enemy location with robust artillery fire and an economy of force element. In a later conversation, Blanford opined that this approach might have failed. He thinks the VC on Hill 150 would have found a way to maneuver off their positions and threaten us from the rear or a flank.

Regardless, our battalion commander and S-3 had to deal with a continuously evolving battle that unfolded unexpectedly and piecemeal. They had two major fights ongoing, involving two of the three rifle companies. They had to consider the strong possibility that our base at Loc Ninh would soon come under attack: that the actions and Hills 150 and 177 were just feints to draw off their forces and attention from the perimeter at Loc Ninh. Uncertainty is the twin of war. The battle unfolded slowly and ambiguously. First reports indicated that we were opposed by a squad, then a platoon, then one company, and finally a battalion. It took several hours for our higher headquarters to appreciate the VC intent, and by then we were well into the fight.

Imperfect knowledge of the enemy is the hallmark of warfare. It is what makes it so difficult and bloody. The enemy operates from behind a curtain. We cannot see what he is doing; we can only guess. It is said that when Napoleon was reviewing his staff's recommendation for a new general, he inquired, "Is he lucky? I want lucky generals."

The division had been in several large-scale battles which concluded successfully. A review of these battles explains why our fight for Hill 150 was so difficult. The VC attacked us in almost all our previous battles, while we were relatively static. This allowed us to conduct a well-coordinated *defense*, bringing to bear our superior firepower. We were mobile in the fight for Hill 150, and the VC were relatively static. We were attacking. We had no experience in conducting a World War II-type coordinated *attack*.

Had we known that we would engage a well dug-in VC force, rather than search a village, we would have mentally and physically rehearsed for that mission. Blanford never had the luxury of meeting with his platoon leaders, face to face, explaining what he wanted done and how, and soliciting their input and opinions. He did it under fire, on the radio, in real-time. We planned while we were operating. Thus, we had plenty of heart and desire for the attack, but no preparation based on rehearsals or practical experience from previous engagements. The fight for Hill 150 was the first of its type. And it was painful.

After the fight for Hill 150, division tactics emphasized the use of firepower, rather than direct assault, to reduce an entrenched enemy force. In World War II, our artillery was very busy conducting counter fire against enemy artillery. Company size units could not count on artillery support for every attack. In those cases, they adapted and learned to do without. In Vietnam, the enemy had no artillery, per se. Thus, we were able to "over-use" our artillery to support attacks that previously, in accordance with doctrine, would have been conducted without its benefit.

Six months after this fight, in early December 1966, Brigadier General S. L. A. Marshall (Retired), a noted military historian and analyst, conducted a ninety-day study of over 100 small unit actions in Vietnam. Some of his findings are particularly germane. Concerning our botched ambush and wretched marksmanship, which so concerned Blanford, we were apparently in good company. Marshall records:

When suddenly confronted by small numbers of the enemy, the Americans firing their M-16s will in the overwhelming majority of cases miss a target fully in view and not yet turning. Whether the firing is done by a moving point or by a rifleman sitting steady in an ambush, the results are about the same—five total misses out of six tries...The fault much of the time is that out of excitement the shooter points high...[51]

Nor were we alone in our difficulty in assaulting the fortified position on Hill 150. Again, Marshall writes:

The record of US Army operations in South Vietnam demonstrates one fact: a company sized attack upon an enemy fortified base camp or semi-fortified village held in equal strength by NVA or VC main force, with a determination to defend, and not subjected to intense artillery and/or air strikes beforehand, means payment of a high price by the attacker. The result of such an attempt is either ultimate withdrawal by the attacking force, too often after excessive loss, or belated reinforcement and a more prolonged involvement than was anticipated or is judicious.[52]

---

[51] Brigadier S.L.A. Marshall (Ret,) *Vietnam Primer*, (Washington: Department of the Army, 1967) Lesson Five—Rates of Fire.
[52] Marshall. *Vietnam Primer*, 7-9.

The VC fought well and accounted for much of what went against us in that fight. The 1st Battalion, 273d Regiment was accorded the honorific "The Loc Ninh Regiment" for its valor against the 1st Infantry Division in the Loc Ninh area of operations.[53] But besides the unavailability of artillery support and poor marksmanship and fire distribution, there was intelligence failure. Our Division should have known of the presence of such a large, capable VC force. There was a Special Forces detachment at Loc Ninh. They should have had agents and sources in place to warn us. Intelligence gathering was one of the Special Forces *raison d'être*. But even here, the "blame trail" is convoluted and barely discernible. Perhaps some VC officer, Blanford's counterpart, finally tired of writing to mothers about why their sons died at the hands of the American imperialists. Perhaps he decided to take drastic action to dissuade anyone from even thinking about revealing his unit's presence. Maybe the execution of the schoolteacher and other village leaders that we discovered shortly after the fight for Hill 150 was a manifestation of this decision. Under this scenario, it is not difficult to understand how intelligence on the enemy might be hard to come by.

With respect to leadership, Alpha Company had committed and competent personnel. One example represents this quality: on one patrol, during a rest break, two newly assigned replacements sidled up to each other to share a cigarette and some idle chatter, breaking the rule to always maintain a five-meter separation between men. Their platoon leader, Sergeant Hale, had previously ordered the prescribed interval to preclude multiple casualties in case of a grenade or mortar attack. He remade his point, this time physically. He struck them both in the face with his open hand. He told them next time they bunched up he would beat them senseless with a hand grenade. The two soldiers looked to me for sympathy and intervention. They received neither. I thought American military cemeteries would be a lot emptier if only there were more Sergeant Hales.

---

[53] History of the 273d VC Regiment, US Army Vietnam, G-2 Section, 5 Feb 1970, 11.

Blanford made good decisions; sometimes, these were matters of life or death. Early in the fight, a soldier from Smith's platoon, Specialist Henry Burch, suffered a gunshot wound to the leg. Smith requested permission to evacuate the man back to the airstrip. Blanford said no. He reasoned, correctly, that it would take two soldiers to carry the man, and since there were VC swarming about, an additional two soldiers would be required to act as bodyguards. Thus, four soldiers out of platoon strength of about thirty would be taken out of the fight, weakening the remainder of the platoon and subjecting themselves to attack by a larger VC force. The decision went down hard. The wounded soldier subsequently died. Yet, it was the correct decision, and we were lucky to have men of Blanford's caliber and character to make it.

Blanford was not a hypocrite. When he was wounded, he did not demand attention. I subsequently observed other wounded who caused considerable commotion. Blanford, however, kept his pain and worries to himself. He did not burden or distract me from my primary mission of obtaining artillery support. Blanford's memory of his being wounded is telling. The few words he uses speak volumes about command responsibility, leadership, and affection for his soldiers:

When I was hit, I felt the blood running off the back of my head. I felt I was going to die. But since I was the company commander, and all Alpha belonged to me in the sense that my children belonged to me, all I could think of was that I had to die in a manner that would not upset the kids in the company.[54]

Ending with an assessment of human performance, let me state that the soldiers of Alpha Company had the will to fight, were obedient to orders, and were steadfast under fire. We suffered three killed (Miller, Burch, and Pitt), four seriously wounded (Ray Blanford, Jimmy James, Harold Grimes, and Conrad Billet), and five lightly wounded (David Nelson, Cleveland Walton, Galen Taylor, Eugene Tactay, and Curtis Sullivan). Our soldiers were responsible for everything that went right at Hill 150; they fought diligently and resolutely.

---

[54] As related to me by Blanford in 2005.

As for my performance, since I was inexperienced, no one expected much more from me than I had produced. Without the help of my RTO, Specialist Dooley, and the division artillery commander, I would not have achieved even that modicum of effectiveness. I was in a "learn by doing" mode that day. This was my first "close-in" fire mission. I nearly caused a friendly-fire situation by confusing the reference lines along which the adjusted artillery fire would move while I "walked" the rounds onto Hill 150. I was lucky it all worked out.

Style-wise, my behavior left room for improvement. My abysmal M-16 marksmanship under stress, my order to engage non-existent snipers when Blanford was shot, and my self-congratulatory over-exuberance when the artillery finally rained in on Hill 150 are moments that I would just as soon forget.

No action was taken against the surviving CIDG (Nung) platoon who quit the battlefield under fire. I was initially furious. First Sergeant Lindquist later told me that during the Korean War, he had seen several US Army units "bug out"[55] to the rear under fire. Things like that happen. Some men reach their limits and break, and the whole unit reacts, like a herd, reducing itself to the lowest common denominator of personal irresponsibility. We never again worked with the CIDG for the remainder of our time at Loc Ninh.

---

[55] The term "bug out" probably derives from early WWII when the Russian Army deployed along the Bug River in Eastern Poland, fled before the German Army, during the opening days of Operation Barbarossa.

CHAPTER 17

GETTING TO KNOW YOU

"Even a child is known by his doings."
PROVERBS, CHAPTER 20, VERSE 11

In late July, I am promoted to captain and transferred within the 3rd Brigade to the 1st Battalion, 16th Infantry as the fire support coordinator. As I change my domicile from the western to the eastern side of the base perimeter, I become responsible for three FO parties, one in each of the line companies, and for planning artillery fire support for the battalion's operations.

The FOs have fought several battles together in the past year. They are glad to be alive and naturally suspicious of any parvenu who might threaten their continued survival through either excess zeal or stupidity. They want to do a good job, but they all look forward to soon being rotated back to their respective artillery batteries to serve as FDOs or XOs—jobs that are many times safer and more luxurious than that of an FO. They are OCS graduates my age and older. Their lives have been more difficult than mine; they have worked harder than I have for what we have achieved. We all know that. Since they are experienced and know what they are doing, I decide to leave well enough alone. Soon they will be replaced by fresh, incoming lieutenants, and I will have my new team. Thus, within a few days, everybody settles down, secure that there will be no dramatic changes.

I am temporarily billeted in the battalion aid station until a soon-to-be departing officer vacates a sleeping tent. There I meet a Jewish medic. He is assigned permanent latrine duty. This means he has to remove the waste barrels beneath the wooden seats, add diesel fuel, burn the contents, and replace the sanitized containers. It is a distasteful and smelly duty. It is assigned to soldiers on a rotating basis, to ensure equity. But he has it as his permanent duty. I make discreet inquiries as to why. I am told he "refuses" to go out on patrol in the bush. His "refusal" is based on a psychological claim that he cannot handle the stress: that he will be a burden rather than an asset and will, therefore, get others hurt. The claim is credible enough to save him from a court-martial, but not assignment to the humiliating position of permanent shit can burner. I am relieved that I detect no anti-Semitic undertones. They are trying to embarrass him into action. I also try to "save" him. I tell him that I, too, am Jewish and that we have a responsibility to do our share. I explain how the soldiers need and revere the medics who accompany them on patrol. I explain how noble it is to be a combat medic—how the medics give life back to the seriously wounded.

He seems to hardly listen. My experience is that no soldier lacks a sense of self-preservation. But this is counter-balanced by an equally strong sense of avoiding shame and the disapproval of peers. Most soldiers navigate cautiously, and successfully, between these two poles. This soldier has an overabundance of the survival impulse and a deficit of self-respect. My dislike for this man's behavior is balanced with pity. I can see his future. Long after the present danger is past and little comprehended by those who were not there, he will have to explain to his children what he did in Vietnam. That will not be a good day.

The battalion commander, Lieutenant Colonel George M. Wallace III, is also newly arrived. He is about forty-three years old and a graduate of the West Point Class of 1945. He had served previously in Iran with the Military Assistance Advisory Group.[56] He is, in theory, old enough to be my father, and that, besides his rank, sets the conditions under which I form my first impression. Wallace strikes me as "patrician," descending from a

---

[56] In 1953, the CIA enabled the Iranian Military to stage a coup d'etat against the Prime Minister, Mohammad Mossadegh, and install the Shah as the head of state of a pro-American dictatorship. Until the Shah was overthrown in 1979, the American and Iranian Militaries maintained close ties.

well-established army family. He never claims or hints as much; my opinion is based on observing his deportment. I later learn that his father was a career artillery officer. Wallace is lean, fit, all business, and has an eerie penchant for detail. He is not the type of officer who makes mistakes nor tolerates others who do. Wallace was an intramural boxer at West Point; his nose is slightly off-center. There is something about boxing that prepares a man well for combat. I think it is the self-discipline required of football players to both train and then function past the point of pain and exhaustion. Like the football player, the boxer knows he will be hit hard and must perform, nonetheless. Boxing is a perfect physical metaphor for the self-discipline required in combat.

I feel I am in good hands with Wallace, but I place myself in his gun sights within days. In early August, we are preparing for a battalion-level search and clear mission of a rather large village thought to contain local and transient VC forces, weapons, and rice caches. The basic concept is for us to helicopter into an LZ, actually, a clear zone all around the village, surround it quickly, and assist Vietnamese police forces in searching and questioning its inhabitants. Along the spectrum of difficulty and danger, this particular mission type ranks relatively simple and safe.

I plot the artillery preparatory fires, but since the LZ is close to and all around the village, I plan to have the artillery "on call," and executed if we receive fire while landing. Wallace seems satisfied with this approach until about sixteen hours before mission execution when he receives fresh aerial photographs of the village and surrounding area. The photographs reveal a massive earthen berm surrounding the village, which does not show up on the maps we have heretofore used for planning. The berm is about two meters high and thick, making the village now look more like a fort.

Wallace is concerned that if the village is hostile, the berm can cover a large force firing on the helicopters as we land. He wants me to place artillery fire *on the wall* to "keep their heads down" during the helicopter landings. We will be in the command-and-control helicopter, and I will adjust the fire, as necessary. I explain that it is impossible to keep all the artillery fires exactly on the berm itself. Due to inherent materiel and ballistic variables, some rounds will fall "short," and others will go "long." Both types of error will cause some rounds to land in the village. He looks at me as if to infer the question, "Aren't the lives of our men more important?" while asking explicitly, "Isn't there some way to ensure the artillery stays on the wall?" I try to explain all about dispersion around a mean value, standard deviations, and range probable error. I try to explain there is no way to make the howitzers and their projectiles any more accurate than they are. I tell him it's all just a matter of statistics. He tells me that statistics are my problem; saving the soldiers' lives is his. We are verbally jostling for the moral high ground, and he is slightly ahead.

LZ operations are very dangerous. The helicopters are most vulnerable when they come for a landing. They come in slow, with their noses flared up; they are sitting ducks. Each helicopter will carry a pilot, co-pilot, two door gunners, and about seven infantrymen. The infantrymen must exit the helicopters from both sides. Thus, we are limited in the number of rifles we can instantaneously bring to bear to counter a potential ambush. That is why we normally use artillery to "prep" the LZs—firing into the surrounding wood lines to suppress and break up possible ambushes. That is to say, we normally assume an ambush situation, and use artillery fire as a prophylactic. But this particular case is different. The LZ is around a village. And, although the village is more like a fort, we have no way of knowing if that fort is designed to protect them from the VC or advantage them if they are VC.

I reiterate that I will gladly adjust the artillery in if we do indeed take fire from the village during the landing phase of the operation. He tells me that will not suffice. He wants the wall suppressed; he will brook no unnecessary casualties amongst our men. He tells me to work it out, or he will find someone who will.

I go back to my corner of the CP to develop a solution. I look at the map. I picture where the artillery is positioned and relook if there is any way I can plan the fires to minimize the range dispersion on all four walls of the berm. I conclude there is no way to accomplish that. Then I think of the consequences. If I use artillery to suppress the berm and the village is not hostile, many civilians might be killed. This is not a good outcome. If the village is hostile, and I am late in adjusting the artillery to suppress the VC fires, we will take unnecessary casualties. This also is not an acceptable outcome.

What Wallace and I need is the ability to see the future. We both need to know if the village is hostile. But that is not knowable now. That is why we are going on a search mission in the first place. We suspect the village may be hostile or harboring hostiles. We are not sure. And it has been our experience that some Vietnamese officials would declare a village "hostile" for any number of reasons, including a village's refusal to pay "protection money" to line the officials' pockets.

In a highly agitated state, I dissect the issues over and over, trying to work out a winning strategy. Then I realize that it is not about my "winning" or saving my career and reputation. It is about doing the right thing. I call my RTO to drive me up to the artillery CP. It is now about 0100 in the morning. We are due to lift off at 0600. The artillery battalion commander, Lieutenant Colonel Charles Daniel, is asleep. No one wants to wake him. I insist. They submit. We talk. He listens, saying nothing. I am sure he will have me replaced. Then he speaks the magic words. He says he agrees with me. He tells me that he and Wallace had overlapped at West Point. He tells me he will call him and work it out.

The drive back to the infantry area seems to take forever. We use "black-out-drive" lights, no brighter than dim flashlight bulbs, traveling no faster than fifteen miles per hour. When I arrive at the CP, Wallace tells me it is all worked out to his satisfaction. He tells me the artillery will be in a "lay but do not load" mode of operation. That means all the firing data will be set on the howitzers and the ammunition prepared and standing by the guns. Executing the mission will take only a few seconds if we take fire from the village, and I call for the artillery. He looks me straight in the eye, speaking slowly and measuredly, but I do not detect anger. Even with this workable solution, he could have replaced me. He could have claimed loss of trust or just insisted out of principle and personal preference. He does not. The situation becomes ancient history; we never discuss it again.

The long and short of it is this: the helicopter assault is unopposed; we take no fire from the village wall. We search the village from end to end. We find nothing worthwhile to justify the effort. But imagining a different, more disastrous outcome is just as easy. Years later, as I became more politically astute, I realized that I might have saved both battalion commanders from themselves. If we did fire up that village needlessly, their heads probably would have rolled first. The My Lai Massacre and the general public sensing that the Vietnam War was wrong for America were still several years down the road. Still, I am sure that Colonels Wallace and Daniel thought of this night in very different terms once those factors became operative.

On another operation, I learn more about both of us. We are on a night march to encircle a suspected VC village complex at first light. First, I am afraid of the dark and the danger of a night ambush. But, little by little, I calm myself; we are over four hundred well-armed and lethal men. Besides our own weapons, we have artillery and air support on call. I convince myself that the VC need to fear us more than I need to fear them. I concoct my own version of the Fort Benning saying, "Yea, though I walk through the valley of the shadow of death, I will fear no evil, for I am the meanest motherfucker in the valley."

In an instant, my newfound tranquility is shattered. Wallace's RTO alerts like a hunting dog and conveys to him in a troubled whisper a summary of the radio message just received. I can tell it is not a routine update. It is something bad. I switch my PRC-25 to the battalion command frequency to listen in on the hush-toned conversation that follows. The words paint a heart-rending picture—our point man was crossing a large stream and accidentally shot his slack man in the face as he reflexively pulled the trigger on the .45 pistol held in his waving hand. Then I am sucked in the actual scene, as Wallace rushes forward to assess the situation, taking the command group with him. When we arrive, the human dimension amplifies the tragedy the radio words convey. The wounded man is moaning pitifully, and his comrades are trying to both comfort and quiet him to preserve our noise discipline. The soldier who had shot him is inconsolable, in a state of shock.

The surgeon studies the wounded soldier and bandages his head. Wallace then takes the surgeon aside, and they confer in private. The next thing I know, the wounded soldier, still moaning, is being lifted onto a stretcher to be carried along with us on the night movement through the jungle. He will not be medically evacuated by helicopter until we reach our objective at daylight.

The man keeps up a steady, plaintive wail for the remainder of the march. It almost unhinges me; I am flooded anew with fear and foreboding. If I could have transported myself anyplace else, I would have done so. By the time we reach our objective, the soldier is silent. He no longer needs medical attention. He is dead. I am full of anger and resentment toward Wallace. I seek out the surgeon and ask about the decision he had helped make. He tells me that the soldier, despite what it seemed, felt no pain, for the bullet had damaged a good part of his brain.

Furthermore, he related, the man had no real chance, even if he had been immediately evacuated. Thus, Wallace had made a tough but correct decision. He had to weigh the evacuation of the soldier with the increased probability that such an operation would have alerted the VC to our presence and placed the whole battalion and its mission at risk. And I learn I will need a lot more hardening before I am ready to command soldiers in combat.

The S-3, Major Tony Jezior, joins the battalion shortly after I do. He is about thirty-three years old and a graduate of the West Point class of 1955. He is a large, physically imposing man who was on the boxing team at the Academy when boxing was still a collegiate sport. He is the heavyweight to Wallace's lightweight. Where Wallace is reserved, Tony Jezior is animated and open. It is easy to discern when he is not happy. Tony grew up in Cleveland, Ohio, in a Catholic, working-class neighborhood where his father ran a tavern. While one would not want to cross Wallace for fear of a good ass-chewing, crossing Jezior could well result in a good ass-kicking.

Jezior likes chess. Often, while out on an operation, we play after we attend to all our tasks, usually around midnight or later. He has a small portable set in which the plastic pieces have little pins beneath them to fit into holes in the board. Our chess parlor is a small, four-man "Hex" (hexagonal) tent illuminated by a Coleman gas lantern. The tent serves as our field CP, where we take turns manning the command radios and maintaining the Battalion Daily Journal, into which we record all significant events. The tent is sealed to prevent light emission, which might attract sniper fire. Thus, the interior is very hot; there is no ventilation, and the gas lantern adds to the accumulated heat. In spite of this, the chess games are a welcome and relaxing respite.

Jezior had done a lot of professional reading on insurgency warfare before he joined the battalion. I can only surmise that he had read that oral hygiene was important in the jungle; the man makes an industry of brushing his teeth. Many nights when I am so tired, I go to sleep with all my clothes on and my teeth *au naturelle*. But not Tony. He always brushes, and with a vigor that seems out of place. The only time I ever brushed like that was in high school, before a hot date. In later years, I fell in with women who smoked and drank cheap bourbon, making breath control somewhat irrelevant. At any rate, despite this disparity in our dental habits, I depart Vietnam with the same number of teeth as when I entered.

Throughout most of August, we have numerous routine missions, securing road convoys and sealing and searching villages. Jezior and I indulge in the time-honored contest of who is the better map reader and navigator. In the thick jungle, there is little notable terrain to orient on and correlate with one's location. In these circumstances, navigation is based on "dead reckoning," walking a set azimuth and estimating the distance covered from the start point. The only problem is that walking a straight azimuth in the heavy jungle is virtually impossible. Every minute or two, you are forced to deviate left or right of your marching azimuth to avoid a vegetation obstacle. Some deviations cancel each other out, and some add cumulatively to increase the navigational error. At every rest break, Jezior and I compare estimates of our location. Sometimes our estimates are spot-on; sometimes different by as much as one thousand meters. My ace in the hole is that when we are at variance with each other, I call for a white phosphorus artillery round to land where we definitely are *not located*. When the thick white smoke drifts above the jungle canopy, I take a back azimuth with my compass, adjust the magnetic grid declination, and get a fairly accurate fix on our location. Jezior and I keep ourselves amused and intellectually occupied between this and chess.

I know almost nothing of a personal nature about Wallace or Jezior. I am vaguely aware that they are married but have no idea of their wives' names, whether they have children or brothers. They, in turn, know equally little about me. We never discuss my time in Alpha 2-28th or Hill 150, my tour in Germany, college, or my family. Almost all contact is professional and business-related. Ultimately, all we know about each other is framed within the context of battle and whether we feel safe with the other person. Our backgrounds, our family pedigree, or lack thereof, have little relevance.

Wallace and Jezior are an interesting pair: opposites who work well together. In his fashion, each works to eradicate stupidity and laziness and inculcate within the battalion a sense of attention to detail and strict obedience to orders and instructions. One can think of the VC as the agent of death on the battlefield, but in actuality, absent stupidity, or laziness on the part of some American soldiers, far fewer VC would have succeeded in inflicting casualties. I remember one episode where we helicoptered out on a battalion-size patrol mission only to discover that night that the Bravo Company CO had left his 81mm mortars sitting at the airfield at Lai Khe. Wallace replaced him with a new CO.

Fortunately, actual contact with the enemy is relatively light, though, on one operation, the helicopter in which Wallace, Jezior, and I are riding is shot down. We are flying low just before coming in for a landing into an LZ situated by the Song Be River. We are to conduct a battalion search and destroy operation in a suspected VC base area. I gaze out the door and notice a VC soldier, clad in the black pajama-type uniform, emerge from a "spider hole"—a small foxhole with a thatched camouflage cover. He fires his AK-47 from the hip. I see all this in slow motion before I can bring my M-16 to bear and forewarn the right-side door gunner. I say to myself, "This guy is going to shoot us down." In the next moment, the right door gunner is shot in the thigh, and the pilot throws up his hands to avoid the bullets crashing through the control panel.

The "Huey" is damaged, but the pilot maintains control. We skim along the treetops and make a hard, forced landing at one of our base camps at Phu Loi. In the true tradition of "No rest for the wicked," we rapidly remove the PRC-25 radios from the damaged helicopter and are soon again airborne in a replacement Huey to rejoin the air assault into the LZ. This last experience serves as the final and perhaps key ingredient in the slow simmering "bonding stew" we have been brewing. It comes just in time for the serious battle that soon follows.

Standing in front of battalion CP area, early August 1966, with the most important pieces of my equipment—a map and my helmet in my left hand and a compass on my web belt, secured with a lanyard.

CHAPTER 18

BONG TRANG

"Confusion now hath made his masterpiece!"
WILLIAM SHAKESPEARE, *MACBETH*

On 25 August 1966, our brigade is on an operational standdown in Lai Khe. The 1st Brigade is conducting a routine convoy protection mission to the east of us. The division's soldiers live in base camps. The camps must be maintained and expanded. The soldiers must be fed, clothed, and supplied with ammunition. Base camp resupply is the background rhythm of war. Periodically, supplies are trucked northward from the dock and warehouse complexes around the Saigon port and Tan San Nhut Airbase areas to the forward base camps.

The 1st Brigade units (1-2 Infantry, 1-26 Infantry, and 1-4 Cavalry) are deployed along Highways 1A and 16, which run from Di An to their base at Phuc Vinh. The terrain in their sector is intermixed rubber plantation and jungle. The brigade must provide the engineering working parties to improve the road and clear it of land mines. Infantry units conduct patrols along the route to detect and disrupt VC ambushes. Convoy protection missions are usually mundane, and we are not involved. It promises to be a relaxing day to catch up on housekeeping, administration, and personal chores—a "Sunday on the farm" type of day.

We barely finish breakfast before that promise evaporates. The stage was set the day before with an incidental squad-size action. Late on 24 August, Charlie Company, 1-2 Infantry, commanded by Captain Bill Mullen, dispatched a fifteen-man patrol into the woods west of their assigned sector along Highway 1A to ambush

CHAPTER 18—BONG TRANG

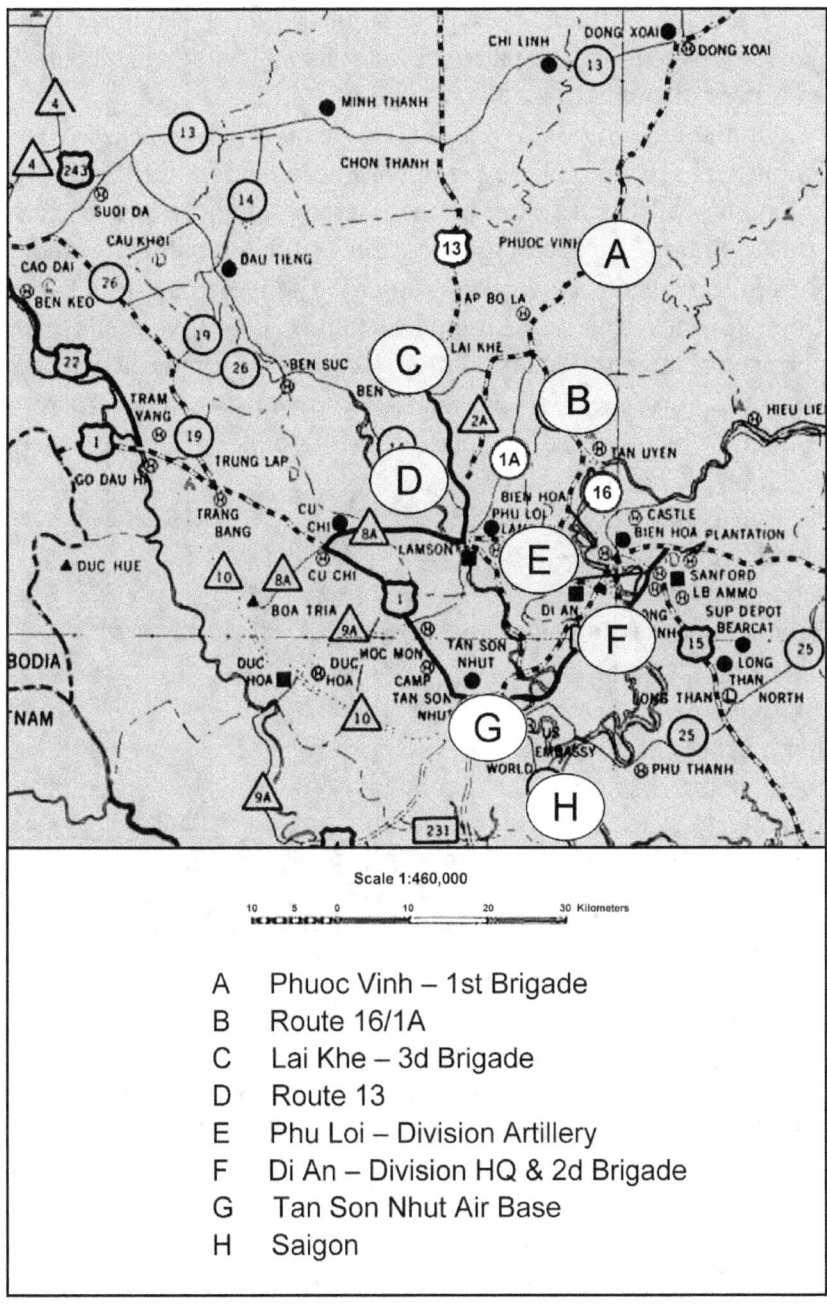

A Phuoc Vinh – 1st Brigade
B Route 16/1A
C Lai Khe – 3d Brigade
D Route 13
E Phu Loi – Division Artillery
F Di An – Division HQ & 2d Brigade
G Tan Son Nhut Air Base
H Saigon

1st Infantry Division base camps and major resupply routes from the Saigon-Di An logistical complex. Adapted by Amy Moore.

a previously identified VC supply point. Because of typical navigational difficulties, the patrol never reached its intended location and spent the night in a defensive perimeter.

On the morning of 25 August, they resume movement to their ambush site. En route, they stumble into a heavily fortified, well camouflaged VC base area, where a fierce firefight erupts. The patrol is outnumbered and outgunned. They suffer casualties and radio for reinforcement and artillery support. The remainder of Charlie Company moves west to extricate the trapped patrol. Mullen's force consists of eighty-five men, mounted on seven modified M113 Armored Personnel Carriers (APCs) known as Armored Cavalry Assault Vehicles (ACAVs), and one M-48 tank of Charlie Troop, 1-4 Cavalry. Each ACAVs is armed with three machine guns (two M-60 7.62mm and one .50 caliber). At about 0800, they fight into a portion of the VC base camp complex, but it is not exactly where their patrol is trapped. Initially, the VC withdraw but soon return and engage Charlie Company in a fierce fight.[57]

Armored Cavalry Assault Vehicle (ACAV). Official US Army photo.

Even with its significant firepower, Charlie Company cannot gain control of the situation. The remainder of 1-2 Infantry is committed. Bravo Company, commanded by Captain Nils Johannsen, and the rest of Charlie Troop, 1-4 Cavalry are sent to reinforce from the northeast. Mullen's company is now in a small open area, eventually designated "The Clearing." It is a clearing in name only. It is relatively free of tree cover, but it is heavily vegetated. And there is room enough for only one helicopter to land.

---

[57] As related in an email by Brigadier General, Retired, Bill Mullen, 7 April 2006. Mullen states that a patrol survivor later stated that the company's arrival succeeded in drawing the VC away from the trapped patrol.

Alpha Company, commanded by Captain John Morton, is ordered to organize a more functional LZ to which casualties from Charlie Company can be evacuated. This area, located about 250 meters east of The Clearing, is designated "LZ Blue."

At about 0900, based on Mullen's report of contact with a large VC force, the division commander, Major General DePuy, commits the remainder of the 1st Brigade and two infantry battalions of the 3rd Brigade: ours, 1-16 Infantry, and 2-28 Infantry. The division is operating under the strategy of attrition: the VC must be drawn into large-scale battles of annihilation. The overall concept of the operation is simple—it is the basic infantry doctrine of "find, fix, fight, and finish" writ large. We are ordered to begin planning for a helicopter insertion just west of the fight and to move east to block a VC escape ("find" and "fix") and "fight" them to the "finish." The 2-28 Infantry is ordered to establish a stationary block to the north; 1-26 Infantry blocks/reinforces from the south, and 1-2 moves in from the east.

However, the actual execution is not as simple as the concept. We are a moving vice, a stationary blocking force. The battlefield is non-linear; there are no front lines, and the reinforcing units are moving toward the enemy and each other. Charlie 1-2 Infantry is deep within a VC base area. Accordingly, the blocking/reinforcing forces must first find the fight, in difficult jungle terrain, which restricts both movement and observation. Thus, we are unaware of the precise locations of other friendly units. The combination of limited visibility and knowledge of the exact locations of units moving toward each other deprives us of our most singular combat advantage—firepower. Under these conditions, safely employing our artillery and air support will be impossible.

Wallace and Jezior study the area maps and identify a suitable LZ about two kilometers west of the ongoing fight. I plan the preparatory artillery fires. Our Bravo Company will be the first to land to secure the LZ; Wallace, Jezior, and I will go in with them. The remainder of the battalion will follow in subsequent lifts. We are then trucked down to the airstrip, where the UH-1 assault helicopters to carry us are still arriving and getting organized. Wallace, Jezior, and I lift off from Lai Khe at about 1130 to function as an airborne command and control element to coordinate LZ operations.

At first, the artillery fires I call for are slow and desultory. We need a more massive and rapid lay-down to suppress any VC around the LZ. I radio back to the FDC to increase the number of guns firing in support to produce a more massive and continuous ring of fire around the LZ. The voice at the other end of my radio seems irritated by my request. He gives the impression that I am disturbing his routine. He is one of the "old" holdovers from the original artillery cohort who has not yet rotated. I will discuss this with the new artillery battalion commander when I return.

Meanwhile, there is a bit of confusion in getting the first lift on the ground. I receive a radio message stating "rounds complete," meaning no more artillery shells (rounds) are in the air or forthcoming. Wallace directs our UH-1 down to mark the landing site with a smoke grenade. But, as we descend, more artillery shells detonate in the near tree line. This forces us to exit the landing pattern. It takes a few minutes for me to re-coordinate the cessation of the artillery fire. Immediately after that, there are reports of VC on the ground. I am obliged to request additional artillery fires, having just raised hell on the radio regarding the artillery fires not being turned off per the "rounds complete" transmission.

I adjust the artillery preparation for a few minutes more, and then we land with the first wave. We move with Bravo Company eastward into the tree line to secure the LZ. They report several VC killed by artillery. The Bravo Company FO party RTO, Corporal Miller, shoots a lone VC who darts across his path. I have no idea what the VC was doing. I can only imagine that he did not see, hear, or reason well. He was, accordingly, "Darwined" into extinction. Miller is allowed to keep the VC's Chinese SKS carbine as a trophy. We later "promote" Miller to serve as my RTO. In combat, there are few rewards, and those that occur sometimes defy explanation. But being an RTO for a captain is a step up from being one for a second lieutenant. It makes Miller happy.

We come across a badly wounded VC whose stomach has been sliced open by a large artillery fragment. His intestines are strewn about on the ground around him. Wallace reacts based on a tale related to him as a cadet by a colonel who had fought against the Moros in the Philippine Insurrection.[58] He directs that the VC's intestines be cleaned off as best as possible, reinserted, and bound up with a pistol belt. The VC is then evacuated. We later learn that he survived and proved to be a reasonably valuable intelligence source. Wallace relates that the old colonel had saved himself from a similar wound by wrapping his stomach and intestines with a cartridge belt sixty years earlier. We do not know what any of the dead and wounded VC were doing in the vicinity of our LZ. Perhaps they were part of a reconnaissance element, perhaps couriers, or perhaps just there by accident.

By 1200 hours, the remainder of our battalion has landed, and we begin moving eastward to join the fight. We normally travel in the jungle with the battalion in a single column formation: a long, single file of soldiers. This lets us move relatively easily and quickly along narrow jungle paths in heavily vegetated terrain by letting the soldiers play "follow the leader." It also facilitates silent, yet effective, communication by using hand and arm signals or whispers, which can be quickly relayed up and down the column.

The drawbacks to the formation are that because there are so few soldiers immediately to the head, it puts limited "eyes forward" to search for signs of the enemy, and especially ambush "tells." It also places limited firepower to our front, which is acceptable only if contact with the enemy is not expected. In our current situation, contact with the enemy appears imminent, and we need maximum firepower to our front.

Additionally, the location of all friendly units is fluid and uncertain. Normally, I would adjust artillery fire a few hundred meters to our front and exposed flanks as we move forward. But, because of the uncertain location of all friendly units and because we are moving toward each other, I cannot use the artillery in the "reconnaissance by fire mode" just described.

---

[58] After the Spanish American War of 1898, the United States acquired the Philippine Islands. A resistance movement opposed American colonialism. This conflict ended in 1902, but Moslem Filipinos, called Moros, in the Sulu Archipelago, continued the resistance until 1916.

To compensate for this and increase our available eyes and firepower forward, Wallace chooses to move to contact with two companies, each in column, abreast of each other, and the remainder of the battalion following behind the leftmost (northern) lead company. Each lead company deploys two platoons in column, abreast of each other, with the third in trail. Thus, the battalion has four platoons' worth of firepower to its front, rather than just a point squad. The reconnaissance platoon is deployed to screen our northern flank. Our battalion XO and the 1st Brigade S-3 are in separate H-13 light observation helicopters to help us navigate and accurately report our location.

The initial movement off the LZ is the high point of organization and planning. From here on, things degrade rapidly. Command and control and situational awareness—knowing who is where, doing what—are problematic. We are moving into a complex and ambiguous fight. By 1200 hours, as we move to the east, five company-size units of the 1st Brigade are either at or moving toward the main battle area, arriving from the west and south. Add our three companies to this mix, and you have eight company size units converging from different directions, only generally aware of each other's locations, if at all. The battle is being fought by the individual company commanders, "guided" from above by a few senior leaders riding in their H-13 light observation helicopters.

There is a big difference in how things are perceived from the air by those who aid our navigation, versus those of us on the ground executing the movement. In the air, one can easily form a sense of organization and control that does not match the reality on the ground. The aerial observer has only a secondhand feel for the intensity of the fight, the spirit of the unit, and the difficulty in movement and observation presented by the terrain. Soldiers in our lead platoons use machetes to clear a way through the thick brush. The triple-canopied jungle allows minimal sunlight to penetrate. The jungle is a natural maze. It is a world of shadows and vegetative obstacles. As if the "friction" of the jungle were not enough, there are the sounds of weapons fire, mortar and grenade explosions, smoke, frantic radio transmissions, and shouts simultaneously assaulting the ground commander's senses. A well-intended

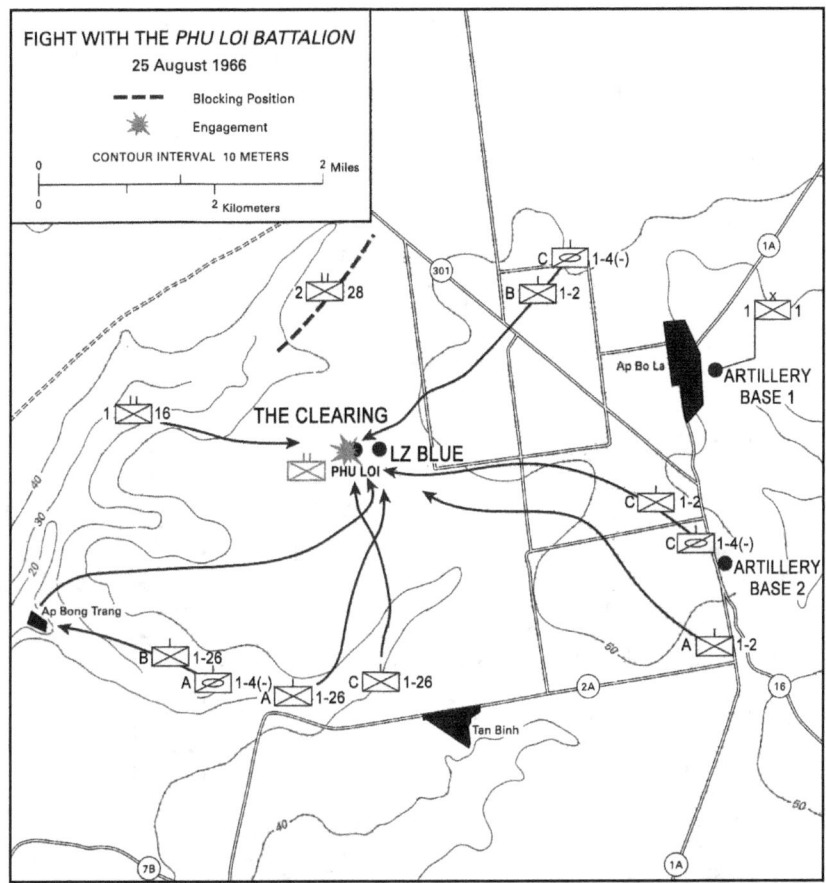

Movement of units toward The Clearing. From Stemming the Tide, *Center of Military History, United States Army.*

man in a helicopter telling a unit moving through heavy jungle terrain to change direction is akin to a financial advisor telling you that you should buy low and sell high to build wealth. In both cases, the trick is not knowing what needs to be done but how to do it.

Wallace likes to position himself (and by extension, Jezior and me) up front in a battalion march, usually with the lead platoon of the lead company. But he has recently been cautioned by our brigade commander not to place himself in such an exposed position. Wallace complies, literally, and now situates himself just behind the second (vice the first) platoon of the Bravo Company on the northern flank. Despite the aerial navigation aid, the battalion formation proves difficult to control. The four lead platoons from two different companies become periodically intertwined. At one point, Wallace, Jezior, our RTOs, and I find ourselves on the formation's extreme southern (right) flank, having followed a portion of a Bravo platoon which "drifted" off its intended course.

Map Symbols/Terms

Military Units

Function

| Airborne Infantry |
| Airmobile Infantry |
| Armor |
| Armored Cavalry |
| Cavalry (Aerial Reconnaissance) |
| Field Artillery |
| Infantry |
| Marine Infantry |

Size

Platoon	•••
Battery, Company, or Cavalry Troop	I
Battalion or Cavalry Squadron	II
Regiment	III
Brigade	x
Division	xx
Corps	xxx

Examples

Company C, 1st Battalion, 18th Infantry	C ⊠ 1–18
2d Battalion, 35th Infantry	2 ⊠ 35
1st Brigade, 101st Airborne Division	1 ⊠ 101
Headquarters, 1st Cavalry Division (Airmobile)	⊠ 1 CAV

CHAPTER 18—BONG TRANG

As we move east, the situation at The Clearing deteriorates. Charlie 1-26 Infantry, commanded by Captain Jim Madden, links up with Mullen's company at about 1300. Madden and Mullen confer on mounting a coordinated attack. The situation is complicated by the fact that Bravo 1-2 Infantry has not yet joined up, and its exact location is uncertain. Any attack, by either fire or maneuver, must take this into account.

The attack is never accomplished. Madden is wounded. Johannsen (CO, B, 1-2 Infantry) is also wounded when his company finally breaks through, with only fourteen infantrymen left standing. To add to the confusion, an Air Force HH-43 "Huskie" rescue helicopter from a unit code-named "Pedro" is shot down by ground fire, and a mini-operation is mounted to save its crew. In the end, Charlie 1-2, Bravo 1-2, and Charlie 1-26 Infantry, along with Charlie 1-4 Cavalry fight from their current locations against an unseen but well dug-in enemy.

Bravo 1-26 Infantry, under the command of Captain George Joulwan, is task-organized as Team Bravo, consisting of two rifle platoons mounted on the M-113 ACAVs of Alpha Troop, 1-4 Cavalry. They initially move west toward the village of Bong Trang, for which the battle will be later named. A VC prisoner previously indicated they would try to evacuate their wounded to this village. Alpha 1-26 Infantry is dispatched along a road almost due south of the ongoing battle, with the same mission. Neither finds any sign of VC activity, and they later move northeast and north respectively, to join the fight at The Clearing.

At about 1400, Berry lands his H-13 helicopter and begins to sort out an ever-evolving series of complications—the units in contact are not so much attacking as they are fighting their way in and then defending themselves and caring for the wounded. New units are close by, moving in to join the fight, but in reality, being forced into the same reactive pattern as the men they are reinforcing, thus adding to, rather than relieving, the confusion. And the VC are fighting aggressively but are largely unseen.

By 1530, we fight our way into a system of trenches that seem to comprise an outlying position of the main VC base camp. We find many rice sacks, but actual contact with the VC is still relatively light. At 1600, our Alpha Company and, shortly after that, Bravo Company link up with the 1st Brigade units at The Clearing. It has not been a rapid ride to the rescue. Between the difficult terrain and minor encounters with the VC en route, it has taken us four hours to cover two kilometers—we have moved at the rate of one kilometer every two hours. By contrast, a person with a pulse and 98.6-degree body temperature can probably walk at the rate of one kilometer in thirteen minutes. We moved at one-tenth of that speed.

The scene at The Clearing is chaotic. There is a smoldering M-113 ACAV, whose ammunition load had been detonated by a VC rifle grenade. Nearby is the wreckage of the Air Force HH-43 "Huskie," recently downed by small arms fire. The various radio networks produce a cacophony of reports of units under fire, trying to organize themselves coherently while battling an unseen and entrenched VC force. I take all this in and shake my head. It is going to be a bad day.

Colonel Berry is still at The Clearing, trying to establish order. Some soldiers have temporarily "left" the fight and taken refuge in the heavy vegetation. Berry works to return them to fight. Companies of different battalions are intermingled or give that

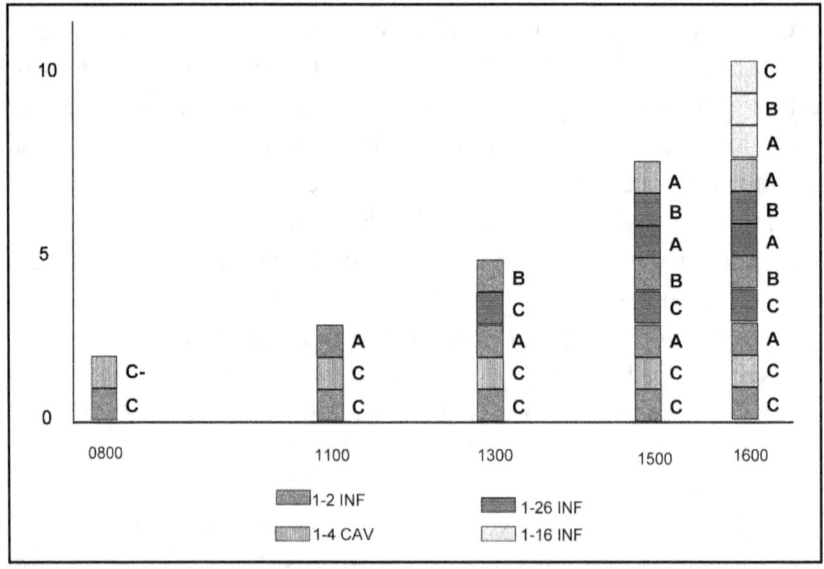

Time-sequenced buildup of company size units at "The Clearing."

impression. The commander of 1-26 Infantry, Lieutenant Colonel Paul Gorman, is reputed to have stated that after he arrived at The Clearing, he encountered soldiers from Charlie Company of all three battalions, plus Charlie Troop of 1-4 Cavalry within a few meters of his location.[59]

Part of Gorman's observation can be explained by the fact that these companies are at reduced strength because of casualties taken in the ongoing operation. Therefore, they occupy less space on the ground than they would at normal strength, making it easy for a man to travel only a short distance to encounter all of them. Size notwithstanding, the companies are in proximity to each other by virtue of their piecemeal arrival under fire. Furthermore, evacuation of the wounded detracts from focusing solely on organizing and maneuvering to defeat the unseen enemy. These factors combine to produce a disordered battlefield. By 1600, nine rifle companies and two armored cavalry troops from four battalions are located near The Clearing.

Berry and Wallace confer calmly. To preclude the VC from slipping away, Berry wants to move rapidly to contain the elusive and aggressive VC force confronting us. However, rapidity at the tactical level in the jungle is difficult to achieve and control.

Berry's basic concept of the operation is to form a 360-degree seal around the ill-defined VC base area. To complete the seal, we are directed to "attack" north, establish the boundaries of the VC force, and effect the seal in our sector. Since we are attacking to the east, we have to turn ninety degrees in heavy jungle, with limited visibility, and sort out our men from those of 1-2 and 1-26 Infantry.

Given the multitude of inter-mixed rifle companies operating in a relatively small area, we need a clear set of doctrinal coordination measures, such as battalion boundaries, objectives, and fire

---

[59] Cantigny Military History Series, Blue Spaders, Cantigny First Division Foundation, 169. Mullen places Gorman's observation in perspective: Mullen's Charlie Company arrived in the fight mounted on the ACAVs of Charlie Troop, 1-4 Cav. They were then reinforced by Charlie 1-26. Finally, George Wallace's 1-16 Infantry arrived on the scene with its Charlie Company last in line. When the lead elements of 1-16 attacked north, Charlie 1-16 was situated closest to The Clearing.

coordination lines. These are not forthcoming. Wallace attempts to bring his little piece of the operation under control. He speaks on the radio with his company commanders in a calm, cadenced voice that connotes a degree of control, which at the moment is illusionary but serves to steady the battalion. Wallace keeps working through the problems of establishing some semblance of control using our radios to put together a coherent view of the battle based on probing questions to those in direct contact with the VC.

We attack to the north, with two companies abreast. Bravo Company, commanded by Captain Quentin Seitz, is on our west flank, and Alpha Company, commanded by Captain Peter Knight, is on the east. Charlie Company follows and supports Alpha, and the command group follows Bravo. As we move northward with Bravo, we enter a second set of VC trenches and take casualties from accurately placed VC grenade launcher fire. To add insult to injury, we also take .50 caliber "friendly fire" from the M-113 ACAVs and M-48 tanks of 1-4 Cavalry. The heavy .50 bullets can travel over three miles. It takes us a few minutes to get this potentially lethal situation corrected.

Wallace and I are crouching behind a giant anthill for cover, going over our maps, trying to sort out who is where so I can bring our artillery support to bear. Two soldiers pass by, carrying a wounded comrade. As the VC fire intensifies, they drop the wounded soldier and seek shelter in a nearby trench. The wounded man cries out, under these trying circumstances, somewhat hysterically. Wallace goes to quiet the wounded soldier and get the other two back to carrying him. As soon as he departs the cover of the anthill, a VC 12.7mm machine gun opens up, cutting down a tree that had been directly behind his head. When Wallace returns, I point this out. He seems momentarily irked that I should bother him with this triviality, and then nonchalantly takes note of his good fortune. At this time, I become conscious of a reporter from a news team that has been with us since we left Lai Khe. He is crouched down in a VC trench. He is sucking on his knuckles. His face has the look of a man contemplating unfathomable confusion and danger.

As the battalion continues northward, Alpha Company comes under heavy 57mm recoilless rifle, 12.7mm machine gun, grenade launcher, and small arms fire from well-entrenched and camouflaged VC forces just north of The Clearing. Alpha Company maneuvers eastward to meet the VC attack. We lose contact with them, pass to the west of their fight, and rapidly continue northward, unopposed. In the process, we snagged one of Alpha's line platoons, which moved northward with us.

Alpha Company is now operating in the immediate vicinity of the much-decimated Charlie 1-2 Infantry. Knight confers briefly with Mullen, who passes on what information he has, and Knight presses forward to develop the fight. Knight soon has all three of his remaining platoons committed, and all three platoon leaders are eventually wounded. Knight is killed as he is leading his men forward against a well-camouflaged VC machine-gun bunker. I am right by Wallace when this news is radioed in. Wallace takes it hard. So do some of Knight's soldiers. The loss of their platoon leaders and company commander momentarily unhinges them. Mullen finds them to be moving rearward. He stabilizes them, gives his helmet to one who has "lost" his, and sets them on a new course back into the fight.[60]

The Charlie Company Commander, Captain Carroll Wilson, is seriously wounded in the hand by a large grenade fragment and is evacuated. Sergeant First Class Fairburn then takes charge by organizing a company perimeter and taking a patrol forward to evacuate the wounded from Alpha Company.

Knight and I had shared a two-man tent for a week or two while he was assigned to battalion staff awaiting an opening in Alpha Company. At night, before turning in, we would sit at a small handmade table, robotically cleaning our M-16s and Colt .45s and checking our ammunition magazines for corroded bullets, all the while bullshitting the time away like two college roommates as if there were no war at all. I liked him; he was easygoing, but I could tell he was a tough, battle-hardened veteran.

Lieutenant Chris Needels, the weapons platoon leader in Alpha Company, is lightly wounded in the action that sees Knight killed. As the last officer standing, he assumes command of Alpha.

---

[60] Based on email correspondence with Mullen.

Like me, he knew Knight only briefly, but it was enough to take the measure of the man. Below are extracts of his recollection of Knight and the circumstances of his death:

As we came closer, the intensity of fire was beyond anything I had ever experienced...within minutes Lieutenant Smith, whose platoon was with Knight and some other soldiers returned from The Clearing. Smitty (Lieutenant Smith) passed me holding his hand to an abdominal wound while informing me that Captain Knight was dead...I would have followed Knight anywhere, and I suppose we did. Although he was in command for only a few days, I got to know him as well as circumstances would permit. He told me about his wife and his son, Chris. He had already commanded a company and was on the promotion list to major, but he still wanted to lead a company in combat again.

This one engagement is emblematic of the entire fight. We have three battalions of infantry, 1-16, 1-26, and 1-2, being fed into the battle, *usually one platoon at a time*. Approximately one thousand US infantrymen are being employed thirty at a time. The VC battalion never feels the full, massed effect of the US force. And because our forces are so close to each other and the VC, we never get to use our superior artillery to full advantage. In our eagerness to close with the VC, we have hobbled ourselves. And we are paying for it.

Wallace stops for a map check and is informed by the assistant division commander in an H-13 that we (the command group and Bravo Company) are well north of and separated from the remainder of our battalion. Additionally, he is informed that a sizeable VC force is now between us and the main body south of us. We have no direct evidence of this, but Wallace acts as if it is so. We move south, cautiously, with Wallace way upfront to achieve maximum control and situational awareness. After moving about four hundred meters, we meet up with part of a platoon of our Alpha Company just as darkness begins to fall.

About this time the VC break contact. All goes silent—the sounds of battle are switched off. Gorman and his command group reach The Clearing. Berry returns to his headquarters at Artillery Base 1, leaving Gorman in command at The Clearing.

CHAPTER 18—BONG TRANG

The plan is to contain the VC force for the night. In the morning the attack will continue, commencing with an air-delivered napalm attack. The terrain to the east and south of The Clearing is rubber plantation and roadways. We have a military presence along the roads, and the rubber plantation affords relatively poor concealment. The VC will not favor a breakout in those directions. Accordingly, the emphasis is placed on the west and north, where the jungle terrain affords the VC better concealment, and a chance to make a direct run for the Cambodian border, approximately thirty-five kilometers (less than a one-day march) to the northwest. There they can rest and refit while we observe the sanctity of the international border.[61]

To produce the containment, the 1st Brigade forms three separate night laagers. The companies of 1-2 and 1-26 Infantry and Charlie and Headquarters Companies of 1-16 Infantry form one laager, under command of Gorman, positioned roughly at the 4 to 8 o'clock positions around The Clearing. Bravo Company, the Alpha platoon, and the Command Group of 1-16 Infantry form a second laager at the 11 o'clock position, about four hundred meters north of The Clearing. The 2-28 Infantry forms a third, at about the 12 to 2 o'clock positions. The airstrike will come in from the west through the "9 o'clock slot" between our laager and Gorman's.

We finally gain a more coherent view of the enemy situation based on radio traffic between the command groups. The VC camp contains several large fighting bunkers, capable of holding upwards of twenty soldiers each. The roofs are reinforced with two to three-inch logs and compacted earth. The major portions of the bunkers are underground. The firing embrasures are only a few inches off the ground, and the surrounding vegetation has been carefully "tunneled" to create clear fields of fire not visible to a soldier standing upright but subjecting him to withering fire when he instinctively "hits the dirt." The bunkers are joined and surrounded by a complex network of trenches. Artillery would not be as effective as napalm

---

[61] Mullen states that this was confirmed by a company commander from the Phu Loi Battalion who was captured in 1968. He reported to interrogators that his unit recuperated in Cambodia after the battle.

in penetrating the camp's fortifications. The napalm will either kill the VC outright or cause them to hunker down in their bunkers and trenches and abandon their firing positions long enough for an infantry assault to go in and complete the job.

The Bravo soldiers on the perimeter set out their claymore mines, trip flares, and establish listening posts. Wallace, Jezior, and I sort out where our forces and other elements of the 1st Brigade are located so I can plan the H and I fires for the night. I plot these fires on likely avenues of ingress/egress from the VC base area to preclude or make any attempts by the VC to withdraw, reinforce, or reposition their forces difficult. The H and I fires will be delivered at irregular intervals to preclude the VC from "timing" them. I then coordinate with the Bravo FO on his plans for artillery defensive concentrations and illumination for our laager. I also talk on the radio with the Alpha and Charlie FOs to obtain their status and understand what fires they are planning and executing, under the operational control of 1-26 Infantry. Wallace works the radio to better appreciate our units' locations and status and establish a sense of cohesion for our separated and somewhat depleted battalion.

I am in a bigger, more confusing battle than the fight for Hill 150 in June. But the only VC I have thus far seen are dead or badly wounded, and they posed no threat to me. I have not had any need to bring my M-16 to my shoulder. Thus, I do not feel personally targeted. Once again, as at Hill 150, I feel emotionally detached from the battle. I am having an out-of-body experience. I am in the fight, but not a part of it. I am watching myself plan, coordinate, and adjust artillery fires. I am an outside observer of my reality. The confused situation is a blessing. It keeps me from worrying about myself. It makes me focus on my responsibility as an artillery officer, and my mind is devoted to problem-solving rather than worry.

As things settle out, the news reporter asks Wallace, in a hopeful tone, if we have the VC surrounded. Wallace replies with a straight face, "Affirmative." The reporter later asks Major Jezior to show him on the map where we and the VC are located. Jezior points out how the VC force probably surrounds our little night

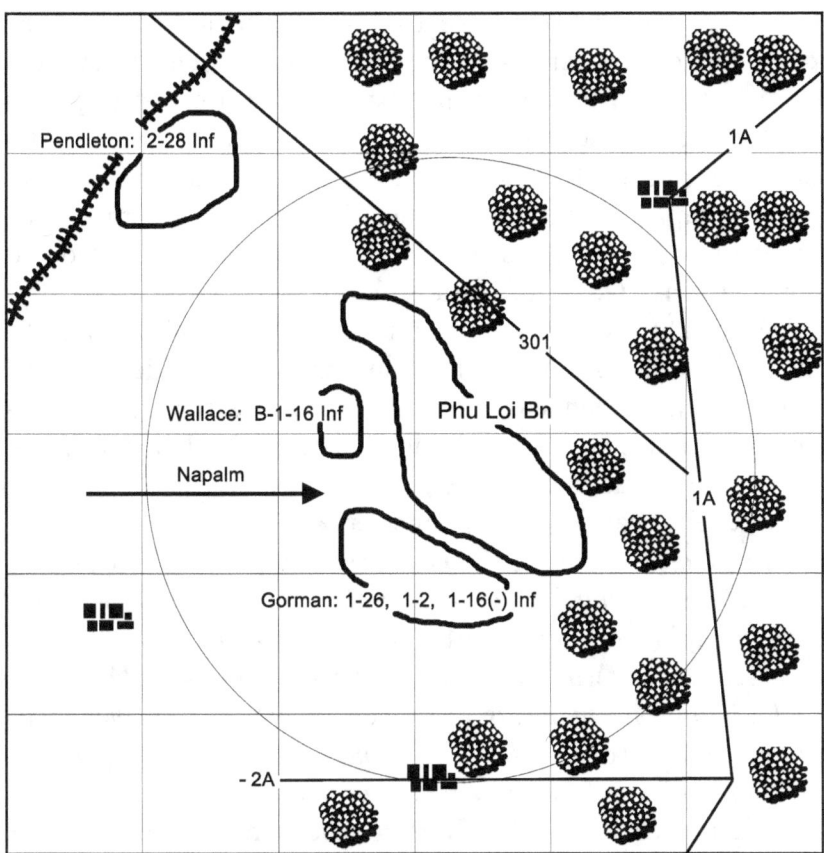

Locations of units on morning of 26 August, prior to napalm strike.

laager. The reporter's hope is dashed. As if to punctuate the point, later that night, our perimeter is probed by a small VC force. The fight is light enough to suggest it was an accidental contact by a wayward VC unit, moving in the dark to escape or rejoin its parent unit. Incidents like this are repeated throughout the night.[62]

At first light on the 26th, we start moving toward Gorman's position. At 0700, the airstrikes are brought in. Flights of F-4

---

[62] Later battle reports indicated that many more of the surviving VC and their wounded than we originally imagined succeeded in exfiltrating the battle area that night. Out of 500 men in the Phu Loi Battalion, US reports indicated somewhere between 149 and 271 were killed. South Vietnamese reports put the number of VC killed at 171.

Phantoms deliver twenty-two canisters of napalm. During the runs, the soldiers remain in the captured VC trenches and destroyed bunkers, observing the results. Twenty canisters are on the enemy; two are not. One errant napalm bomb bounces off a tree, ricochets ninety degrees, and splashes Gorman and his command group. Miraculously, Gorman suffers only a burned map. The twenty-second canister falls short, killing two and wounding fourteen.[63] Our headquarters company commander, Captain Ed Boroski, is seriously burned about his face and upper body. Sergeant Fairburn is also burned but manages to retrieve several of his likewise wounded comrades. In the process, he receives additional burns to his body. Fairburn will be awarded the Silver Star for this and his actions the day before.

Needels recalls the napalm incident as follows:

Tragically, a stray napalm bomb hit our position. It was truly surreal—a blinding flash of light, an intense moment of heat, and a feeling of the air being sucked out of our lungs. And as quickly as it happened, it was gone, with many wondering what had hit us. Sadly, it took only moments, as soldiers on fire ran from the impact point...I tackled one soldier on fire and smothered him with a poncho to put him out. I wonder if he ever made it.

Wallace, Jezior, and I arrive at the scene immediately after the napalm strike. An F-4 makes a strafing run, dumping 20mm cannon fire right in front of us, sending our soldiers diving for cover. The forward air controllers and S-3 Air do their best to identify the targets and mark friendly locations, but the VC are very close to our lines. The F-4s are moving at about three hundred miles per hour. Small features on the ground, such as trench lines and humans, are a blur. When the separation distance between our forces and the VC is small, friendly fire incidents are almost guaranteed. Between the VC and "friendly fire," we have, in less than twenty-four hours, lost three of our four company commanders.

After the napalm attack, both 1-26 and 2-28 Infantry go in to clear out what remains of the VC force. There is some confusion

---

[63] John M. Cartland, *Stemming the Tide*, (Washington, D.C.: Office Chief of Military History, 2000), 325-333.

over which battalion is where, and 2-28 Infantry fires into the 1-26 Infantry area. Fortunately, no friendly casualties are produced.

At about 0900, we are ordered to attack southeast to re-engage the VC who either escaped or were not contained in the seal. We encounter several stay-behind ambush and sniper teams, which we overcome with artillery fire but fail to make significant contact with the main enemy force. One of our elements takes friendly fire from 1-26 Infantry, which is operating just north of us. When Jezior learns of this, he becomes quite heated and starts to berate the 1-26 Infantry command element via radio. Wallace helicopters to Gorman's CP, and they review the battalion boundaries and fire coordination lines and ensure they are properly posted to their maps.

Later in the day, one of our patrols, led by a survivor of the Charlie 1-2 Infantry ambush patrol, finds the bodies of six members of the original fifteen-man patrol. On the radio, we hear that the other nine had emerged a few hours earlier from the VC bunker where they had taken refuge and made their way to Gorman's battalion.

That night, we set up a defensive perimeter. In the early evening, in heavy rainfall, we receive incoming rifle and RPG fire. The troops are wet and exhausted. Fire is coming in, but we have no firm targets to engage. Trip flares are going off all around the perimeter, indicating enemy presence, but we cannot see them. Luckily, the real estate situation is well sorted; we know where all our forces are located. We can safely use our artillery. The company FOs and I have several artillery battalions in support, and we do not waste them. I move to the edge of the perimeter to coordinate the FOs. We "pass" the fires around from company to company, encircling our battalion perimeter with a moving, close-in, protective wall of artillery fire. It breaks up the possible VC attack before it can get started. More than that, the artillery helps solidify our spirits. Everyone is now working as a team. The howitzer gunners are servicing the guns all night; the fire direction crews are computing the firing data; the FO parties and I are adjusting the fires. In their widely scattered fighting positions, we give the soldiers a sense that something good is being done for them.

Several soldiers start a small fire in the morning, using empty mortar ammunition crates to dry out their wet clothing. I join in. Our battalion command sergeant major fulminates that our campfire will attract VC fire. He probably expresses pent-up emotions from the previous day; his argument makes little sense. It is daylight; the campfire is a tactical non-issue. His occupation with minor matters is a sign that the danger is past; the battle is over.

This is how the fight is officially summarized: one hundred seventy-one VC killed, forty-one US killed, and one hundred wounded. The statistics confirm the statement attributed to Arthur Wellesley, the Duke of Wellington, after the Battle of Waterloo, "Next to a battle lost, the greatest misery is a battle gained."

Award ceremony at Lai Khe, early September 1966. Division Commander, Major General William E. DePuy presenting me with the Bronze Star for Valor, 1st Oak Leaf Cluster and Air Medal. Official US Army photo.

CHAPTER 19

MAKING MONKEYS

"I presided over this very gory and unsuccessful operation."
MAJOR GENERAL WILLIAM DEPUY

Let me make two obvious assertions. First, the battle could have been better conducted. Second, the enemy played a large role in causing the difficulties we faced. The VC Phu Loi Battalion was experienced and well-led. They had prepared an extensive network of hidden trenches and bunkers. They engaged our M-48 tanks and M-113 ACAVs with light infantry weapons. We had elements of four US infantry battalions arrayed against them, with air and artillery support, yet the VC offered effective resistance for ten hours. Notwithstanding our hasty reinforcement and limited employment of artillery, a lesser-quality enemy force might have been more easily overcome earlier in the fight.

Captain Jim Madden, the CO of Charlie 1-26, eventually met one of the VC company commanders from that fight. Madden, who was twice wounded and evacuated on 25 August, was in Vietnam on a second tour, again with the 1st Infantry Division. The VC company commander had been seriously wounded, evacuated to Cambodia for treatment and rest, and captured upon returning to combat in Vietnam. He switched allegiance, in theory at least, and worked on a special task force that Madden commanded. Madden describes the man as thoroughly professional and technically competent.[64] This competency was undoubtedly derived from the experience of continuous service in infantry units

---

[64] Jim L. Madden, unpublished manuscript, C Company, 1-26th Infantry, 25-26 August 1966, 2002.

in persistent combat. In comparison, US officers were on twelve-month rotations, of which usually no more than six months were spent in line units. Other competing assignments, as well as career development policies, operated to deprive US combat units of equal, long-term leadership experience.

Shortly after the battle, Wallace spoke with General DePuy. He proposed that the senior leaders in that fight caucus to analyze what happened and why, and to generate lessons learned to be applied in similar situations. This after-action review never occurred, at least not as proposed. But thirteen years later, in 1979, DePuy, then retired as a four-star general, upon being interviewed by Bill Mullen, then a student at the Army War College, had this to say about the events of 25 August 1966:

Suffice it to say that Bill Mullen's patrol got into the middle of a VC base camp, and then his company went in to rescue the patrol, and his battalion came to reinforce him, and then I brought in other battalions. Paul Gorman's battalion, the 1st of the 26th Infantry, came in from the south. 'Goony' Wallace's 1st Battalion, 16th Infantry, came all the way across from Lai Khe, while Elmer Pendleton's 2d of the 28th Infantry, came in from the north and tried to block that escape route. We tried to get all around the camp because, obviously, the patrol reported there were a lot of enemy. It turned out to be a battalion-sized base camp. Gorman's move was only partially successful. 'Goony' Wallace's move was a disaster. Elmer Pendleton was positioned okay, but they didn't go out his way. The 1st of the 2d Infantry, when it came in, was not well in hand. I presided over this very gory and unsuccessful operation. The VC made monkeys of us... [65]

Mullen, intending no disrespect whatsoever, related to me on 7 April 2007, that it might have been more accurate for DePuy to have stated that we had made monkeys out of ourselves.

When he assumed command of the Division in March 1966, DePuy had already served two years in Vietnam as the J-3 of

---

[65] Romie L. Brownlee and William J. Mullen III, *Changing An Army, An Oral History of General William E. DePuy, USA Retired* (Carlisle, PA: United States Military History Institute; Washington, DC: United States Center of Military History, 1979), 157.

the Military Advisory Command, Vietnam (MACV), the highest operational headquarters in the country. He had developed an opinion, born of experience, of how the war should be conducted henceforth, and used his command of the 1st Infantry Division as a laboratory and bully pulpit:

It was my idea to go after the Main Forces wherever they could be found and go after them with as many battalions as I could get into the fight...To do that required a very agile and fast-moving division...My initial efforts were to create just such a division. I took it as my main mission to defeat or disrupt the activities of all the VC Main Forces north of Saigon... [66]

DePuy's precepts shaped the battle. The senior leadership's initial operating premise, based on long experience with VC "hit and run" tactics, was that the VC would attempt to withdraw. This had to be precluded to set the conditions for a decisive battle with the US forces. Adherence to this concept of operations led to the rapid insertion of US units to surround the VC, fix them in place, and then finish the fight.

Contrary to expectation, in the early phases of the fight, the VC battalion either made no effort to flee the battlefield or reasoned it was too risky, with so many US forces moving about in all directions. For whatever reason, they decided to stand and fight. Whatever VC movements detected by the US forces were probably misinterpreted as VC escape attempts. These movements may have represented localized tactical repositioning of VC elements to engage the US forces more effectively.

The division's senior leadership required almost ten hours to develop an accurate picture of the enemy situation and craft an effective response late on 25 August. In the interim, the initial concept of blocking a VC retreat remained operative. This led to the hasty insertion of multiple battalions from converging directions. The terrain was not conducive to control. The hurried efforts to prevent the perceived VC retreat produced a disordered and crowded battlefield. This condition made it difficult to establish a safe separation of US and VC forces and define an area where massive

---

[66] Brownlee and Mullen, Changing An Army, 138.

US firepower could be employed. Two companies were already there when our battalion started moving eastward to the battle area. Another company was moving in from the northwest, yet another from the south, and a fourth company from the southwest.

Generals and colonels see a fight one way, junior officers another. Lieutenant Tom Galvin, a platoon leader in Bravo Company 1-26, was seriously wounded, clearing a large VC bunker. Today, he describes the piecemeal insertion of individual rifle companies as they arrived on the scene as the equivalent of a large barroom brawl into which several hundred reinforcements are fed one at a time. Galvin's statement can be paraphrased as follows:

The VC never had to *deal with four to five rifle companies; they just had to deal with one platoon at a time. They would shoot up an attacking platoon and shift their fires and dispositions slightly to shoot up the next platoon in line.*

The senior leadership thought they were directing the battle and effecting the encirclement with battalions. In actuality, no one was entirely in charge of anything. Company commanders were maneuvering and committing their platoons in response to "facts on the ground"—terrain and the very local enemy situation. Their platoon leaders were doing likewise, often further modifying, by necessity, what their company commanders intended. Battalion commanders were caught in the middle. They received orders from brigade and division and attempted to reconcile these orders with the reality on the ground, as reported by their company commanders, platoon leaders, and sometimes their squad leaders. By and large, the battle was being fought at the platoon level by a very few platoons at a time. The cumulative mass and shock action of several battalions' worth of platoons was not achieved. The senior leaders' failure to appreciate this precluded the development of orders to mount a coordinated, deliberate attack, with associated control measures to enable our superior firepower's safe and effective employment. Rather than a criticism, I offer this observation as an example of commanders' difficulty in "seeing" a fight for what it is versus what they have preordained.

DePuy was certainly neither wrong nor alone in his desire to engage the VC in decisive combat. Several years later, another famous division commander, Major General Melvin Zais, of the 101st Airborne Division, had this to say after he was criticized for incurring heavy casualties while assaulting Hamburger Hill (Hill 937) in May 1969:

That hill was in my area of operations, that is where the enemy was, that's where I attacked him...If I find him in another hill...I assure you I will attack him...It is true that hill 937, as a particular piece of terrain, was of no particular significance. However, the fact that the enemy force was located there was of prime significance.

Victor Davis Hanson places both DePuy's and Zais's comments in a multi-year context, as he explains in *Why The West Has Won*:

...the American military during the first few years in Vietnam still operated with a sense of invincibility. In their eyes, the problem in Southeast Asia was not defeating the enemy, but finding him and then coaxing him to come out and fight, where he would then be promptly destroyed through overwhelming American firepower.[67]

At the tactical level, most US soldiers, NCOs, and junior officers performed superbly. The fighting men of the 1st Brigade team temporarily destroyed the operational effectiveness of a first-rate VC battalion. The soldiers fought doggedly and bravely against a seasoned VC force, which mounted an aggressive and determined defense on its home turf. Wallace's battalion fought and stumbled through a confused and disordered battlefield, did all that was asked, and endured high casualties with a laconic reserve that the Spartans could envy.

Wallace led and commanded from the front. He positioned himself where he could see, understand, and influence our battalion's actions. My most vivid recollection of that day is his face. It is the classical picture of troubled thought and determination. His photo could have been on file in Hollywood Central Casting as an actor ready to play any number of similar roles—the dedicated but perplexed doctor trying to save a beloved patient for whom no treatment protocol seems yet to work, an overworked defense

---

[67] Victor Davis Hanson, *Why The West Has Won* (New York: Doubleday, 2001), 390.

attorney sifting over and over through a plethora of conflicting evidence arrayed against an innocent man consigned to death row, or, as himself, a commander trying desperately to minimize the damage to his battalion, while still accomplishing the mission assigned.

Jezior, too, never portrayed the slightest hint of despair. He worked relentlessly to support Wallace. My efforts were less expansive. I concentrated on blotting out the confusion and mayhem about me that was beyond my responsibility and capability to rectify. I focused on trying to understand where our battalion elements, other battalions, the artillery units, and the VC were situated to gain an appreciation of where and when I could bring in artillery support. I set myself a modest goal and did it marginally well.

In spite of Wallace's and Jezior's efforts, and the fighting spirit of our soldiers, our battalion's contribution was problematic. We lost several key leaders in the fight and recorded only a few confirmed VC killed in action. Man for man, we lost more than we gained. Perhaps we served best by distracting the VC and limiting their ability to maneuver and mass against the other brigade units.

The division's shortcomings in the Battle of Bong Trang and the fight for Hill 150, which occurred forty-four days earlier, share much in common. Both were meeting engagements conducted concomitantly to "routine" operations, which portended minor prospects for major combat. At Hill 150, we started the day on a village search and clear mission, and unexpectedly transitioned into a frontal assault on a dug-in VC company. At Bong Trang, a patrol effort, coincidental to a road-clearing mission, led to a two-day battle against an aggressive and well-dug-in VC battalion. The US forces were surprised by a determined enemy willing to engage in direct combat in both fights. In both fights, the US forces deployed and maneuvered in a manner that initially negated the effective (and decisive) use of superior US air and artillery fire support.

Both fights ended with the employment of superior US fire support means after the battle lines had been tidied up, and both fights entailed near or actual loss of friendly life from the decisive fire support delivered close in.

The similarity in problems with those of the 11 June fight in the Loc Ninh Plantation suggests some deficiency in the division's ability to conduct an operational analysis. Indeed, no one can claim the division leadership was intellectually deficient. After the battle of Bong Trang, General DePuy promulgated several changes to division tactics.[68]

The noise, smell, confusion, and suffering of the battle were reduced to numbers in the reports that ensued. A total of forty-one US soldiers were killed, and another one hundred wounded. The 1st Brigade team killed one hundred seventy-one VC: one hundred one from the Phu Loi Battalion, sixty from its attached C62 Company, and ten laborers. The number of VC wounded is unknown.[69] The number of VC dead briefed well at MACV Headquarters and reflected favorably on our division. That "reflected glow" covered up a lot of mess.

---

[68] Examples are the use of "clover leaf" patrol techniques, modification to the construction of infantry fighting positions, and a five-minute standard for artillery response to calls for fire.

[69] Mullen relates that it was later determined that many VC wounded were safely extricated from the multi-battalion "seal" on the night of 25-26 August. It was further learned that the number of wounded VC overwhelmed the VC hospital system in that area of operations. Mullen further states that he is sure the majority of VC dead were caused by infantry and crew-served weapons, mortars, and artillery. This belief has credence; I do not recall recovering many "charred" VC after the 26 August napalm strike.

CHAPTER 20

CHANGE

"Every body continues in its state of rest...unless it is compelled to change that state by forces impressed upon it."
ISAAC NEWTON, PRINCIPIA MATHEMATICA

In early December, I am summoned back to my parent artillery battalion to take command of its headquarters battery. This is the plum, career-enhancing assignment I have shamelessly coveted. The headquarters battery is the only command a sane battalion commander could assign me. The line batteries do the actual shooting, and their commanders must be technically qualified in artillery gunnery and cannon procedures, skills I lack from an air defense background. The headquarters battery, which provides support and services to the battalion, has artillery experts assigned to those positions requiring it. All I need to provide is a decent degree of leadership and organization. But a headquarters battery is a political minefield. Line batteries have a single captain, and he is god-like. Headquarters batteries have many captains serving on the battalion staff and two majors, the XO, and the S-3. All these officers "share" the battery's soldiers; they are mine to command but work for the aforementioned officers. Innumerable conflicts are associated with priorities for the soldiers' efforts and how they should be disciplined and promoted. Luckily, I commanded an air defense headquarters battery in Germany, and have a reasonable chance of success based on lessons learned from previous mistakes.

Lieutenant Colonel Charles Daniel, Jr. commands the battalion There is a lot to say about this man, all of it good. He is dignified, convivial, caring, and a thoroughly competent professional. Daniel reminds me of Beaver Cleaver's father, Ward, dressed out in a helmet rather than a man's hat. Daniel is an "Army Brat." His father was a career officer. Born in 1925, he entered West Point in 1943 and graduated in 1946. He served in the Korean War as a battery commander in the 39th Field Artillery Battalion, supporting the 15th Infantry Regiment of the 3rd Infantry Division. Daniel is also brilliant. He received a Master of Science degree and completed the required Ph.D. level coursework in nuclear physics from Tulane in 1963.

In August 1966, he is in Vietnam, assigned as my third battalion commander in as many months. The first commander rotated after a normal tour shortly after the fight for Hill 150. The second commander was replaced after only a week or two in command. There was a firing battery error, and several Vietnamese civilians were killed. There was pressure from division headquarters to have the battery commander relieved and admonished. The battalion commander demurred. Daniel later told me that the battalion commander had an advanced degree in law and thought about assigning culpability in a more legalistic context than his superiors. At some point, the division threw down the gauntlet—relieve the battery commander, or you will be relieved. The battalion commander stood by his convictions and was soon gone. While his courage was admirable, one had to question his military wisdom.

Even while still assigned to 1-16 Infantry, I saw quite a bit of Daniel. He sincerely cared about soldiers. He would helicopter into our field CP to ensure we received the best artillery support possible. Under Daniel's direction, artillery responsiveness improved dramatically, without any noticeable increase in "incidents" that the previous regime labored so mightily to avoid. I liked him immediately and looked forward to serving under him.

But Daniel is conducting an internal uphill fight to remodel the battalion. The pressures of war and the dangers of combat have a way of influencing behavior by setting free "demons" within us that are, in peacetime, held in check. In the extreme, war can induce psychopathic responses like the My Lai Massacre. In our case, the response is much more benign. In the battalion, we have a certain degree of "looseness" in the behavior of certain officers, manifested by an over-familiarity with the enlisted soldiers, an indulgence in drink, and "fraternization" with the local women. Daniel later tells me that he had to admonish and eventually replace one of the line battery commanders who habitually played poker and gambled with his enlisted men. As I said, war can create a sense of shared danger and equality, sometimes translating into blurred distinctions in the chain of command. A commander must be able to keep a reasonable distance from his soldiers. Often war requires the issuance of orders that are tantamount to telling soldiers that they must "eat a shit sandwich." It is difficult, if not impossible, to effectively enforce such orders if the officer or the soldiers think of each other as equals or friends. An officer should love his men but at a distance. Daniel does this well; no one doubts his deep affection for his soldiers, but all understand he is still their commander.

I find several less than fully motivated staff captains in the battery. When it comes to their comfort, however, their energy levels are high. They devote inordinate effort to bettering their living conditions (which by infantry standards were already lavish). They are preoccupied with constructing wooden huts, obtaining mattresses, furniture, tape decks, etc. Almost immediately after my arrival, I am offered the opportunity to "buy" the wooden "hooch" (hut) built by the former battery commander. I decline the real estate investment opportunity and choose to live in a GP small tent, which I share with my XO. We sleep on army folding cots and use the standard-issue air mattress and poncho liner as bedding. Our furniture consists of two metal folding chairs and a homemade table. We continued to live in this tent even after wooden barracks were finally constructed for the soldiers.

These captains are divorced from kinship with the infantry. Some of them are married and appear to be carrying on with the young Vietnamese village girls hired to clean their sleeping quarters or serve as waitresses in the battalion club. Given my low tolerance and transparent disdain for unprofessional behavior, I am soon at "war" with this clique. I go out of my way to ensure that no resources or services intended for the primary benefit of the enlisted soldiers are diverted for their personal use. I also notice that they tend to "sleep in" and come to breakfast after posted dining hours, demanding to be served by the enlisted orderly. I put a stop to that practice by enforcing the posted dining schedule. I inform the enlisted mess personnel that they are to follow my orders and brook no bullying from the latecomers.

The two majors in the battalion are an interesting pair of opposites. The XO, Major Bob Schneider, is devoted to Daniel but is not an artillery expert. He is responsible for the smooth administrative and logistical functioning of the battalion; he supervises the staff and is the official "enforcer" for the low-performing staff officers (who fear him as much as they dislike me). The S-3, Major Rinker, is a West Pointer with a rather short temper but is my hero. He knows artillery backward and forward, but that is also his bane. He is ultraconservative when it comes to its utilization. He would reserve artillery support for only the most essential missions. He does not want to take unnecessary risks in chancing an artillery incident. The less we shoot, the lower the odds of an incident. In a way, he is protecting Colonel Daniel; a previous commander had been replaced because of an artillery accident.

In addition to Schneider, Daniel has the full support of the battalion's senior enlisted soldier, Sergeant Major Koshiama. This man sets the tone and example for all the battalion's soldiers to follow. He is aligned with Daniel in an almost feudal or tribal way, which in combat is the best of all bonds possible. I, too, form an easy alliance with Koshiama, which enables me to quickly effect some changes in the battery's culture essential to improving its combat posture. For example, when I arrive, several senior NCOs have taken the habit of treating Sunday as a day off. They wear civilian clothing, rest, or visit with friends in other units. I stop this silliness; Koshiama supports me, leaving no room for the NCOs to complain or appeal. I also start a strict regime to service our trucks and jeeps daily, repair and strengthen the bunkers along our internal perimeter, conduct convoy counter-ambush battle drills and weapons training, and widen the road network within our area. All this takes the soldiers away from their staff officers for several hours a day, but Schneider and Koshiama back me 100 percent, again leaving no room for complaint or appeal. Change is not accomplished easily, but I am resolved to get it over with as quickly as possible. After a few hard weeks, the battery takes on a more professional mien.

Dooley, now a sergeant, reappears in my life. He is standing before my desk, somewhat at attention, with his new leader, a very strict, by-the-book all spit-and-polish captain, formerly from the 82d Airborne Division. He is now assigned as the Artillery LNO for one of the Infantry battalions—the same job I held just previous to assuming command. He tells me he is on the verge of recommending Dooley for court-martial for insubordination. I smile, inwardly. Dooley speaks, without permission, and requests he be given a new captain to work for. Now, I am laughing inwardly. Without much effort, I separate Dooley from a probable court-martial and have him replaced and reassigned. True to form, Dooley manages to neglect to say thank you.

On 13 February, we deploy with the 3rd Brigade on Operation Tucson, which is intended primarily to pre-position forces for an upcoming, but still secret, operation code-named Junction City. Major Schneider, the line battery commanders, and I are helicoptered into our battalion's area of operation to lay it out for the main body, which will arrive later by road convoy. Having emerged from my assignment with 1-16 Infantry without a scratch, I entertain the thought that I am now safe. Artillery units are still the "rear area." As an analogy, you can think of artillerymen working in a thunderstorm. They are technically vulnerable to a lightning strike. But you can describe the infantrymen as running through the storm with a lightning rod in each fist.

We occupy our first position without incident. That night it is decided to move the battalion to a different position, several kilometers further south.

On 14 February, at 0500 in the morning, I lead a small convoy of jeeps and three-quarter-ton trucks down a dirt road on the eastern edge of the main Michelin Rubber Plantation. We are the advance party. Our mission is to conduct a reconnaissance of a new artillery position, map out where the guns and FDC will go, and then guide the main body to the designated locations. Our headlights are on, and we are traveling at high speed. We are not trying to be unobserved. The theory is that if we move quickly enough, the enemy will not have time to organize an ambush or lay mines. And if freshly planted landmines exist, they should be made more evident by our headlights.

I am in the first jeep. Ahead of me are four M-113 ACAVs belonging to a mechanized infantry platoon of the 2d Battalion, 2d Infantry. They provide counter-ambush security and will subsequently secure the outer perimeter of our new position. The main convoy is still in the assembly area. They will pace their movement based on the situation as we radio it in. They will join us when all is secured, and the new positions are staked out.

I do not expect any problems. The decision to relocate was made just hours earlier. We have done little to alert the VC of our intentions and have found no evidence of enemy presence in our immediate area. There is no way they could have had the time to send in forces and prepare to ambush or disrupt our convoys.

It does not take long for reality to trump theory. I hear the dull retort of an explosion. I know that sound and what it connotes. A moment later, the radio confirms that the lead ACAV has struck a mine. It has thrown a track and is temporarily out of action. Now, three ACAVs are in front of me. As we pass the disabled ACAV, we see the crew laboring to replace the thrown track. It is arduous work. A short time later there is another explosion. It is a repeat performance. Now, two ACAVs are in front of me. This incredible sequence repeats itself twice more. We are in line for the next landmine and have about two more kilometers of road to cover. The landmines are blowing the tracks off the relatively heavy ACAVs; they will not be so kind to our little, open, M-151 jeep. The floor of the jeep has a layer of sandbags as minimal protection against blast damage from landmines, and we are sitting on, rather than wearing our flak jackets. But the real danger from a mine is more insidious. The blast will blow you from the open vehicle. You will be propelled up, vertically. In the process, you may have your legs cleaved at the knee as they fail to clear the front dash panel.

Soldiers in the front seat, so-called assistant drivers or "shotguns" (so named in reference to those who protected the stagecoaches of the Old West, armed with a shotgun and sitting next to the coach driver) soon learn to sit with their legs tucked up by their butts, heels on the seat rather than on the floor. First Sergeant Troy Eads rides in the back seat, manning the radios and the M-60 machine gun. He will have a hell of a tumble if thrown from the jeep, but his legs are quit from being severed. My driver has no choice; he must keep his feet on the floor to manipulate the clutch, brake, and gas pedals. Since he is driving for me, it would be poor taste on my part to attempt to protect my knees.

We three, "the next in line," look at each other in the dim light of the beginning of morning nautical twilight, BMNT as we call it, the time when the sun is twelve degrees below the horizon, giving off just enough light to distinguish shapes. My driver must be wondering how he allowed himself to be drafted when everyone else found a way out. Our silent grousing is for naught. No more landmines exist, or our jeeps and light vehicles are below the weight threshold at which the mines' pressure plates are set to fuse. We arrive at the new position without further incident.

My men secure the perimeter while the other parties commence to stake out the positions for their howitzers. In the center of the clearing is a stucco-like building that looks like an old country church. I think it will make a good location for the battalion FDC. It is roomier than the GP Medium Tent we usually use for that purpose, and it has an actual floor that will help keep things clean. Additionally, it will afford some protection from mortar fragments should we be attacked, and it will be easier to control light emission at night. I leave my driver with the jeep to tend the radios and take two senior NCOs with me to clear the building. Accomplishing that without incident, I walk outside and start to relax. I glance across the dirt road and see my driver boiling water in his canteen cup. I contemplate the simple pleasure of a leisurely instant hot cocoa and C-ration chopped ham and eggs breakfast on the hood of our jeep—a war-zone tailgate party.

I pause to talk with a small group of fellow artillery officers who have just arrived with the main body. I tell the "next in line for a mine" episode with relish. I hardly take notice of the approaching M-48 tank from the division cavalry squadron escorting the still-arriving artillery column.

Suddenly, I am knocked down. My ears are ringing. I feel like I have been punched in the face. I am trying to figure out which artillery officer hit me and why. When I regain my senses, First Sergeant Eads places my field dressing on the right side of my face. Out of my left eye, I see the M-48 with its left track blown off by a landmine. The driver and tank commander are on the ground, injured. Within minutes, a medical evacuation helicopter arrives to take the wounded to our brigade aid station at Lai Khe. As we lift off, I see the medics tending to the other wounded. Some, like me, have head and facial wounds; others have their pants down around their ankles. The medics are picking bits of metal and gravel out of their rear ends. They look absurd.

The situation presents an interesting variation on the "game theory" of risk and reward applied to one's body. A wound to the rear end is relatively risk-free—it will not cost an eye. But later on, there is little reward. In fact, one may suffer a future loss in the form of mild embarrassment in explaining how one came to be wounded. A facial wound, on the other hand, has lots of risk. But if one is lucky and the eyes spared, ample reward and dash will be associated with the retelling.

I am flown to the Third Field Hospital in Saigon, where my "wound" is debrided and sutured. I spend four days in the hospital and then rejoin my battalion for Operation Junction City, which commences on 22 February 1967.

One of the other artillery officers wounded by the mine blast is Colonel Lawrence Caruthers Jr., the new division artillery commander who took over from Colonel Camp in September 1966. He is struck in his face by rock, debris, and fragmentation. After a quick verification of seniority among the artillery battalion commanders, conducted by radio, Colonel Daniel is designated as the acting division artillery commander, and he retains this position until Caruthers is released from the hospital and returned to duty on 11 March.

CHAPTER 21

"SERVABO FIDEM"

Latin, "I will keep faith."
MOTTO OF THE 33RD ARTILLERY REGIMENT

Junction City is a multi-division, multi-phase operation conducted along the Cambodian border in War Zone C, Tay Ninh Province. Its purpose is to eliminate the Central Committee of South Vietnam (COSVN), the overall military headquarters of the Viet Cong. It is believed that the 9th VC Division is based in this area. The operation is named after a small Kansas town near Fort Riley, the home of the 1st Infantry Division.

One group of this force forms a 60-kilometer-long inverted "U" cordon to seal the battle area and conduct search operations in sector, while a second group is to search for and attack the VC units within the cordon. The 1st Infantry is responsible for the eastern and northern legs of the cordon. The 25th Infantry is responsible for the western portion. On the east, the seal begins at Nui Ba Den Mountain (elevation 986 meters) and runs north along Route TL-4 to Katum City. My brigade, the 3rd Brigade, mans this portion of the cordon. In the vicinity of Katum, the 173rd Airborne Brigade, under the operational control of the 1st Infantry Division, mans the seal, continuing to the northeastern portion of Route 246, which runs parallel to the Cambodian border. The 1st Brigade of the 1st Infantry Division and the 196th Separate Brigade take up positions along the remainder of Route 246. On the west, along Route 22 toward Tay Ninh West, the 196th Brigade and 3rd Brigade of the 4th Infantry Division complete the inverted U. Both of these brigades are under the operational control of the

25th Infantry Division. Finally, the 2d Brigade of the 25th Infantry Division and the 11th Armored Cavalry Regiment will enter the cordon from the open southern end and search and attack to the north. A total of thirty thousand US soldiers in eighteen maneuver battalions and thirteen fire support bases (FSBs) are deployed for the opening phase of Junction City, the largest operation of the war to date.

The operation commences on 22 February. Some battalions conduct multiple helicopter assaults into their assigned areas on the cordon. The 3rd Brigade units advance by road north on Route TL-4, establishing fire support bases between Nui Ba Den

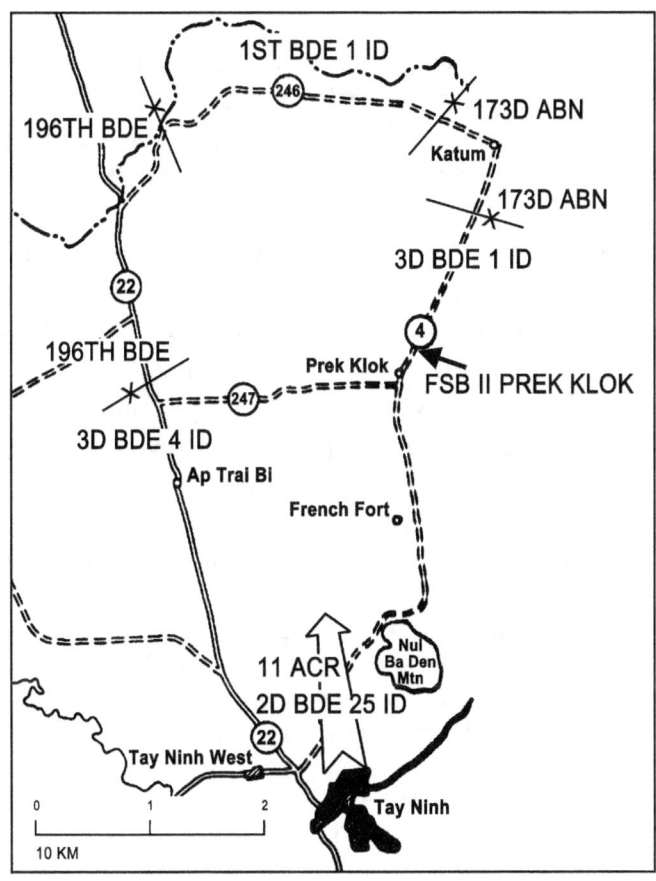

Junction City Area of Operations.
Adapted from official operational graphics.

Mountain and Katum City. Additionally, a battalion of the 173rd Airborne Brigade is parachuted into its area in the first combat parachute assault since the Korean War. None of the battalions make contact with the enemy.

Our battalion was pre-positioned at Souida on 21 February. On 22 February, we follow the 1-4 Cavalry and 2-2 Infantry along Route TL-4 (Axis Iron). At 1400 hours, my battery, Bravo, and Charlie batteries occupy Fire Support Base (FSB) II, located along Route TL-4, thirty-five kilometers north of Nui Ba Den Mountain. At 1500 hours, our Alpha Battery continues north for several more kilometers to occupy FSB III, just south of Katum City.

FSB II is protected by Alpha and Charlie Companies of 2-2 Infantry (Mechanized) in ACAVs. Additionally, we have elements of the 168th Engineer Battalion, whose mission is to construct a C-130 capable airstrip and Special Forces/CIDG camp. The area we occupy is named Prek Klok, after the large stream by that name, which runs parallel to and east of TL-4, astride where our firebase is located.

The first few days pass quickly. We are busy preparing the firebase for defense. In my battery, the FDC, where all the battalion artillery fire missions are processed, is the "queen bee" of the hive. It receives the priority of effort to keep it safe and functional. The FDC tent must be partially dug in below ground and the remainder heavily sandbagged to hip-level above ground. Likewise, we must construct fighting positions and bunkers around the FDC to form an interior perimeter that ties in with the fighting positions of 2-2 Infantry.[70] Sleeping tents must also

---

[70] Under General DePuy, the Division perfected a fighting position known as the "DePuy" bunker. This bunker had a large earthen berm to its immediate front to protect it from head on, incoming fire. The soldiers who manned it fired forty-five degrees out to the flanks, tying in their fires with similar bunkers on either flank. The rear of the fighting position also contains a mass of earth to protect those inside from friendly fires directed from behind to counter an enemy penetration of the perimeter. Now, under new leadership, we are instructed to produce the "Hay Hole," named for General Hay, who has his own design peccadillos. Personally, I do not see any difference between the two; my battery just continues to construct the bunkers as usual, except now we say we are building "Hay Holes."

be sandbagged and sloped pits with sandbag parapets are prepared for our jeeps and three-quarter-ton trucks. Field phones must be run between the fighting positions, the FDC, and the battery command posts. Finally, newly joined soldiers must undergo live-fire familiarization with their personal and crew-served weapons.

When the initial fortification frenzy is completed, life settles into a less demanding regimen. First Sergeant Eads and I rise at 0400 and begin our morning routine. We inspect the soldiers manning the perimeter bunkers, ensure that those awaking in the sleeping area are correctly uniformed and shaved, and have cleaned their weapons. Then, we check our reserve ammunition levels, accomplish communications checks on our radio and wire networks, and supervise vehicle preventive maintenance by the drivers. When this is completed, we have breakfast at 0730. The remainder of our morning is filled with administrative routines and the anticipation of lunch.

The 2-2 Infantry dispatches units to conduct limited search and destroy operations in sector, or escort convoys traveling along TL-4, which bisects our ever-improving perimeter. They return to base before dinner to reestablish the outer perimeter. Our two firing batteries conduct a daily registration and then shoot missions throughout the day and night in support of Junction City. The sound of outgoing rounds becomes part of the aural landscape. The continual din is not even noticed; indeed, what would now be noticed is its absence. After dinner, my first sergeant and I conduct a second perimeter, soldier, communications, and ammunition check. We usually are asleep by 2100, rising at 0400 to repeat the daily protocol; our fail-safe alarm clock is the "mad minute" conducted by 2-2 Infantry, whereby all perimeter bunkers open fire with all weapons into the surrounding wood line for a minute or two, at first light. This drill aims to break up or disrupt any attacking force that might be in place.

Throughout the day, convoys arrive and depart the perimeter. Artillery ammunition must be restocked daily. We have twelve 105mm howitzers, each firing about seven rounds an hour, one round every eight minutes, day after day.[71] We are fortunate to have a consolidated battalion mess section, providing three hot meals a day for upwards of three hundred soldiers. There is a constant need for water and rations to sustain the fighting force. After several days, the novelty of the new position has worn off. The fine line between routine and boredom is breached, and we begin to schedule our meager pleasures around meal hours.

On 28 February, Bravo Company of 1-16 Infantry engages in a day-long battle, five kilometers south of us, resulting in friendly casualties of twenty-five dead and twenty-eight wounded (out of estimated field strength of about 100). A later sweep of the battle area reveals one hundred sixty-seven enemy dead. A prisoner captured shortly after that tells that he is an assistant company commander in 2d Battalion, 101st Regiment, of the 9th Viet Cong Division. Apparently, Company B intercepted this force as it was positioning itself for an attack on a US convoy along TL-4.

There is no further enemy contact, which is disconcerting, given that the massive operation focuses on locating and destroying the VC headquarters and associated field forces. I spend a portion of the day "listening to the radio." I tune my jeep-mounted VRC-47 radio to various infantry frequencies and monitor their reports and orders. It is dull radio. We assume our position now serves as "bait" for a VC attack rather than a firebase to support the original mission.

The tense waiting period for the VC attack is made worse by the heat. The average high is ninety-seven degrees Fahrenheit with a relative humidity of 71 percent. This equates to a Temperature Humidity Index ("feels like temperature") of about 124 degrees. Tempers flare. Rinker is in high dudgeon. One morning at breakfast, he discovers a wheat weevil in his muffin. He explodes, berating the poor soldier whose misfortune is to be on KP. I observe the spectacle like a dog watching television, trying to understand what the human is doing and saying. I'm not fond of biscuits; I

---

[71] During Phase 1 of Junction City, 22 February-14 March, the battalion fired 59,312 rounds of 105mm howitzer ammunition: *Lessons Learned, Headquarters 1st Infantry Division After Action Report—Operation Junction City,* 8 May 1967, 167.

am contented with and grateful for toast. Furthermore, when I was with 2-28 Infantry, after trundling through a riverbed, I watched in fascination as Blanford's RTO picked a live leech from his penis. A dead weevil in a biscuit pales in comparison.

Another time, at lunch, when the day is approaching peak heat, Rinker, watching a gun crew from a nearby howitzer, jumps up and loudly announces in a prosecutorial manner that the gunner had not leveled his sight before firing.[72] The battery commander of the accused, a mere captain to Rinker's majority, jumps up from the bench and states that his gunners are well trained and disciplined and Rinker had, therefore, not properly observed the event. They stand face to face like young boys in the schoolyard, yelling at each other, "Yes, he did," "No, he didn't," repeatedly. When the next rounds are fired, all four of their eyes are focused on the poor gunner, oblivious to the attention he is attracting. The gunner levels the sight. The captain asks Rinker if he is able to see that. Rinker storms off, leaving his meal half-eaten.

The days drag on, and the tension does not abate. We take the role of being a VC target system in stride, even though the senior leadership at brigade and division, which assigned us this role, are not residing with us. We rehearse the headquarters battery "reaction force" to counter any perimeter penetration or otherwise respond to a serious attack. The force has about thirty soldiers, composed primarily of the reconnaissance and survey and communications sections. The men make up an interesting tapestry. The reconnaissance and survey soldiers are the brightest. Their primary job is to precisely locate points on the ground from which a common grid can be established to allow the massed fires of several artillery units on a target using unobserved fire techniques. To accomplish this, they are equipped with standard survey equipment: rods and chains to measure distance, theodolites to measure direction and elevation angles, and astronomical, trigonometric and logarithmic tables to process the survey data into precise points on the ground. However, we usually do not require their services since we use observed fire techniques and

---

[72] The howitzer sights are set at the prescribed elevation, and the gunner must verify this setting by observing that the level bubble is centered.

conduct daily registrations to accomplish muzzle velocity deviation corrections. Nevertheless, I have them survey in our location to combat the boredom. After a day of measuring and calculating, they announce, "The survey will not close." That means they cannot make the physical and mathematical locations of the starting and ending points coincide. It is as if they drew a giant polygon of control points on the ground, except that it has an opening: the endpoint will not close on the beginning point. The communications soldiers are relatively low-skill workers whose primary job is to string field phone wire from point A to B. They are almost as prone to silly error as the infantry heavy mortar crewmen. But, in combat, as in hard work, they are steady and uncomplaining.

Before I go to sleep each night, I take off my jungle uniform jacket and hang it from a support loop on the inside of my hex tent. On the left pocket is a cloth insignia of our regimental crest, worn by all soldiers in the battalion. It is a golden lion, recumbent, on a red background. Beneath is a banner in Latin with the regimental motto. It reads, *Servabo Fidem*, "I will keep faith."

CHAPTER 22

PREK KLOK II

"There's a real danger in doing a sequel..."
DONNIE WAHLBERG, ACTOR

There is an element of playing with history and time shifting in assigning numerical adjectives to the names of battles or wars. The men who fought with General Pershing in 1917-18 were engaged in the Great War. This war was retroactively renamed World War I to form a chronological sequence after World War II. At the time The Hundred and The Thirty Years Wars were being fought, they were not so named. It would have been impossible to assign them durations until after they were finally concluded. On 10 March, the inevitable attack on our firebase is named the Battle of Prek Klok II. The formerly unnamed battle fought by Bravo Company, 1-16 Infantry, on 28 February, several kilometers south of our base and near Prek Klok stream, is named the Battle of Prek Klok I.

On the evening of 10 March, two companies, Alpha and Charlie, of 2-2 Infantry are manning our perimeter. Alpha Company is positioned east of TL-4. Charlie and the artillery are on the west side. At 2030 hours, a listening post from Alpha encounters three to four VC. This otherwise minor incident is taken seriously because we are poised to receive an attack. The 2-2 Infantry commander orders a "mad minute" of fire into the wood lines to spoil any VC attack that may be forming. Nothing further develops from this situation, and I retire for the night at about 2130, somewhat unconcerned.

At about 2200, I awake to the unmistakable sounds of incoming mortar fire. I put on my jacket, boots, helmet, and web gear and

Headquarters Battery area, Fire Support Base II, two days before the battle.

move to the CP bunker adjacent to my tent. There, I am quickly joined by First Sergeant Eads. My driver follows, bringing the field phone from my tent to the bunker, where wires are already laid for it. Our jeep mounted radio is wired into the bunker, too, so we have excellent communications with the FDC and several of our bunkers, which are also pre-wired for field phones.

The incoming mortar rounds continue at about the rate of six to seven a minute, or once every ten seconds. After several minutes of this, First Sergeant Eads and I conclude that if there is to be an associated ground attack, we will be safe in our current position but otherwise unable to influence our men effectively. Our bunkers are relatively proofed for indirect fires, but not, despite our best efforts, well suited to provide for observation and situational awareness. Were our men to remain in these bunkers after the mortar attack, they could be disadvantaged by enemy soldiers who managed to penetrate the outer perimeter.

First Sergeant Eads and I decide to conduct a reconnaissance. My RTO retrieves the jeep radio and places it in a pack frame, and the three of us leave the bunker to ensure our soldiers are correctly positioned to meet the expected ground attack. As we move westward toward the external perimeter, VC green tracer fire, low to the ground, screams across our front. This fire is contrasted with outgoing red tracers from 2-2 Infantry.[73] The combination of incoming, knee-high tracer fire and exploding mortar rounds, ranging from 120mm to 60mm, gives rise to a sobering moment

---

[73] US forces utilize a red tracer element composed of strontium salts in small arms ammunition. The Communist Bloc nations manufacture their tracer ammunition using barium salts, which give off a green glow.

of hesitation. The bunker from which I had recently departed suddenly seems much safer.

The firing and commotion are more severe to the east, where the main attack seems to be taking place, though that is small comfort to me. As we continue to move toward the perimeter, we are joined by our communications sergeant, a grizzled veteran of the Korean War. A mortar round strikes a nearby bunker. Two soldiers manning the fighting position are wounded. We extricate them, render preliminary first aid, and radio for a medical evacuation helicopter, several of which are already orbiting our position. After the medical evacuation is completed, we deploy ourselves behind a fighting position on the external perimeter. We coordinate with those inside who are manning a ground-mounted M-2 caliber .50 machine gun. I then radio back for the remainder of the battery reaction force and position them to our right and left behind the fighting positions on the perimeter.

At about 2230 hours, the mortar barrage lifts, and we take a ground attack from the southwest, which originates from the wood line 200 meters out from the perimeter. It seems suicidal.

About thirty ACAVs and six to eight other supporting armored vehicles are around the perimeter. These vehicles are positioned at about a 50-meter interval. Each ACAV has one M-2 heavy machine gun and two M-60 medium machine guns. Each other type armored vehicle, such as those used to tow disabled ACAVs, has one M-2 heavy machine gun. Thus, there are at least ninety-eight machine guns around the outer perimeter, not counting those of the two artillery batteries, my battery, and the engineer soldiers within our base, which adds about twenty-five more M-60s. Many of the 2-2 Infantry's machine guns are dismounted each night from their vehicles and dug into ground-based fighting positions with overhead cover, where they can more effectively place low grazing type fires, parallel to the ground. A triple concertina-type barbed wire obstacle is fifty meters in front of the bunkers and dug in ACAVs to impede and slow down an infantry assault. Finally, we are within range of the howitzers of at least two other FSBs, not counting the contributions of our own howitzers and the mortars from 2-2 Infantry. On the northwestern portion of the perimeter, C

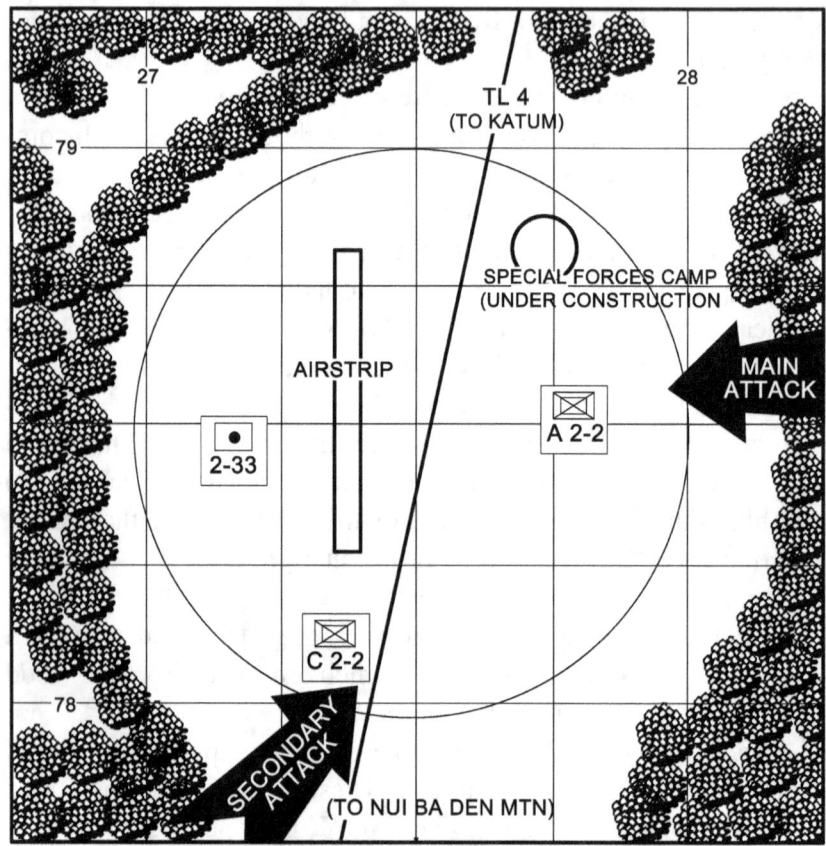

*Disposition of units at Fire Support Base II,
Battle of Prek Klok II, 10 March 1967.*

Battery levels its six howitzers and places direct fire into the wood line a few hundred meters away to break up any possible VC attack in its sector.

The preliminary thirty-minute VC mortar barrage was relatively intense. It consisted of 166 60-120mm mortar rounds. Placed in perspective, this was about equal to the average twenty-four-hour output of one of our howitzers. However, it fails to suppress the defenses. About four ACAVs have been hit, both by mortars and RPGs, but the casualties are relatively light since most of their machine guns and crews were in their ground-fighting positions. Upwards of twenty soldiers are initially wounded, and an RPG round has passed, harmlessly, through the canvas walls of the

FDC tent. But the defense is viable and growing stronger by the minute. The division designates TL-4 as a fire coordination line. Our own artillery, plus that from close by firebases, is employed west of TL-4. Tactical airstrikes and helicopter gunships are being directed east of TL-4.

If they ever had one, the VC moment of opportunity is passed. The only way they could have succeeded was to rapidly penetrate our perimeter during the initial mortar barrage. They would have had to create a small gap by targeting a contiguous cluster of bunkers and ACAVs to accomplish this. But the opening barrage, while initially unsettling, was not massive enough to disrupt movement or precisely enough targeted to take out a specific sector of the perimeter. Our defense's coherence is unaffected, and the terrain provides ample fields of fire on a force originating from the surrounding wood lines. Finally, while night and darkness can wreak psychological paralysis, our men are relatively static and thereby minimally impacted by the natural fear of the night.

The VC ground attack in our sector is easily defeated, if not entirely wiped out. In the morning, at first light, 2-2 Infantry sweeps the perimeter and finds 197 VC dead and five wounded who are taken prisoner. Our own losses are disproportionately light: three killed and thirty-eight wounded. Many of the VC dead are bandaged. It seems that they were wounded in one phase of the ground assault, medically evacuated and treated, and then re-inserted for a second, or even a third push. They were good soldiers—dangerous ones. I am glad they are no longer viable.

CHAPTER 23

CHICKENS, PIGS, AND BICYCLES

"Everything that can be counted does not necessarily count; everything that counts cannot necessarily be counted."
ALBERT EINSTEIN

Prek Klok II was the third and most successful in my series of firefights. Paradoxically, it was the least exciting and least dangerous. Had Blanford been there that night, he would have found the situation so well in hand that it would have been unnecessary to roust himself from slumber and put on his trousers.

Although it was "drama–lite," Prek Klok II came closest to representing the ideal fight espoused by Major General DePuy. It was a carefully prepared, well-defended, relatively static defensive position, with ample fire support at its call against which a VC attack could be broken.

Nonetheless, little of the battle is recorded. The existing operational reviews of Operation Junction City gaff the participants with its disproportional recording of trivial facts and events. The official Lessons Learned After Action Review expends more space and words in enumerating the quantity of VC chickens, pigs, and bicycles captured (pages 16-17) and US paper cups and plastic knives, forks, and spoons issued (half of page 54) than to describing the battle itself (9 lines, page 5).[74]

Perhaps it is instructive to consider what the VC might have done differently to make their attack successful. First, the VC

---

[74] *Lessons Learned, Headquarters, 1st Infantry Division, After Action Report-Operation Junction City* (Washington, D.C.: Adjutant General's Office, 8 May 1967).

mounted two attacks on the perimeter: a main attack on the east and a supporting attack on the southwest. The VC had used this technique previously, to good effect, and did so again in the future. Indeed, there are many examples in all nations' military histories of the successful employment of supporting attacks to enable the success of the main attack. This just was not one of them.

In this case, the supporting attack may have detracted from the mass and shock value that the main attack could have generated. "The defense" was declared by Clausewitz to be the stronger form of warfare than the attack. While the defender is forced, in relative terms, to defend everywhere, the attacker may concentrate his forces at a single point. Supporting attacks are usually designed to deny the defender the freedom to shift forces to meet the main attack. However, in this case, the supporting attack may have been counterproductive. Had the VC made the main attack more forceful and their mortar and RPG attack more focused in its targeting, they might have been able to breach the perimeter in a narrow sector. This breach could have then been exploited to compromise the integrity of the defense and sow a degree of confusion, if not panic, among the defenders elsewhere on the perimeter once the breach became common knowledge.

From my perspective, the supporting attack in my sector was a squandered opportunity. It brought the VC no apparent benefit, and was, quite honestly, easily defeated. I think our perimeter was just too strong with regard to a large number of machine guns which were well sited to place a massive volume of interlocking grazing fire against the VC attackers.

None of the VC mistakes detract from the skill with which the US force prepared the defensive perimeter or their steadfast and aggressive reaction during the initial VC mortar and RPG barrage. There are anecdotal stories of some soldiers "hunkering down" in their fighting positions to minimize their exposure to the incoming VC barrage, particularly among those in the inner perimeter who had no immediate responsibility or possibility to meet the attack. But their behavior can be explained as instinctive and natural—the urge for self-preservation is genetically ingrained. Given this instinctive impulse, the behavior of the soldiers on the outer perimeter, the men of 2-2 Infantry and the 2-33 Artillery, is all the more commendable. They did not hunker down; they manned their weapons and placed effective fire into the attacking VC force. I would suggest that the VC hopes of success were predicated on more American soldiers opting for self-preservation and laying low in their "fighting" positions, rather than aggressively manning their weapons.

While the VC may have miscalculated the size and effect of the supporting attack, they did not want for fighting spirit. As mentioned in the previous chapter, many of the dead VC in my sector were bandaged. Some were still resting on the triple concertina wire obstacles in front of our perimeter. To this day, I can picture them and speculate that they had partaken in at least one previous attempt to breach our wire, were wounded in the process, returned to their attack position, bandaged, and sent back into combat for a subsequent assault. Behavior like that bespeaks enormous self-discipline and dedication. These VC soldiers were competent and dangerous foes.

EPILOGUE

MOVING ON DOWN THE ROAD

"Life is a series of collisions with the future."
JOSE ORTEGA Y GASSET, PHILOSOPHER

Home, 1967. At left is my Aunt Bea, the American-born daughter of my grandfather, the Russian Cavalryman.

The battles of Hill 150, Bong Trang, and Prek Klok II are historically insignificant. They compare well with the unobserved labor of ants in a world of giants. These battles defy meaningful descriptions to non-soldiers holding Hollywood-induced notions of war. But that does not detract from either the soldiers' performance or the magnitude of the personal danger they faced. It matters little whether they were engaged in an enormous, pre-planned battle destined for fame or fending off an unforeseen ambush at an unnamed crossroads that will rank in the last decimal place of history. The disparity in historical context is a distinction without a difference. It is like being out in a rainstorm; after a certain point, more rain will not make you any wetter. A death is a death, and a missing eye is a missing eye.

The Loc Ninh Plantation itself became a macabre parody of an annual football bowl game. There were four more significant battles fought there: once in 1967, twice in 1968, and finally in 1972, when North Vietnamese tanks overran it. These battles produced countless American casualties, as well as two winners of the Congressional Medal of Honor, one posthumous. On 11 June 1966, Alpha Company enjoyed the dubious honor of playing in the opening game of the "Loc Ninh Bowl."

I thought it would be interesting to learn what "Loc Ninh" means in English. I asked my barber who had served with the Vietnamese Special Forces. He knew where Loc Ninh was and there were big battles, but he was clueless about what the name meant. He asked his compatriots; they did not know. I asked a Vietnamese American Naval Officer with whom I worked and who had an older sister who was well-educated. She knew. When French Christian missionaries arrived in Indochina in the early eighteenth century, they changed the former Chinese based alphabet to the western-based one we use today, and transliterated old place names. Accordingly, Loc Ninh does not translate; it means nothing.

~

The Special Forces camp established at Prek Klok in March 1967 was officially designated A-334. It was abandoned nine months later, in December 1967. The holding of that terrain and the ensuing battle of Prek Klok II were for naught, except to serve as a killing ground.

~

After the fight at Hill 150, Blanford recuperated, with verve. When the division commander, Major General William E. DePuy, visited him in the hospital to award him the Purple Heart, he was informed that Blanford was "off-campus," in Saigon, enjoying a steak dinner with some of the hospital staff. He was chauffeured to the occasion in a Cadillac ambulance, with his own attending nurse. Earlier, upon hearing of Blanford being seriously wounded, DePuy is reported to have opined that he had lost one of his best company commanders. I am sure DePuy left the hospital more convinced than ever that indeed he had.

Ultimately Blanford was assigned as an ROTC instructor at the University of Illinois, in Urbana, where he was presented the Silver

Blanford receiving Distinguished Service Cross at University of Illinois, 1968. His first wife is to his right. From Ray Blanford personal collection.

Star for his leadership and bravery at Hill 150. This interim award was pending final action on his nomination for the Distinguished Service Cross (DSC). Later, the approved paperwork for his DSC was discovered lying around in some bureaucrat's desk. Blanford was asked if he would like to have the DSC, the nation's second-highest award for valor, presented in a ceremony at the university. With characteristic nonchalance, he declined, saying that the civilian faculty would have trouble understanding why he was being given a second award for the same thing. Thus, they handed Blanford his DSC in a small, private ceremony.

Blanford returned for a second, in his words, "uneventful" tour in Viet Nam in 1968. He remained in the Army until 1974, retiring medically as a Major. He went back to school, earned a master's degree and served with the Veterans Administration as a counselor.

As a civilian, he remained tough as ever. In 1993 he was diagnosed with colon cancer and given eighteen months to live. While on this "borrowed time," he crashed an ultra-light aircraft into some trees, necessitating the emplacement of an eight-inch steel rod in his spine. In 2000, he suffered a heart attack, which required bypass surgery. Pursuant to this procedure, the doctors discovered a growth near his larynx. He underwent radiation and chemotherapy, which resulted in a stricture of his throat and difficulty eating solid foods. All of this is in addition to his missing right eye. He set a new standard for understatement when he told me in 2010 during a First Infantry Division officer reunion dinner that he was doing fine.

Ray Blanford cashed in the last of his nine lives on 10 October 2015. In early 2016, Richard Kolb, the editor of the *Veterans of Foreign Wars* magazine, contacted me, searching for Ray Blanford. He was preparing an article on forgotten battles of the Vietnam War which should not have been forgotten. He had determined that Hill 150 was one such battle and wanted Blanford's input. Kolb was late by just a few months and got my input instead. Blanford remains everything a good soldier needs to be. He is buried in Arlington National Cemetery, a few miles from where I live.

~

In the winter of 1972, I read in *Time* magazine that my tough-as-nails RTO at Hill 150, Robert Dooley, had been killed in the line of duty, as a police officer in Detroit. There is a picture of the slain officer. It does not take much imagination to see a more mature, aged version of the man I knew in 1966. I think to myself that it is cruelly ironic to have survived the war only to be killed six years later on the streets of his hometown. He was a good soldier and taught me how to be an FO. Combat did not outwardly affect him. The most rattled I ever saw him was when he wrote three different girlfriends love letters and later realized that he had stuffed them into the wrong envelopes.

But the report of his demise is erroneous. In 2003, I contacted the 28th Infantry Regiment Association to obtain information on former members of Alpha Company. I received a listing of soldiers who had, at one time or another, been active in the association. The name Dooley is there. I learned two things. One, his first name is Robert. Two, he is alive. I call. He tells me, very briefly, that the *Time* article confused his name and picture with his partner. The gunman seriously wounded him; his partner was the one who was killed. I ask if he remembers anything of the battle of 11 June and if he is interested in being interviewed by me. "No," he quickly replies to both questions. I ask if he is bitter. He says, laconically, he is not: that the fight was long ago, many things have happened since, he has had bad experiences with writers, and he has gotten on with his life.

In 2007, reviewing newspaper archives and corresponding with an author of a book about racial strife in Detroit, I learned more about Dooley. The gunshot wound left him blind in one eye and paralyzed from the waist down. In December 1972, he was assigned to a plainclothes police unit that was involved in tracking down three Black militants who had previously wounded four members of his unit. Dooley was part of a team that surrounded a house in which the suspects were located. Dooley was shot, and his partner killed. The author, operating under the premise that the Detroit police were "out of control," portrayed Dooley's unit in a highly critical manner. Thus was born his hesitation for further interview.

Armed with this new information, I phoned Dooley and assured him he had nothing to fear in talking with me about Hill 150. True to form, he asked me, "What part of 'no' don't you understand?"

Robert Dooley died on 15 September 2012. His obituary states that he finally succumbed to the gunshot wound to the head he sustained as a Detroit police officer. Like Blanford, he practiced a quiet grace and courage in adjusting to adversity, spending the last forty years of his life partially paralyzed and blinded in one eye. He and Ray Blanford set a high bar for me to meet in dealing with my comparatively minor problems.

~

Late one night, in a bar in Tel Aviv, while serving as a "non-kinetic" US Army military contractor for a bilateral military exercise with Israel, I exchanged war stories over cognacs with a work colleague, a former infantry officer. I related the Battle of Hill 150 and the teacher's execution. He was a friend. We had a history and could trust each other. He listened, occasionally nodding his head, knowingly. When I finished, he simply said, "You got her killed."

~

Sometimes the location of a wound is much more important than its seriousness and can lead to love and marriage. The medical evacuation route is a long and complicated path. Carol, my wife-to-be, was an Army nurse. I met her at Fort Bliss, in El Paso, in 1968, when I was attending the final phase of the Artillery Advanced Course. She was working on a surgical ward at William Beaumont General Hospital, caring for officers who were medically evacuated with long-term, slow-healing wounds. Some had been in the hospital system for over a year. She was dating a captain recently discharged from her ward at the time. He had been shot in his posterior aspect.

Carol, El Paso, Texas, April 1968, two weeks before marriage.

I wanted that nurse, so, all being fair in love and war, I proceeded to undermine his position. My facial wound was obvious; the "dueling" scar was quite dashing, so I asked her to consider the probable situations under which a soldier could get shot in his rear end. We were married, much to our children's shock at the telling, a little over six weeks later. It would have been a bit earlier than that, but for the fact that Carol missed her appointed pre-marriage license blood test by a few days. But, if her former beau had been even so

Promoting Carol to first lieutenant, 1969, El Paso, Texas. Official US Army photo.

much as only nicked anywhere on his ventral aspect, my children might have had a different mother.

~

After graduating from the Naval War College in June 1983, I was assigned as the G-3 (operations officer) of the 32d Army Air Defense Command, stationed in Darmstadt, West Germany. Upon promotion to colonel in late 1984, I became the chief of staff. We had four air defense brigades, a support group, and a signal battalion to execute our Cold War, NATO air defense mission, in the context of what I described in Chapter 6, though on a much grander scale and at a higher level of responsibility. The work, while at times grueling and contentious, was mostly pushing paper. Nonetheless, on occasion, danger was briefly interjected—and by my own hand.

In late September 1984, my G-3 directorate was tasked to dispatch a three-man team to Beirut, Lebanon, to develop a defense protocol for the US Embassy, which had already been twice suicide-bombed, at a loss of 34 US personnel, and less than a year after the suicide bombing of the US Marine Corps Barracks, causing 241 US military deaths.

Thinking it would be poor taste to send my men into harm's way while I hung back, I made myself a member of this threesome. Our assignment was to assess the threat of an aerial attack on the embassy, believing the Hezbollah terrorists would seek to employ a new and surprising method of attack as we continually strengthened our defenses against a

US Marine Corps Barracks Beirut bombing, October 23, 1983. USMC photo.

ground assault, and then develop a workable, low-profile, defense architecture for this possibility.

Beirut, in addition to the aforementioned suicide bombings, was a long-term war zone. Israel had invaded in 1982 to uproot the Palestine Liberation Organization, which had taken up residence in Beirut and used it as a base for its terrorist operations. Additionally, there was an ongoing muti-faction, multi-year civil war between the Maronite Christians and Suni and Shia Muslims, with Iran covertly aiding the Shia (Hezbollah) faction. Portions of the city were war-ravaged while others, only minutes driving distance apart, were unscathed and luxurious. Just navigating to and from the embassy and across city districts was a challenge. We had to pass through multiple sectarian check points, manned by well-armed, ill-tempered, evil-looking men. It reminded me of the worst version of my hometown Bronx where various ethnic gangs controlled their streets, and woe unto the person being on the wrong block at the wrong time. But in a more lethal sense it was the urban equivalent of the vegetative jungles of Vietnam, and the threat of sudden violence hung over us like an invisible, perilous mist.

We wore civilian clothing and rode in a Volkswagen van. We were protected by our embassy-issued identification badges and a Maronite CIA mercenary bodyguard. We were, by embassy policy, unarmed, and as far as I could tell, probably the only unarmed folks in the whole of Beirut. I decided to remedy that situation. Our military lead was the Chief of the Office of Defense Cooperation (ODC), who had been one of my instructors at the Artillery Career Course when I was a very junior captain, just returned from Vietnam. Even then, he was a legend in his own time, an infantry officer with three tours in Vietnam and wearing multiple awards of the Silver Star and four of the Purple Heart. I prevailed upon him to arm us as a fail-safe against kidnapping and long-term exploitation as political pawns. He saw the logic in this and provided each of us with a standard issue Colt .45 pistol, which he ordered we keep out of sight. We accomplished this as best we could by carrying them inside our trousers, in the small of our backs, covered by a loose-fitting shirt with the tails out—the universal concealed-carry uniform of the day. Our embassy lead, the Regional Security Officer, was aware of this policy infraction, but chose to look the other way.

Within two weeks, we completed our assessment without excess drama or incident. After coordinating our findings and recommendations with the embassy staff and the ODC Chief, we returned to Germany to PowerPoint-brief our superiors. The return itinerary was the reverse route from which we had entered—by helicopter from Beirut to Larnaca, Cyprus, and onward by special mission aircraft to Brindisi, Italy, and finally, Stuttgart, Germany. At Headquarters European Command in Stuttgart, as we took our PowerPoint presentation up the chain-of-command, we spent more time making it "sexy" than we had in formulating the actual underlying defense architecture. One night, after yet another laborious but meaningless slide revision session, I briefly entertained the wish of being instantaneously transported back to the sanity of Beirut.

US Embassy, Beirut, April 1984.
US Government photo.

In May 1986, at the age of forty-four and almost 23 years after attending Airborne School at Fort Benning, I elected to jump again, on very short notice and way out of practice. A young lieutenant, the aide to our deputy commanding general, arranged for our commanding general and several of his staff to qualify for the German Army paratrooper badge. I am not sure how I allowed myself to volunteer. There was some element of fealty; I was

*Qualifying as German paratrooper, Bruchsal, Germany, 1986.
I am third from left.*

our commanding general's chief of staff. But, by and large, I just heard myself inexplicably saying "Yes" when logic and maturity demanded a "No, thank you."

At any rate, I did it. We jumped from UH-1D helicopters, like the ones I had ridden in Vietnam. The exits were relatively easy and quiet. The landings were quite another matter. The ground winds were just below the maximum value for safe parachute operations, and I was unquestionably well below the desired experiential threshold. I bounced hard on the first two landings and split my chin on the third and last jump. The German medic who treated me decided to test his English while applying a butterfly compress to my minor injury. He asked, "When in America had you first jumped?" I replied that it was November 1963. He seemed a bit puzzled and then responded, "I was in 1963 not yet born." Concurrently our German hosts began serving champagne to the American jumpers. I downed two flutes, rapidly.

~

The Army presented opportunities for me and my family that might otherwise have eluded me socially and economically. We learned to sail, and I held office in a military yacht club. We rode in military stables and owned and kept horses. In the Pentagon, I played squash and served on the board of governors in the Pentagon Officers' Athletic Center. My family skied in Germany, Austria, Switzerland, and Italy. We trekked the Alps "hut to hut." While stationed in West Germany, we traveled throughout the Continent and Great Britain. All this was not too shabby for a Bronx boy who had only occasionally gone farther than a subway token could take him.

Winter break from school in Germany, 1987. Skiing in Cortina D'Ampezzo, Italy. Left to right: Leslie, Carol, Mark, and Libby.

~

Concerning CCNY, my feelings evolved. I came in contact with officers who had attended classical football dormitory colleges. They seemed more socially advanced than I and benefited from widespread, well-organized alum support groups. At first, I was envious and then resentful that CCNY was not a "real college." But eventually, I learned to appreciate that CCNY had provided me with a world-class education. Furthermore, I met officers who had worked through college year-round in a manner I had previously thought impossible. Their examples convinced me that I was ultimately responsible for my college choice and experience.

The hallmark of CCNY was the high admittance standards, and the excellent nature of the education received. However, the social unrest deriving from the Vietnam War and a stoked awareness of racial grievance combined to shatter this hallmark. In 1969, Afro-American and Puerto Rican students at CCNY set fires in Shepard Hall and "seized" the South Campus. This was done to force the college to drop the stringent entrance requirements, which the rioting students felt disadvantaged them and their class. The college capitulated. In 1970, it adopted an open admissions policy that allowed the entrance of formerly disqualified students. In 1972, the college terminated its ROTC program to complete its self-destruction.

By the 1990s, CCNY had gradually reclaimed a semblance of admissions sanity and was on the path to restoring some of its former fame for academic excellence. In 2008, several ROTC graduates formed a ROTC alumni sub-group. I joined and became a board member. One of the first acts by the group was to dedicate a plaque to honor the six ROTC graduates and one ROTC faculty member killed in Vietnam. The plaque is mounted in the college administration building.

In the summer of 2013, ROTC returned to CCNY. One of our most notable alums, Retired General Colin Powell, our former Chairman of the Joint Chiefs of Staff and Secretary of State, spearheaded the effort.

Plaque honoring CCNY students and faculty killed in Vietnam. Photo courtesy of Allen Rothman, CCNY, '68.

~

When my book was still in edit, I contacted the girl central to the dream from the fight for Hill 150—the dream that turned what could have been an eternal nightmare into a more pleasant memory. The concept of a long-distance reunion seemed safe enough; we were both married grandparents in our sixties. I wanted to discuss the dream, and because I remembered her as a budding intellectual, I wanted her views on some of the sociological issues we had both experienced and which I had addressed in the Parkchester chapter. It did not go well—it was a classic case of "you can't go home again." Perhaps there was the issue of discomfort. Even though it was a "nothing happened" dream, it probably caused a problem I should have foreseen. At any rate, her tepid reaction made me realize the dream had long since served its purpose, and its reconciliation with reality was, in retrospect, predictably doomed to be disappointing.

~

My three children came of age in a much more open society than I did as a youth. They accept as fact my description of societal values and behavior patterns of my times, but they cannot relate to it. For example, our son earned admission to both West Point and Annapolis. I suggested he select West Point because I was prejudiced towards the Army and believed the Navy to be stodgier and more conservative than the Army, and perhaps more inclined to harbor antisemitic feelings. Our son chose Annapolis. I often asked him whether his being Jewish was a problem. After I had posed that question once too often, he replied that I was the only person concerned about his religion!

Mark Kurtz, Plebe Summer, 1997. Personal Photo.

~

Since this memoir was first published, I have learned more about my ancestry. I contacted Kurtz family researchers in Israel, Argentina, and the United States. Together, we reconstructed our origins in Poland as small-scale farmers who kept chickens, cows, and horses and sold eggs and butter at the village market. My ancestors lived in a farm-cluster known as Wieglie, close to the village of Stoczek, and the record-keeping municipality of Wergow. My grandfather, Isidore, emigrated to New York City in 1907 after his wartime military service, because he was not the eldest son, and could not, by tradition, inherit the farm. This was in addition to the deteriorating condition of Jews in Poland starting in 1905, as discussed in Chapter 3. His family, including my father, at the age of three, followed in 1910. Another brother, Charles, emigrated to Mobile, Alabama. Other family members later went to Salta, Argentina, and El Paso, Texas. Had my grandfather "stayed on the farm," he and his family would surely have perished in the opening weeks of World War II when the Nazis began murdering Polish Jews wherever they found them. However, there is an amazing story of survival. One Kurtz family member was in the Polish Army when the Russians invaded Eastern Poland in 1939 and occupied Stoczek before it was taken by the Germans two years later. The Russians detained him and his wife and subsequently sent them to Siberia as laborers. They survived the war, lived in DP camps in West Germany, and eventually emigrated to Israel by way of Paraguay. The preservation of this history gives life back to my family members—especially those consumed in the Holocaust.

~

History and insights as a soldier have provided perspective on my understanding of the Jews' response to their slaughter in the Holocaust. At Hill 150, the schoolteacher, her father, and other village leaders were executed at the edge of a drainage ditch. There were no signs of resistance. In 1940, the Russians shot 22,000 Polish Army officers, political leaders, and intelligentsia and buried them in a mass grave in the Katyn Forest. There is no evidence of resistance, even though many were trained military men and leaders.[75] In December 1944, during the Battle of the Bulge, seventy-eight US soldiers were captured and murdered by the 1st SS Division at Malmedy, Belgium. There is no evidence of resistance.[76] Approximately 156 Canadian and British soldiers were executed by the 12th Panzer Division at Normandy in June 1944 without signs of resistance.[77] Knowledge of these massacres has made me less judgmental of the Jews slaughtered in like manner throughout Eastern Europe. Unarmed people have few options in their moment of peril. When I was a youth, I thought it was a simple and required decision to fight back in the face of slaughter. Now I understand. Now, I pray never to be tested.

~

---

[75] Timothy Snyder, *Bloodlands, Europe Between Hitler and Stalin*, (New York: Basic books, 2010), 287, 396.

[76] Richard J. Evans, *The Third Reich at War*, (United Kingdom: Penguin, 2008), 44, 658.

[77] Howard Margolian, *Conduct Unbecoming*, (Toronto Canada: Toronto University Press, 2000), 120.

In the Introduction chapter, I reference having served in two armies, the Draft and the All-Volunteer Army of today. In actuality, I served in a third army—the army resulting from the anti-Vietnam War protest movement, the racial strife which dominated American society in the late 1960s and early 1970s, and rampant drug abuse. The army I knew in 1966-67 and described in this memoir was totally different from the one I knew on my second tour in Vietnam in 1971. How all this happened in a matter of a few years is a subject worthy of deep study, well beyond the scope of this epilogue.

After graduating from the University of Texas at El Paso, with an MS in aeronautical engineering in late 1970, the Army returned me to Vietnam, in accord with a logic known only to them. Our daughter, Libby, was eighteen months old, and Carol was three months pregnant with Leslie, our second daughter-to-be. I was initially assigned to the staff of the 101st Airborne Division at Hue-Phu Bai, in the northern part of Vietnam. In mid-1971, I was re-assigned as the operations officer (S-3) of a Duster battalion[78] deployed on the US Marine Corps firebases along Route 9, in the North-South Vietnam DMZ, where the North Vietnamese were plentiful and well-armed.

Our routine missions were base perimeter defense and road convoy protection. The soldiers were, by and large, not happy campers. Some combat units were already being re-deployed home to the United States, making those remaining to feel like losers. Life on the firebases was austere and dangerous—while ground attacks, like that at Prek Klok II were rare, daily rocket attacks were commonplace. There were no females to offer sexual relief from the tensions of war: that relief being provided by alcohol and drugs. Many of the soldiers flaunted traditional military standards and courtesies. I did not abide this behavior and made the junior leaders do their job in enforcing traditional standards of appearance, behavior, and obedience to orders. Therefore, I was not necessarily a welcome sight when I helicoptered into remote firebases to see how things were going. One night, I was

---

[78] The "Duster" was a M-41 tank chassis with a twin 40mm Bofors gun turret.

M-42 Duster of my battalion, 1971, on a Marine firebase, along Route 9. USMC Photo.

symbolically fragged[79] with a CS gas grenade, as opposed to a lethal fragmentation grenade. It was thrown by someone into my temporary sleeping quarters to dissuade me from maintaining professional standards. By contrast, in 1967, such military standards and missions would have been just routine. I was not dissuaded. A short time later, while correcting the sloppy appearance of a gun crew, a soldier asked if I had not "gotten the message," implying he was the one, or knew the one, who had tossed the CS grenade. I took him aside for a one-on-one chat, with no witnesses. In the genre of gangster movies, I made him an offer he couldn't refuse. I then passed his name up the chain of command and to the Military Police. Thereafter, grumbling continued, but threats to my life ceased.

The volunteer army concept was adopted in 1974 to reverse this martial deterioration. Nonetheless, it took many years to weed out the worst of the previously recalcitrant soldiers and develop recruiting incentives sufficient to attract quality personnel

---

[79] Fragging was the act of killing, with a fragmentation hand grenade, officers and NCOs judged to be too strict and professional in keeping the unit operational. It is estimated that about 800 such cases occurred with about 86 resultant deaths.

to replace them. When I took command of a battalion in 1982, the situation was still somewhat tenuous. Manpower was scarce; the Army was having trouble meeting recruitment requirements. It tended to scrape the bottom of the barrel, so to speak, to find the needed manpower. Accordingly, some of my soldiers had arrest records (but not conviction records) for serious crimes. Our armored-tracked vehicles required many hours a week of extensive and unglamorous maintenance. The rule of thumb was two hours of maintenance for each hour of field operation. However, many of our soldiers could not read the operator and technical manuals essential for the successful conduct of this function. Substance abuse, both alcohol and drugs, ran rampant. Then there were vague, unverified, stories of officers, always somewhere else other than on our base, being assaulted or placed in wall lockers and thrown from windows. However, when I took command of a brigade in 1987, the Army was, finally, well in hand. That command was a breeze.

~

When I retired from the Army in 1993, I took a job as a military contractor supporting the US Missile Defense Agency in Washington, DC. For many, this resulted in consignment to a cubicle wasteland, processing paperwork and building Power Point presentations. Luckily, I was assigned to a division tasked with preparing our combatant commands for their receipt of the soon-to-be deployed ballistic missile defense systems.

We accomplished this by having the combatant commands "test drive" their new systems in specially designed ballistic missile defense exercises. This entailed setting up a sophisticated, troops-in-the-loop, Monte Carlo, distributed, interactive simulation, whereby the actual weapon systems, with real operators, saw a simulated, but real to them, incoming ballistic missile attack. They responded, and the engagement outcomes were evaluated to yield the result—kill or miss. In this manner we were able to develop tactics, techniques, and procedures to determine what to defend and how, and methodologies to manage our interceptor inventories. Additionally, we refined timely early warning systems for these attacks.

Part of my job was devoted to the multi-phase planning processes for these exercises, preparing instructional material to aid the introduction of these new systems and conducting a daily post-battle assessment of which of our defense methodologies worked and which had to be modified for the next iteration. Carol was sometimes able to join me, at our expense, and explore these countries on her own, whilst I worked. At worst, we saw each other for late suppers; at best we had a weekend together. In this manner, Carol got to explore Seoul, Amsterdam, Berlin, Prague, and Jerusalem, often on her own, using local transportation.

This work was rewarding in and of itself, but the events evolving from the October 7, 2023, Hamas attack on Israel yielded job satisfaction beyond all description. From about 2003 to 2016, I was deeply involved with the European Command (which then had responsibility for Israel) in a ballistic missile defense exercise series held every other year in-country. In this series, we war-gamed the coordination and integration of US missile defense systems with those of the Israel Defense Force (IDF) in response

With my IDF counterpart, Brigadier General Eitan Yariv, dressed up for a Dining In, 2016.

to attacks from countries geographically equivalent to Iraq and Iran. Throughout all these years, my IDF counterpart, Brigadier General Eitan Yariv, remained a constant and trusted comrade. In 2024 and 2025 Iran launched ballistic missile and drone attacks on Israel in support of Hamas and Hezbollah. All our previous work came together, with US, IDF, and other allied forces defeating these attacks in a well-coordinated and integrated air and missile defense architecture. And Eitan Yariv was on duty in the IDF command center, implementing the lessons learned from our exercise series. It is rewarding to look back and realize we helped lay the foundation for this great achievement.

~

In December 2014, with Christmas music playing softly over the public address system, I found myself at George Washington University Hospital, somewhat numb, sitting in a circle with five others—my wife, Carol, a working nurse; a radiologist; an oncologist; a urologist; and a patient care coordinator—discussing my treatment options for prostate cancer. It had taken seventeen years of inconclusive test results and four negative biopsies before my cancer was diagnosed. It is a given medical finding that exposure to the Agent Orange defoliant employed in Vietnam is carcinogenic, and a very disproportionate slice of Vietnam veterans developed prostate cancer.

Thus, I began a two-year treatment adventure, whose efficacy, ten years later, seems good, but we do not know how long it will take to declare victory with finality. I continued to work as a military contractor until 2018. Now, I hike, fly fish, weight-lift at Golds, and keep our home and landscaping in good repair.

After my most recent annual checkup, I asked my doctor to define success. He replied, sardonically, that unambiguous success will be declared when I die from something else first.

~

Finally, a seemingly trivial shopping fact serves to place the defining year of my life in an absurd perspective. I can go to the

Army PX at Fort Belvoir, Virginia, just a short drive from where we live in Alexandria, and purchase clothing and sports apparel made in Vietnam. Other stores nearby do the same with furniture. It is as if there were never an eight-year war.

AFTERWORD

THE NEW ANTISEMITISM

*"Villainy wears many masks;
none so dangerous as the mask of virtue."*
WASHINGTON IRVING

Israel's response to the Hamas terror attack on October 7, 2023, sparked a wave of antisemitic protests on college campuses across America. This openly expressed hatred was unlike anything I had encountered before. What was more perplexing was how it was framed as an act of virtue in support of the oppressed. It was as if all the English literature departments had conspired to twist Shakespeare's words to read, "Cry oppression, and let slip the dogs of antisemitism."[80]

As I struggled to understand this phenomenon, I began to realize that it had been developing for decades and was foreshadowed by the Vietnam War. This afterword aims to explore how and where this antisemitic sentiment originated and its connection to the war that profoundly impacted my life.

Upon returning from Vietnam in 1967, I was stationed in Oklahoma and West Texas, where I attended Army schools. During this time, I was largely shielded from the civilian world. However, I could not watch the nightly news without seeing reports of violent anti-Vietnam War demonstrations occurring on college campuses, led by passionate student political activists. Their extreme actions included the seizure of campus buildings, disruptions to academic routines, and the bombing of a research building at the University of Wisconsin-Madison, which resulted in the death of

---

[80] Shakespeare, *Julius Caesar*, Act 3, Scene 1, Mark Antony speaking, "Cry havoc, and let slip the dogs of war."

a faculty member. When the Army sent me to graduate school in 1969, their primary concern was not which school was the best, but rather which campus was the safest.

A variety of factors drove the anti-war activists, and there was some ambiguity regarding whether they wanted the war to end or if they supported North Vietnam's victory. The movement was primarily led by Students for a Democratic Society, which embraced a New Left philosophy advocating anti-imperialism, anti-capitalism, activism, and resistance to traditional forms of authority. While some participants were genuine pacifists, others were motivated by self-interest, particularly the desire to avoid disruptions to their life plans—such as being drafted into the U.S. Army. Many women joined the movement out of concern for their boyfriends, hoping to protect them from the dangers of war. In this sense, they represented some of the movement's most altruistic and sincere members.

This anti-war activism occurred simultaneously with violent, arson-fueled riots by Black anti-establishment activists in our major cities. The combined actions of both movements contributed to an impression of disorder and chaos, similar to that seen after October 7.

After the war, not a few of these anti-war activists found succor on our college campuses. While completing their educations, they also embarked on a multi-generational campaign—a Long March[81] through our universities—to validate themselves, identify social justice issues, and legitimize extralegal action in pursuit of their remedy.[82] The current cohorts of university leaders and

---

[81] A reference to the Chinese Communist Army's retreat in 1934 to save itself from annihilation by the Chinese Government, and later to return victorious in 1949. Today, the term is used as a metaphor for long-term strategic survival under arduous conditions.

[82] Guenter Lewy, *Campus Intolerance/Then and Now, The Influence of Marcusian Ideology*, (Council of Trustees and Alumni, Institute for Effective Governance, February 2018), 1-4, https://www.goacta.org/wp-content/uploads/ee/download/campus-intolerance-then-and-now.pdf.
Margherita Gobbo and Marco Rizzi, "From Vietnam to Gaza: Evolution and Impact of Student-Led Anti-War Movements," *Mondo Internazionale,* 6 July 2024, https://mondointernazionale.org/focus-allegati/from-vietnam-to-gaza-evolution-and-impact-of-student-led-anti-war-movements.

activist students involved in the new, virulent antisemitism are their ideological and biological offspring.

The Hamas terror attack on Israel included murder of adult civilians, infanticide, rape, immolation, arson, and hostage taking of both those alive and, grotesquely, those dead. It was an ugly, heinous attack that should have deeply offended American sensibilities. Instead, it produced on American college campuses and in our media a surplus of justification and support. This represented —and continues to represent—a staggering misalignment of our national moral compass.

A similar failure of another nation's moral compass resulted in mass murder. A visit to the United States Holocaust Museum starts on the top floor. There, one can trace the role a years-long, systematized, and normalized antisemitic propaganda campaign played in setting the conditions for the genocide of European Jewry. This antisemitic campaign involved the press, books, pamphlets, and the cinema—the mass media of the time. It is a lesson we must internalize.

Kurtzes were murdered in the Holocaust, especially those who stayed on the family farm, which my grandfather was too young to inherit. I was only three years old when World War II ended. Jewish youth of my age, presenting no economic value to the Nazis, were gassed immediately upon arrival at the death camps. Therefore, I take institutionalized antisemitism personally and am honor-bound to address it.

To be sure, antisemitism has always been with us. It is described as the oldest and most enduring hatred. It has been justified under a variety of explanations—the Jews killed Jesus and renounced his teachings, the Jews spread the Plague, the Jews are communists, and, contradictorily, the Jews are exploitative capitalists. The only things that change are the excuses that are in vogue and how strong society's moral guardrails are at containing them.

For example, many prominent student anti-Vietnam War activists were Jewish.[83] There was an Army report showing a direct correlation between the percentage of Jews on a campus and

---

[83] Mordecai Specktor "'60's Jewish radical," *The American Jewish World*, May 9, 2024, https://www.ajwnews.com/60s-jewish-radical/.

anti-war activity on that campus. Its primary purpose was to identify ROTC units at risk and secure campuses for Army graduate students. This information had the potential to inspire antisemitic comments. Although we all abhorred the anti-war movement, I never heard anyone make any direct or derogatory mention of this Jewish connection to the anti-war environment. I do not doubt for a second that many were aware of this Jewish nexus, but I suggest our then-operative societal norms inhibited its hostile expression.

Accordingly, "October 7" serves to demarcate antisemitism in American culture into two cases. The first being the antisemitism our societal elites formerly condemned, and the second being the antisemitism to which an influential segment now subscribed. I grew up in the era when our body politic abjured antisemitism, based on conscience and moral clarity. There was antisemitism, to be sure, but it was neither celebrated nor normalized. Therefore, this period serves us well as a starting point for comparison with the antisemitism that emerged after October 7.

Having previously addressed the fistfight antisemitism I knew as a youth, I will continue with a description of the antisemitism, or scarcity thereof, I encountered in my thirty years in the Army, from 1963 to 1993, and onward as a military contractor until 2018.

Despite warnings from relatives who had served in World War II that Jews would not be welcome in the career Army, and despite my preparations, both mental and physical, for this eventuality, reality was a pleasant surprise. My religion hardly ever came up, and I did not encounter any *overt* anti-Jewish animus directed at me. However, I am not a Pollyanna; I overheard, from time to time, fellow officers expressing non-favorable Jewish stereotypes or using terms such as "to Jew someone down." On one occasion, I had to offer to fight two fellow officers who were mocking the Jews. They begged off, apologized, and claimed I was being unfair because they did not know I was Jewish. Obviously, the absurdity of their defense eluded them—claiming, in effect, that they never would have expressed their antisemitism in front of *me*, had they known I was Jewish. And some people did not like me, for no discernible reason on my part. However, that dislike never translated into adverse action. And if it were in fact based on my being Jewish, that factor was never expressed directly, because society judged openly expressed antisemitism to be beyond the pale.

In the big picture, my religion did not hinder my career. I passed through a series of highly competitive selection processes. I was promoted early, "below the zone," to major and colonel, selected for battalion and brigade command, graduate schooling, the Naval War College, and tours in the Pentagon with the Joint Chiefs of Staff and the Army Staff. Not being selected for promotion to brigadier general was due to my failure to appreciate the value of networking and politics, and an over-reliance on merit to further my career.

When I encountered antisemitism, it was non-institutional, attitudinal, and non-threatening. Notwithstanding, it was at times hurtful. For example, as a lieutenant, I was dating a colonel's daughter. She was nice; I liked her. And she liked me. But this was long before the feminist movement, and girls her age from military families did not usually date just for fun. Every lieutenant was a prospective husband and entrance into the social milieu of an officer's wife—balls, parties, luncheons, charities, teas, and postings to exotic places. After our second date, she told me her family thought we should all go to church this coming Sunday, and then to brunch at the officers' club. I painfully understood the near-subtle effort to indirectly sort out a non-prospective husband, by virtue of religion, without directly asking. Accordingly, there was no church, no brunch, and, by awkward mutual consent, no third date.

It is also possible, in some cases, that I may have missed an antisemitic intent, while in others, I may have overdiagnosed it. A single vignette illustrates the mostly nebulous nature of the antisemitism I encountered. In 1987, our corps was on a military exercise in Germany, mentally rehearsing our war plan to reinforce NATO in the event of a Warsaw Pact attack. For a time, we were in the vicinity of Bergen-Belsen, the concentration camp complex in Northern Germany where Anne Frank had died. In 1952, the German government designated the camp as a national monument.

Our corps commander, a three-star general, was keenly aware of the geography and military battles fought in this area during World War II. Still, he never indicated that he knew or cared about being so near the camp. Nonetheless, I visited Bergen-Belsen, as did many other US Army soldiers and even whole units bivouacking nearby. And it was stark. There were fourteen earth-berm mass graves, containing over 22,000 bodies of dead Jews, and one could envision the huge grid of inmate barracks that were burned to the ground by the British to contain the spread of typhus when they liberated the camp in early May 1945.

One night, he invited an influential German female publisher to dinner to explain our mission, in the hope that she would write favorably about our corps. During the meal, she related being a nurse in Berlin when the Russians conquered it in 1945. She told of starvation and her rape by Russian soldiers. I silently sympathized with her and admired her strength in rising above this trauma. I was, however, put off by my commander's verbal reaction. He ardently expressed his approbation and sympathy for her ordeal. He was wining and dining her, but I could not help but notice how this contrasted with his previous lack of acknowledgement of the suffering of the Jews nearby. I mused whether it betrayed a type of complex antisemitism, whether it was just politics, or both.

Years later, I learned that he was a member of an American influence group composed of former high-ranking military and civil leaders to foster strong security ties with Israel. Furthermore, he was a signatory on letters to Congress and the President promoting support for Israel. It was not what I had expected.

The Army also placed in perspective my teenage encounters with antisemitic Irish toughs in the Parkchester playgrounds. The Irish I met in the Army were friends, and more. Captain Moran, my ROTC Summer Camp tactical officer, was Irish. He was not only bias-free but also aided me. I attended the Basic Course at Fort Bliss and Airborne School at Fort Benning with an Irish West Pointer from Parkchester. We got along fine together. It was hard for me to believe we originated from two different "tribes" in Parkchester. Another Irish West Pointer, Dick Gilligan, was my best friend in graduate school and mentored me through the intricacies of non-linear differential equations and FORTRAN programming. Without his help, I never would have graduated. Mike McConnell was the chief of staff of the 1st Cavalry Division when

I was a battalion commander. He looked after me; I was one of his protégés. After his promotion to brigadier general, he continued to take an interest in my career and was instrumental in my selection as a brigade commander. When I was assigned to the Pentagon, he sponsored my membership in the tony Army-Navy Club in downtown Washington, DC.

My experiences are far from universal. Others had more serious antisemitic episodes and consequences than I did. Sometimes this age-old hatred resulted in violence and murder, such as the 2018 Tree of Life Synagogue shooting by a right-wing extremist in Pennsylvania, resulting in eleven dead congregants. But—and this is a big "but"—such occurrences were universally condemned by a broad spectrum of mainstream American society and the media.

This stands in sharp contrast with the lack of broad condemnation of the post-October 7 antisemitic outbursts across the United States. The American university system emerged as the *sine qua non* for this phenomenon. And following in close second place was the American media universe.

Almost immediately after the Hamas atrocity, about thirty-four Harvard student organizations published a letter blaming Israel for provoking the assault by denying the Palestinians statehood. Harvard President Claudine Gay demonstrated moral fluidity in addressing this matter. First, she stated only that the letter did not speak for Harvard. After an outcry from some faculty members and alums, she found her voice to denounce the Hamas terror attack. Somehow, she felt compelled to append her approbation of terror by stating that the letter was a First Amendment exercise of free speech. That she was not shocked to discover that her institution had created an environment in which its students felt free to justify rape and murder begs the question as to her personal feelings about this matter. We can speculate whether or not she would have defended as free speech a letter blaming the LGBTQ+ communities for their own oppression. Then she concealed the names of the signatory groups to shield them from any accountability. This stood in contrast to Harvard's later failure to protect its Jewish students from harassment and actual assault, which followed the letter's publication. From this point on, numerous campus protests erupted, in some cases resembling riots. The anti-Jewish animus they nurtured eventually produced violent and lethal outcomes.[84]

An investigation by the House Committee on Education and the Workforce found that elite universities failed to protect Jewish students, made astounding concessions to the organizers of illegal encampments, failed to discipline antisemitic conduct, and considered Congressional oversight a nuisance at best and with open hostility at worst.[85] Claudine Gay appeared before this committee in December 2023. There, she continued her display of ethical ambidexterity by failing to condemn as hate speech the calls on her campus for the death of Jews. Her testimony was so disastrous that she was forced to resign shortly thereafter, in January 2024.

The university-wide atmosphere we observe today did not arise spontaneously. Over time, our most prestigious institutions have instilled in their students the belief that "the ends justify the means," leading to the acceptance of illegal acts when they are perceived as promoting desired social justice outcomes. In a manner reminiscent of George Orwell's novel *Nineteen Eighty-Four* and its concept of "Newspeak," these institutions have used language to shape and control thought. They have redefined heinous crimes such as rape, murder, arson, and hostage-taking as forms of "resistance" to oppression. Their narratives have presented Palestinians and Hamas—a designated terrorist organization—as the oppressed, while depicting Israel as the oppressor. This justification has led to the intimidation of Jewish students and faculty members. Accordingly, campuses became theaters of performative, and often violent, expressions of this oppressor-antisemitic ideology.

Columbia University was the first to host anti-Israel rallies, becoming an epicenter, if not a model, for subsequent

---

[84] The murder of two young Israeli diplomats in Washington, D.C., the Molotov cocktail attack on Jews in Boulder, Colorado, and the arson of the home of the Jewish Governor of Pennsylvania.
Michelle Boorstein and Ben Brasch, "How Oct 7 has changed antisemitic attacks in the U.S.", *The Washington Post*, June 3, 2025.

[85] Committee on Education and The Workforce, "Antisemitism on College Campuses Exposed, Education and The Workforce Committee Releases Report," Washington, DC, October 31, 2024, https://edworkforce.house.gov/news/documentsingle.aspx?DocumentID=412025.

nationwide disruptive, violent, and performative antisemitic action. Interestingly, Columbia University already had a history of indiscipline, which may have served as a template for the post-October 7 riot season. In 1968, Columbia University was the scene of a weeklong anti-Vietnam War, anti-segregation riot that included taking a faculty member hostage and occupying Hamilton Hall.[86] Later, in 1985, it hosted violent student activism against South Africa's Apartheid policy.

But its role in defining and redressing in-vogue social justice issues began in Germany, well before the Vietnam War. During the 1920s and early 1930s, the Frankfurt School, a group of philosophers and sociologists, developed Critical Theory to explain why a working-class revolution failed to take root in post-World War I German society, even though conditions were ripe for it. The members of this school saw themselves as agents of change, required to transform society rather than merely study it.[87]

One of the school's key proponents, Herbert Marcuse, emigrated to America to escape Nazism. He found a home at Columbia University, where he continued his analysis of how to effect societal and cultural change. Ultimately, he became known as the "Father of the New Left," whose philosophy, incorporating elements of Critical Theory, substituted the traditional economic and class-based injustices inherent in Marxist theory for social injustices, such as group oppression. In a sense, it was a form of cultural Marxism. The New Left championed the use of aggressive tactics to overcome, as they defined it, societal oppression.[88] As discussed earlier, the New Left led the anti-Vietnam War movement and framed its political rationale.

Later, universities like Columbia also hosted the emerging discipline of postcolonial studies. This area of study gave rise to the colonizer-anti-colonizer construct, which neatly overlapped with

---

[86] Zachary Folk, "Columbia Student Protestors Occupied The Same Buildings in 1968-Here's How The Two Protests Compare So Far," *Forbes*, April 30, 2024, https://x.com/Forbes/status/1785417612609892616.
[87] "Critical Theory (Frankfurt School)," *Stanford Encyclopedia of Philosophy*, December 12, 2023, https://plato.stanford.edu/entries/critical-theory/.
[88] Gobbo and Rizzi, *From Vietnam to Gaza*; Lewy, *Campus Intolerance*, 4-6.

the oppressor-oppressed and anti-imperialism models. These departments were staffed with non-US academics with an Israel-as-a-colonizer axe to grind.

This generalized anti-Israel and antisemitic atmosphere was tolerated, if not endorsed, by its leadership to the degree that its president was forced to resign in August 2024 after an embarrassing, morally ambiguous testimony before the Committee on Education and the Workforce.

Universities host a range of attitudes, values, cultures, and generations. Faculty are not always united with administrators, and student bodies have their own unique values. These values span a spectrum of causes and issues. Arab students, on average, displayed concern for Palestinian rights and statehood, which now translated into a zero-sum game—the creation of a Palestinian state concomitant with the destruction of the only Jewish state. Other groups embraced humanitarian concerns, now focused solely on Gaza. Yet others seemed dedicated to expunging their "White privilege" by railing against White Jewish colonialism. Some participants seemed ill-informed. Gay and feminist groups joined in, even though Hamas had committed horrific acts of rape and would gladly fling gay people from the rooftops of Gaza. The established preoccupation with social justice was selectively and singularly focused on Israel as an oppressor and colonizer. It excluded actual offenders, such as Russia vis-à-vis Ukraine, China vis-à-vis the Uighurs, Myanmar vis-à-vis the Rohingya, Iran vis-à-vis its own citizenry, and any number of tribal-based slaughters occurring on the African continent. The "why" for this unique obsession with Israel may be explained, in part, by "following the money."

There is an indication that Middle East money may have had a role in changing student perspectives on Israel for the worse. Between 1986 and 2021, colleges and universities received $8.5 billion from Arab sources.[89] Qatar was the largest donor, donat-

---

[89] Joe Hutchison, "Cornell, Harvard, NYU, and Georgetown have received billions in funding from Arab countries over the past 30 years," *The Daily Mail,* October 19, 2023, https://www.dailymail.co.uk/news/article-12649249/Cornell-Harvard-NYU-Georgetown-received-billions-funding-Arab-countries-past-30-years.html.

ing $6.3 billion between 1986 and 2024, with more than one-third of this arriving since 2021.[90] The top recipients—Cornell, Georgetown, Harvard, and NYU—were also the campuses where egregious acts of Israel-bashing and anti-Jewish animus occurred. Quantitative analysts often warn us that correlation is not the same as causation. Still, an investigation by the Network Contagion Research Institute found that universities that accepted money from Middle Eastern donors had three hundred percent more anti-Semitic incidents than those that did not.[91]

The most benign justification of the Arab funding is that it represents the exercise of "soft power" to influence American understanding of Arab-centric issues favorably. But in many cases, this money was earmarked for specific chairs, departments, and curricula, fostering pro-Arab, post-colonial narratives.[92] In this way, the academic world became more than a public square for the Arab voice; it became a hatchery for anti-Israel, antisemitic polemic. Our universities' reliance on this funding might explain their feeble response to antisemitism. For example, the Jewish president of MIT, a major recipient of Saudi Arabian money,[93] decided not to expel blatantly disruptive Arab students because it would jeopardize their student visa status.[94]

---

[90] Danielle Pletka, "Saving American Universities Requires Cracking Down on Foreign Funding," *American Enterprise Institute*, August 20, 2025, https://www.aei.org/articles/.saving-american-universities-requires-cracking-down-on-foreign-funding/.
[91] Bari Weiss, "Is Campus Rage Fueled by Middle Eastern Money," *The Free Press*, November 6, 2023, https://www.thefp.com/p/campus-rage-middle-eastern-roots-qatar.
[92] Seth Cropsey, "Arab Money and the Universities," *Commentary*, April 1979, republished February 2026, https://www.commentary.org/articles/seth-cropsey/arab-money-and-the-universities/.
[93] Michael Sokolove, "Why is There So Much Saudi Money in American Universities," *The New York Times*, July 3, 2019, https://www.nytimes.com/2019/07/03/magazine/saudi-arabia-american-universities.html.
[94] Michael Casey, "Tensions running high at East Coast campuses around Israel-Hamas War," *CBS News*, November 10, 2023, https://www.cbs42.com/news/national/ap-tensions-running-high-at-new-england-campuses-over-protests-around-israel-hamas-war/.

There were also homegrown funding streams from various donors, such as George Soros's Open Society and the Rockefeller Brothers Fund, which financed the activist groups and subsequent legal defense costs.[95] This begs the question: what came first—student activism in search of funding, or funding in search of student activism?

There is an interesting intergenerational divide in how the campus demonstrations were viewed. On average, the younger generations were apt to be more critical of Israel and more sympathetic to the Palestinian cause. The older generations, the Silent and Baby Boomer Generations, were wont to view the protests as a threat to Jewish life and safety. Generation X demanded that our educational institutions provide for the safety of its students, who were, in most cases, their children. The Millennials, the students themselves, were focused on diversity and social consciousness, and tended to view the destructive behaviors as merely instances of free speech gone a bit awry.[96]

Ultimately, the protest themes converged on demands that the universities divest from and boycott Israeli industries, calls for a ceasefire in Gaza, for humanitarian relief, and the cessation of Israeli military action in built-up areas (wherein Hamas was embedded). Upon closer examination, these demands served to provide more than humanitarian support for Gaza. On a whole other level, they provided military and moral assistance to Hamas. For example, demanding a ceasefire would not only spare further human suffering but also serve to give Hamas respite from Israeli military action and a time to reorganize and rebuild. An unconditional surrender, by contrast, would have guaranteed an end to Gazan suffering arising from Israeli military action in the built-up areas. And antisemitism may well have served as an adjunct Hamas strategy to make American Jews fearful of supporting Israel, as

---

[95] "Who is Funding US Anti-Israel Groups?" *The Anti-Defamation League*, March 12, 2025, https://www.adl/resources/article/who-is-funding.
[96] Steven Mintz, "Why Gaza became the defining campus flashpoint," *Inside Higher Ed*, March 31, 2025, https://www.insidehighered.com/opinion/columns/higher-ed-gamma/2025/03/31/why-gaza-became-defining-campus-flashpoint.

Columbia University. Photo by Adrian Florido/NPR.

well as pandering to a pervasive Arab hatred for all things Jewish. Calls for an arms embargo on Israel would likewise help preserve Hamas from military defeat.

The activist messaging and dress were the most vexing and belied a sincere concern for Palestinian rights and avoidance of civilian casualties. The activists dressed as terrorists, signaling admiration and approval of rape and murder. The messaging glorified violence and inflicted fear and emotional pain on Jewish students. The slogan "from the river to the sea, Palestine will be free" was especially pernicious. The river is the Jordan, and the sea the

Tulane University. Photo by Ryan Zamos.

Mediterranean; these waters bound the current state of Israel. Thus, the message can only mean Israel and its Jewish people must be removed to make way for the Palestinians. Interestingly, many carrying this signage were unable to correctly identify which river and sea were being referenced in their sloganeering. All they seemed to know for sure was that most Jews found it intimidating. Another frequent message sent was to praise or "globalize the intifada," intifada being Arabic for violent struggle against Israel. To globalize meant to bring its violence to America; to praise it was to justify terrorism. Martyrs is the term used by Hamas to describe its dead terrorists. At George Washington University, the message was to glorify them.

George Washington University. Photo by Gingerjew04 on X.

Israel and Jews on American campuses have been unjustly accused of "genocide," often by individuals who should know better. This accusation is based on Israel's insistence on controlling what aid flowed into Gaza to prevent its exploitation by Hamas. However, this resulted in claims of intentionally causing starvation and attendant deaths among the Palestinians. Claims of *deliberate* starvation (as opposed to hunger) are emotionally charged and originated in institutions and nations with a historical animosity towards Israel. The same is true, perhaps even more so, for claims of deliberately inflicting massive civilian casualties. The Palestinian casualty figures, provided by the Hamas-led Ministry of Health, cannot be independently verified and seem to have been manipulated to influence global public opinion. Examples of this manipulation include miscounting men as women, categorizing adults as youth, counting individuals who died of natural causes, and failing to differentiate between combatants and non-combatants.[97]

---

[97] Andrew Fox, "Questionable Counting: Analyzing The Death Toll From The Hamas Run Ministry of Health," *The Henry Jackson Society,* 2024, https://henryjacksonsociety.org/wp-content/uploads/2024/12/HJS-Questionable-Counting-Hamas-Report-web.pdf.

Beyond its emotive context, the accusation of genocide is historically inaccurate and harmful; it resembles a deceitful form of Holocaust denial. Genocide specifically refers to events like the Holocaust, wherein six million Jews were systematically and industrially murdered. It is both cruel and defamatory to label the descendants of these victims—who are engaged in a conflict they did not initiate—as perpetrators of genocide.

The casualties arising from Hamas's use of civilian infrastructure, no matter how disproportionate, do not legally constitute genocide, as there must be a specific intent to kill civilians for the sake of killing. Nevertheless, it is hard to ignore the disturbing images of suffering in Gaza, especially among children and women. Understanding the context of this suffering is essential—was it intentional or collateral? Did Hamas contribute to these civilian casualties by employing urban warfare tactics? Regardless of the answers, it appears that Hamas has exploited Gaza's suffering; it has influenced public opinion against Israel and reinforced the false claims of genocide.

Nor do the big-picture Gaza population numbers spell genocide. Gaza has the 40th-highest birth rate worldwide at 2% per annum. Overall, the population of Gaza has increased, based on estimates, from 245,000 in 1950 to 2.1 million in 2025.[98]

The protestors and their university supporters claimed that anti-Zionism was not the same as antisemitism. And in the world of ideas and semantics, that *could be theoretically* correct. But the real world tells us otherwise. Palestinian media and discourse refer to Israelis, contemptuously, as "the Jews." In Europe, Jews with no apparent connection to Israel are attacked by members of the large Arab populations therein resident, in revenge for perceived injustices inflicted on their brethren in Gaza or the West Bank.[99] And the campus activists embraced this conflation. For

---

[98] "Gaza Strip," The World FactBook, the CIA, June 4, 2025, https://cia.gov/the world factbook/countries/Gaza-strip/. Accessed December 2025. Site closed February 4, 2026, and no longer exists.

[99] Stanislaw Biachowicz, "Jews in Europe Still Face High Levels of Antisemitism," *European Union Agency for Fundamental Rights*, 11 July 2024, https://www.fra.europa.eu.

example, at Cal Poly, the faculty instructed Jewish students to hide their identity to avoid threatening behavior, rather than protecting them and disciplining those who would attack them.[100]

Given that selective media coverage can either exaggerate or downplay a phenomenon, it is difficult to categorize the extent of campus unrest across the spectrum of American colleges. There are over 2,800 four-year colleges in the United States, and only a fraction of that number reported protest activity. Indeed, those occurring at elite universities, such as Harvard, Columbia, MIT, UCLA, Northwestern, and Tulane, received outsized media coverage. According to a Generation Lab survey of 1,250 students reported by Axios on March 7, 2024, only 8 percent participated in the protests, but 45 percent supported them, and only 24 percent opposed them. To put these numbers in context, Columbia had a total student enrollment of about 35,000 in 2024, so even small percentages of demonstrators quickly add up when the student body is significant.

The news media's role in legitimizing campus pro-Gazan unrest appears to be a natural consequence of precedent and the progressive atmosphere of the journalism schools that resource this profession. During the Vietnam War, our news media grew progressively critical of the conduct of the war. Their reporting increasingly portrayed the war as immoral and unwinnable. Doubtlessly, this contributed to both convincing the American public that the war was wrong and encouraging the anti-war actors to continue.

The media response to October 7 appears modeled after their earlier anti- Vietnam War activism—perhaps more brazenly so. If the university system played a key role in breaking down protective societal barriers holding antisemitism in check, the media world exploited that opening with biased reporting and a seemingly willful ignorance of historical context related to the Israel-Hamas war.

---

[100] Alana Goodman, "Cal Poly Told Jewish Students to Hide Their Jewish Identity to Avoid Anti-Semitic Harassment, Federal Complaint Says," *The Free Beacon*, March 6, 2025, https://freebeacon.com/campus/cal-poly-told-jewish-students-to-hide-their-jewish-identity-to-avoid-anti-semitic-harassment-federal-complaint-says/.

Gaza, 2024. Photo by Yahya Hasouna/AFP/Getty Images

The media weighed in heavily in the battle for assigning victimhood, thereby affecting public opinion. Both Israel and the Gazans suffered greatly, without question. However, Hamas sought to monopolize this suffering for propaganda purposes, and the US media consciously abetted this effort. The print and television news flooded the public with a narrative stream that emphasized Gazan suffering, while ignoring or minimizing that of Israel. Other than Israel producing a video of the Hamas atrocities and concerned Americans hanging posters of the hostages, the victimhood battlespace was dominated by pro-Hamas reportage. In crafting narratives that emphasized Gazan casualties, the news media was also conducting, wittingly or otherwise, an influence operation in support of Hamas—using public opinion to force Israel to cease military operations in the civilian areas in which Hamas had embedded itself. It was as if the media also wanted Hamas to win.

A study conducted by Israel's Bar Ilan University analyzed the content of the New York Times (NYT) digital newsletter, "The Morning," which has a subscriber base of seventeen million, giving it reach and influence. The analysis found serious factual errors in its reporting, inadequate corrections, omissions, misquoting of

Israeli officials, and employment of questionable journalists. The net effect was to produce narratives favorable to Palestine and Hamas, and detrimental to Israel. More disturbingly, the analysis concluded that the NYT employed a group of young, pro-Palestinian and pro-Hamas journalists who challenged authority and intimidated the editors.[101]

Another study of the NYT by Yale professor Edieal Pinker concluded that it overwhelmingly shaped a narrative that produced sympathy for the Palestinians while downplaying Israeli suffering and Hamas's role in causing it. Conversely, it published personal stories highlighting Palestinian suffering nearly daily.[102] The Washington Post was found to be guilty of unprofessional reporting in its disproportionate reliance on "anonymous sources" in shaping anti-Israel sentiment in its reportage, compared with that of its peers.[103]

The "verdict first, evidence afterwards" reportage on the Al-Ahli Hospital "bombing" on 17 October 2023 is a prime example of news media bias producing antisemitic sentiment. Initial press reports, including those by the NYT, stated Israel bombed the hospital and caused upwards of five hundred civilian casualties. But the hospital was, for all to see, undamaged, and the reported deaths were in excess of the hospital's patient capacity and medical staff. A subsequent investigation by Israel, and verified by Western intelligence agencies, revealed that a malfunctioning Palestinian Islamic Jihad rocket, launched at Israeli civilians, hit the hospital parking lot. In response, some news agencies tepidly retracted, or, in the case of the NYT, evasively modified their reporting to

---

[101] Taylor and Francis Online, "The New York Times Coverage of the Israel-Hamas War—errors, omissions, and poor editorial supervision," 3 September 2024, https://www.tandfonline.com/doi/abs/.

[102] The Media Line Staff, "Study Finds New York Times Coverage Skews Against Israel War Reporting," 19 February 2025, https://www.themedialine.org/headlines/study-finds-new-york-times-coverage-skews-against-israel-in-war-reporting/.

[103] Robert Satloff, "Anonymous Sources in Gaza War Reporting: The Washington Post vs Its Peers," *The Washington Institute*, July 29, 2024, https://www.washingtoninstitute.org/policy-analysis/anonymous-sources-gaza-war-reporting-washington-post-vs-its-peers.

indicate they could not discern who to blame. But, by then, the initial reportage had spread rapidly and stoked widespread anti-Israel and anti-Jewish rallies.[104]

The media failed to present key historical background information, such as civilian casualties caused by the Allies in World War II. This background information would have enabled informed, measured judgments about Israel and Gaza. Furthermore, the news media placed the onus on Israel to end the war and end Palestinian suffering. It acted as if the Palestinians had no agency or responsibility to stop their own suffering. They did this by neglecting to mention that Israel left Gaza in 2005, and by 2006, the Gazans elected Hamas, which was pledged to destroying Israel, to govern them. The media also missed stating the obvious—that the Gazans had to have seen, with their own eyes, that Hamas was building tunnels and storing rockets under their homes, schools, mosques, and hospitals, thereby placing them in danger. It never dawned on the media that the Gazans should now denounce Hamas and demand new elections, thereby enabling an end to the fighting. The absence of this context contributed to a portion of American society perceiving Israel as the sole agent of Gaza's suffering.

Social media also played a significant role in promoting antisemitic behavior on campus. For many of Generation Z, social media was also their only source of news, however fact-free it might have been. Social media reduced complex and nuanced arguments regarding Israel and Palestinian statehood to simple-minded but catchy chants, rhymes, and slogans. Social media told people what to think, how to act, what to shout, when, and where. Its carefully crafted algorithms presented susceptible people with mis- and disinformation to further the antisemitic narrative, in what we can describe as digital echo chambers.

The media's focus on civilian casualties, without objectivity and historical context, is worthy of more discussion. It should hardly be a headline that terrible things happen in wartime.

---

[104] Yasha Mounk, "How the Media Got the Hospital Explosion Wrong," *The Atlantic,* October 23, 2023, https://www.theatlantic.com/ideas/archive/2023/10/gaza-hospital-explosion-misinformation-reporting/.

Civilian deaths and damage are, unfortunately, a given and not at all unique to Israel in the history of warfare. The questions to be asked are who is actually responsible for causing the casualties, whether the casualties were collateral or deliberate, and what actions were taken to minimize such casualties.

John Spenser is the chair of urban warfare studies at the Modern War Institute, which is collocated with the US Military Academy at West Point. His thoughts on Gaza casualties are summarized below: [105]

Israel's civilian-to-combatant ratio is still historically low, given the precautionary measures it took. Israel has done more and implemented more measures to prevent civilian harm than any military in the history of urban warfare. Israel's evacuation of Gaza's cities, its limited use of force, and its distribution of maps to communicate with the civilians were all actions taken to minimize civilian casualties. Despite these measures, media and Hamas advocates try to portray some type of illegality by taking the numbers out of context to malign Israel. It is really essential that people understand that these are just forms of lies, damn lies, and statistics.

There is a nuanced, factual, and historical context within which the current war in Gaza must be viewed, especially regarding the highly emotionally charged issue of civilian casualties. Judgments concerning ethics, precedents, and law cannot be made without an accurate fact pattern. But, instead of facts, the media and academe flooded us with agenda-laced narratives—either out of actual ignorance, or by making themselves willfully so.

The media would have us believe that Israel is the first and only nation on earth to cause civilian casualties in a war it did not start. They would like us to be ignorant of the fact that in World War II, the United States and Great Britain decided at the 1943 Casablanca Conference to deliberately inflict extensive damage to German cities in an effort to destroy Germany's economic base, burden its government with dealing with the disruption of civilian

---

[105] Marylin Stern, "John Spenser on Israel's War in Gaza: A Technical Analysis," *The Middle East Forum*, January 24, 2025.

AFTERWORD—THE NEW ANTISEMITISM

Dresden, Germany, 1945. Photo by Richard Peter, Deutsche Fotothek.

life, weaken the German people's war resolve, and to expedite an unconditional German surrender.[106]

America and its allies wrestled with the ethics of causing both collateral and deliberate civilian casualties. They concluded both were necessary to force Germany to surrender and end the suffering for all—the Allies and the German people. A quick review of the Allied bombing campaign over Germany during World War II is, therefore, instructive. This multi-year bombing effort caused extensive civilian casualties and reduced cities to mounds of debris. The German government estimated that 410,000 German civilians were killed in the Allied air campaign.[107] Another 8 million were made homeless.[108]

For example, in 1945, a decision was made by the United States and Great Britain to mass bomb Berlin and Dresden to demoralize

---

[106] Richard J. Evans, *The Third Reich at War* (The Penguin Press, New York, 2009) 441.
[107] German Federal Statistical Office, October 1956, as duplicated in Wikipedia entry, "German casualties in World War II."
[108] Evans, *The Third Reich at War*, 451.

the German populace and hasten the conclusion of the war. Before that, the British adopted a deliberate bombing campaign against fifty-eight German cities to destroy the morale and burden the German war effort.[109] But, in general, America preferred a daylight precision bombing campaign against militarily significant targets, usually located in cities. But "precision" was not achievable,[110] and collateral civilian casualties resulted. Again, this was viewed as necessary to expedite the German surrender and the end of the war.

The situation in Gaza shares similarities with America's experience during World War II. Aachen was the first major city the US Army encountered after crossing into Germany in 1944. Initially, the plan was to bypass Aachen quickly. However, Germany chose to defend the city, viewing it as politically and symbolically important. They deliberately positioned their forces within the urban infrastructure and failed to evacuate all civilians. The US 1st Infantry Division, which I served in during the Vietnam War, took the city block by block and house by house. As a result, Aachen was reduced to rubble, and there were collateral civilian casualties.

*Aachen civilian refugees leaving city, 1944.
Everett Collection, Inc./Alamy.*

---

[109] Donald L. Miller, *Masters of the Air*, (New York, Simon & Schuster Paperbacks, 2006), 54-55, 410-440.
[110] Miller, *Masters of the Air*, 109.

No one claimed America was guilty of war crimes in its pursuit of eliminating the threat presented by Germany. Even the Germans themselves had the post-war grace to recognize that they had brought their suffering upon themselves. America eventually had some soul-searching into its bombing campaign, especially about Dresden, but, by and large, America and the rest of the world concluded that German civilian casualties were caused by Germany's initiation of World War II and its continued resistance to unconditional surrender.

The media and academia would have us not know that the end of World War II produced a flood of refugees of all nationalities, as some fled the Soviet advances into Eastern Europe. Others were expelled as unwelcome ethnic Germans, and some were Jews seeking new lives in Israel and in the West. For example, at the Potsdam Conference in 1945, the Allies punished Germany for a war it had started. They moved Poland's borders westward into German East Prussia and approved the ejection of several million ethnic Germans from Eastern Europe. These refugees were eventually integrated into German life—that is, they did not become refugees in perpetuity.[111] The historical context

German refugees expelled from Eastern Europe, 1945. Alamy photo.

---

[111] Adam Taylor, "The forgotten story of when the Germans were refugees" *The Washington Post*, September 3, 2015, https://www.washingtonpost.com/news/worldviews/wp/2015/09/03/the-forgotten-story-of-when-the-germans-were-the-refugees/.

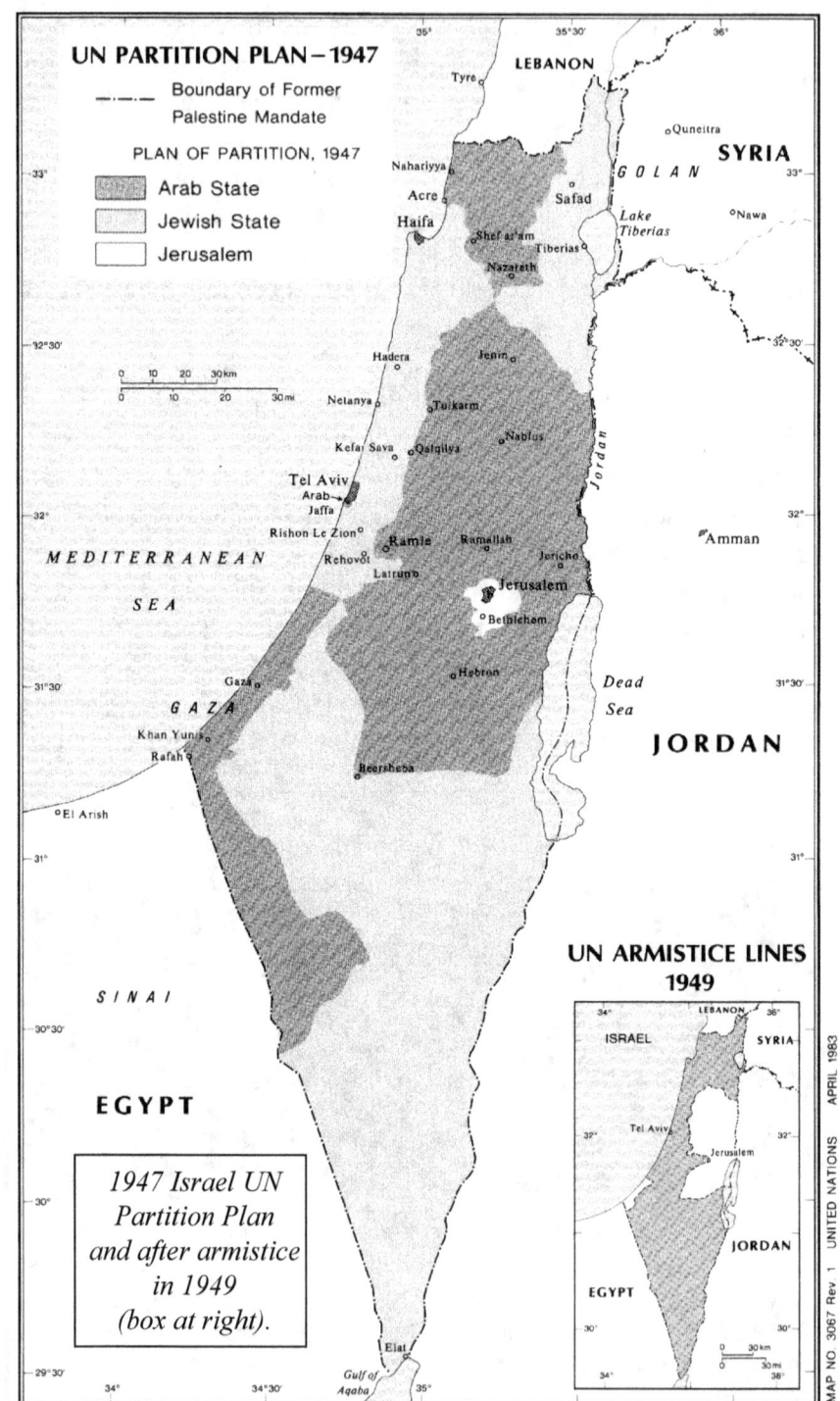

1947 Israel UN Partition Plan and after armistice in 1949 (box at right).

is that from 1945 to 1950, the world witnessed massive refugee movements across shifting national boundaries, an unavoidable consequence of a lost war. The German government estimated that over 1.2 million ethnic German civilians were killed or died as a result.[112]

There are numerous other historical examples of civilian casualties resulting from war, the most obvious today being those caused by Russia's bombing of Ukrainian cities. None of our social justice warriors seem to have the appetite to take on that blatant violation of international law. Again, this only serves to highlight the media's and academe's selective and highly negative preoccupation with Israel, and by extension, the antisemitism it incites.

Regarding the creation of Israel, the media and academe are guilty of a form of intellectual malpractice, misrepresenting history by the process of omission. In their zeal to brand Israel as the colonizer, they failed to acknowledge that Jews had been living in the land of Israel since antiquity. They also totally ignored the actual colonizer, Great Britain, which had ruled this land since 1918 as a protectorate, its prize for winning World War I. Before that, the Ottoman Turks had colonized this land. In 1947, the United Nations (UN) Partition Plan allowed for the creation of *both* an Israeli and a Palestinian state, ending the British protectorate. However, in 1948, after Israel declared its independence based on this plan, the armies of five Arab states invaded to destroy it.

The warring Arab states advised the Palestinians to temporarily flee to avoid the upcoming fight, and some Palestinians were forcibly expelled or induced to flee by Israel. By 1949, Israel had repelled the Arab invasion and secured more areas than allocated initially by the Partition Plan. The Palestinians who had fled or were expelled were not allowed back. Egypt governed the Palestinian enclave of Gaza from 1949 to 1967. Jordan, the next colonizer in line, annexed the residual Palestinian land, known as the West Bank, and held it until 1967, when it too, like Gaza, was lost to Israel in the "Six-Day War." Interestingly, neither

---

[112] German Federal Statistical Office.

Palestinian refugees, 1949. UN archives.

Egypt nor Jordan offered statehood to the Palestinians under their governance.

There was also a parallel flow of Jewish refugees from Arab countries, such as Yemen, Iraq, Morocco, and Tunisia, into Israel. During the period 1948-51, 250,000 Jews from Arab countries entered Israel. They were motivated by both pull and push factors, and the push factors included mob violence and murder. By 1972, 600,000 Jews from Muslim countries had fled to Israel as a result of Israel's victories during the 1956 Suez War and the 1967

Yemenite Jews awaiting flights to Israel. Aden airport, 1949.
Wikimedia Commons.

Six-Day War, and the dangerous conditions this created, as Arab citizens sought Jewish scapegoats for their humiliating defeats. The Jewish refugees were absorbed, painfully for those whose cultures and poverty hindered assimilation into a European-oriented society. But assimilated and absorbed they were, and the refugee camps they had previously occupied were emptied.[113] This is in contrast to both the UN and the Arab states perpetuating the Palestinian refugee problem, quite probably to preserve them as a continuing threat to Israel.

Returning to the world of higher education, in effect returning to the scene of the crime, a personal college experience highlights the role of academia in justifying hatred of the Jews, and that this is nothing new under the sun.

In 1983, I was an Army exchange student at the Naval War College in Newport, Rhode Island. In my small, ten-man Strategy and Policy section, we had a Royal Jordanian Coast Guard officer exchange student. He would frequently travel to New York City to meet with his "mentor," Professor Edward Said, at Columbia University. Said was a Palestinian and a professor of literature, but he was also a founder of the post-colonial studies movement.[114] Said argued for a Palestinian state with the Right of Return, that is, the right of about four million Palestinians resident in Jordan, Gaza, Lebanon, and Syria to return to their "lands" in Israel, thereby effectively destroying Israel as a Jewish homeland. It was the demographic precursor of "from the river to the sea."

The coursework required each of us to give a presentation on strategy and policy. The Jordanian student prefaced his by noting he had coordinated with Professor Said, as if to front-load a sense of intellectual gravitas. But what followed was an embarrassment. Our Harvard-educated professor sat transfixed, staring at his shoes, in what looked to us like profound discomfort. Our

---

[113] Benny Morris, 1948, (New Haven, Yale University Press, 2008), 64, 184, 308, 396-97, 407-416. "Jewish exodus from the Muslim world," Wikipedia, 9 July 2025, https://wikipedia.org/w/indexphp?title=Jewish_exodus_from_the_Muslim_world&action=history.

[114] "Edward Said/American Literary Critic and Philosopher," *Britannica*, June 3, 2025, https://www.britannica.com/biography/Edward-Said.

foreign student contingent was there in furtherance of American political-military relationships with friendly foreign militaries. This student was our guest; accordingly, our professor chose not to intercede and shame him. My classmates and I fidgeted nervously, waiting for the abomination to end. I was personally offended but said nothing, following my professor's non-verbal cue.

The Jordanian student asserted the Palestinians were the actual victims of the Holocaust because it drove the surviving Jews to seek refuge in Palestine, which became, by force of arms, Israel, resulting in the creation of a Palestinian refugee class. But the real assault on our sensibilities was his contention that the Jews were responsible for the Holocaust because they made themselves universally despised by flaunting their financial and intellectual superiority. Thus, these Jewish characteristics caused the Palestinians to lose their homeland and justified the Nazi genocide.

My fellow students and I could only assume that Said implanted this antisemitic thrust. It truly shocked me that a prestigious university like Columbia would countenance the propagation of this type of antisemitism. Afterwards, no one in our section would have anything to do with him, and that reassured me. But if he had made his presentation today, at Columbia, I fear he might have received a round of applause.

Ultimately, the combined efforts of the university and media worlds changed our national political landscape. Sectors of American society previously believed to be supportive of its Jewish members became, at best, passive observers, or at the worst, incubators for this newly released antisemitism. Friends became enemies, and vice versa.

Republicans, heretofore thought of as dismissive of Jews, emerged as their protectors and advocates. The Democratic Party, long viewed as a bastion of Jewish well-being,[115] sent mixed messages. It was an election year, and the party jockeyed to garner both the Jewish and Muslim-American vote. Accordingly, the party could not unequivocally condemn antisemitism without includ-

---

[115] As exemplified by the popular quip, "Reform Judaism is the Democratic Party with Jewish Holidays," and Reform Judaism comprises the largest cohort of "religious" American Jews.

ing, in the same breath, an admonition against Islamophobia—the latter effectively trivializing the former. On 7 November 2023, the House of Representatives censured Rashida Tlaib, a Democrat, for virulent antisemitic speech. But only twenty-two Democrats, a mere 10 percent of their total, voted for this censure.[116] Despite the evidence of its role in promoting campus violence against the Jews, the Democratic Party persists in its leftward drift by failing to discipline and eject its growing and ever more aggressive antisemitic members.

Now, some thoughts regarding Jewish participation in the antisemitic surge. It appears to me that Jewish values and behaviors were part of the problem, and, therefore, must be included in the solution. And the solution set requires a high degree of critical self-appraisal and an appreciation of the need for unity in combating a threat that endangers all Jews, irrespective of political inclination.

Jewish-named campus protest groups were especially problematic. For example, the Jewish Voice for Peace not only advocated for Palestinian statehood but also espoused an anti-Zionist rhetoric, which may well be its core, Marxist value.[117] Rather than demonstrating separately, they joined, openly and loudly, with the pro-Hamas component, thus willingly lending it protection from charges of antisemitism.

It is common in American society to think of Jews as being "smart." But maybe not. Jewish support for Zohran Mamdani as mayor of New York City is a case in point. During his campaign, he clearly expressed an anti-Zionist, anti-Israel rhetoric. The International Holocaust Remembrance Association (IHRA) illustrates anti-Zionism as a possible manifestation of antisemitism. Yet Mamdani received about 33% of the Jewish vote.[118] Some

---

[116] Katy Stech Ferek, "House Censures Rep. Rashida Tlaib Over Israel Remarks," *The Wall Street Journal*, November 8, 2023, https://www.wsj.com/politics/rep-rashida-tlaib-faces-house-censure-vote-over-israel-remarks.

[117] Joshua Muravchik, "Not So Jewish, Not for Peace," *Commentary*, April 2019, https://www.commentary.org/articles/joshua-muravchik.

[118] Samuel J. Abrams, "Two Jewish Moral Worlds: What the Mamdani Election Reveals," *The American Enterprise Institute*, November 10, 2025, https://www.aei.org/op-eds/two-jewish-moral-worlds-what-the-mamdani-election-reveals/.

of this support was from an ultra-religious Jewish community that thinks Israel should be reincarnated only when the Messiah comes. Others were Marxists who believed Zionism conflicted with a unitary focus on class struggle. Yet others, such as Jewish Congressman Jerry Nadler, who openly endorsed Mamdani, were mainstream Progressive Democrats.

Notwithstanding this Jewish support, one of Mamdani's first acts as mayor was to rescind a pre-existing mayoral executive order adopting the IHRA definition of antisemitism. This could easily be interpreted as telegraphing his intent to normalize anti-Israel rhetoric and action in the future. And it places all Jews, including his Jewish supporters, in danger. How is a crowd on an anti-Jewish tear to know which Jews are Mamdani supporters—and would they care?

I am unable to pinpoint why this Jewish-self-destructive behavior pattern obtains. Some would simplistically attribute it to "self-hating Jews." And this may be a part of the explanation. History provides an insight into another dimension of the explanation. Some German Jews, during the early rise of Nazism, sought to portray themselves as "good Jews," as distinguished from the "other Jews" that Hitler despised. It did not avail them. They were either forced to flee their beloved motherland or were consumed in the Holocaust. There were communists of Jewish extraction, "good Jews," who denounced Zionism and affiliation with the Jewish religion and culture. Eventually, the Soviet and Polish Communist Parties purged them by way of nationwide anti-Semitic campaigns. And in many cases, the purges resulted in murder, imprisonment, and exile. It would be wise for Mamdani's good Jews to acquire historical literacy.

We, Jews, are responsible for doing more to protect ourselves, both morally and physically. Starting at home, the battlespace over which we have the most control, we must educate our children and arm them with a robust set of historic and cultural facts that nullify the anti-Jewish, oppressor-colonizer models which they will encounter in our education and media realms. Teaching the Old Testament is a good starting place. We should endeavor to make our children physically resilient and adept at defending themselves from antisemitic hooliganism. To be sure, we need allies in this fight, but we, ourselves, must be strong; we must be worthy allies.

Moving outward, we must engage in what was formerly a trivial political pursuit of electing our local school boards. We must be on guard to ensure that what we teach at home is not contradicted in our local schools. The oppressor-oppressed narrative must not be allowed to permeate our K-12 schools.

Regarding our universities, we alumni should insist on a return to education, not indoctrination. Facts are essential to intelligent debate, and these facts must be presented and argued objectively. Universities must not allow their departments and curricula to be for sale. There must be clear boundaries between the expression of thought and intimidating and threatening behaviors. Student safety must be guaranteed, and violent students must be disciplined. Campuses must strive to be centers of learning, not factories for hateful narratives.

As subscribers and advertisers, with some degree of economic, if not moral, power, we should demand that our printed news media adopt a narrative-free news reporting style—factual, source-verified, and double-checked "news" on the front pages, and opinions on the editorial pages. We have yielded the digital battlespace to the bigots, leaving them free to spread anti-Jewish narratives. Surely our collective cyber savvy can be harnessed to reverse this trend.

The fight against antisemitism must be depoliticized. We must open our threat filters to acknowledge antisemitic intent and action by the Progressive and Socialist Democrats, as well as from the Right, white supremacists, and Neo-Nazis. To deny that Leftist antisemitism exists because we may not like the Republicans in power is self-defeating.

Palestinian statehood must be addressed realistically, without the emotions inherent in the oppressor-colonialist model. The issue is how to produce a Palestinian state that is not resolute in destroying Israel. This is not a quick and easy task.

Finally, American Jews must adopt a sense of unity in combating antisemitism. Jewish humor celebrates our fractious nature. Common themes include two Jews forming three political parties, or a shipwrecked Jew, on a deserted island, building two synagogues—one to pray in and the other not to be caught dead in. These types of jokes, while worthy of a chuckle, should also make it evident that each of us must be part of a unified effort to defend all Jews. To paraphrase John Donne, no American Jew is an island entire of itself.

GLOSSARY

AC-47. A two-engine, DC-3 type aircraft used to provide fire support to soldiers on the ground.

ACAV. Armored cavalry assault vehicle. A modified M-113 with one M-2 and two M-60 machine guns.

AK-47. Russian-designed 7.62mm assault rifle. Very rugged and dependable.

Ambush Patrol. A small group of soldiers, usually five or fewer, set up outside the main Laager or NDP at night to intercept enemy soldiers in the immediate vicinity.

APC. Armored Personnel Carrier / M-113.

Army Brat. A term used, with pride, by the children of career army personnel to describe themselves.

BAR. Browning automatic rifle. A .30 caliber automatic rifle with a 20-round magazine used in WWII and Korea. Replaced in the US inventory by the M-60 machine gun.

BOQ. Bachelor Officer Quarters. On-base housing for unmarried officers. Usually consisting of a bedroom, bathroom, and shared kitchen facilities, if for long-term occupancy.

Ball Ammunition. Regular ammunition, as distinguished from tracer ammunition.

Battalion. A US Army formation commanded by a lieutenant colonel containing four batteries or companies.

Battery. A US artillery unit, commanded by a captain containing about 100 soldiers and six cannon. Equivalent to a company.

Bazooka. A shoulder-fired anti-tank weapon system employing a rocket-propelled-shaped charge projectile.

Below the Zone. Selection for promotion from below the primary year groups under consideration. Usually, about 5% of promotions were below the zone or early.

Body Count. The number of enemy soldiers killed—a key but often inaccurate metric used during the Vietnam War to measure success.

Brigade. A US Army formation commanded by a colonel containing two or more battalions.

Bush. Slang for the jungle.

Butt Pack. A canvas pack worn on a soldier's **Web Gear** in the lumbar region to carry essential equipment.

C-7. A twin-engine army medium transport aircraft called the Caribou.

CH-47. Large multi-purpose helicopter known as the Chinook.

C-123. The Provider. A two-engine air force transport aircraft used for paratroop training and combat resupply.

C-130. Four-engine transport aircraft capable of landing on dirt airfields.

Caserne. German for an army base.

Charlie. Slang for Viet Cong and pronounced phonetically as "Victor Charlie."

CIDG. Civilian Irregular Defense Group. Groups of local Vietnamese recruited by the US Special Forces as mercenaries, who usually lived with their families in the Special Forces camps when not on patrol or interdiction missions along the border areas.

CO. Commanding Officer. Usually referring to a company commander.

Colt .45. Standard issue .45 caliber semi-automatic pistol.

Command Group. The commander, his key staff, and associated RTOS required to accomplish the command-and-control function.

Claymore. A small, shaped charge, anti-personnel mine, firing ball bearing size projectiles.

Company. US Army formation commanded by a captain with about 185 soldiers organized as four platoons and a headquarters element.

CP. Command Post. Location of commander and his key staff.

CS. A strong form of Tear Gas.

Dining In. An Army formal dinner occasion.

Donut Dolly. Slang for a Red Cross girl (serving coffee and donuts).

F-4. US fighter-bomber, commonly called the Phantom, used to support soldiers on the ground.

F-105. US fighter-bomber, commonly called the Thunder Chief, used to support soldiers on the ground.

FDC/FDO/FO. Fire Direction Center. A place where soldiers working under the FDO, Fire Direction Officer, compute the settings to be transmitted to the guns to hit the target radioed in by the FO, Forward Observer.

Fire Team. A sub-element of a squad containing four to five soldiers.

First Sergeant. The senior NCO in a company or battery. Revered for their toughness, wisdom, experience, maturity, and judgment. Roughly equivalent to the fabled Roman Centurion.

FM. Field Manual. Official, authoritative US Army publications containing approved doctrine, tactics, techniques, and procedures for all combat and combat support activities.

Four Deuce. 4.2-inch mortar.

Fourragere. A cloth and metal shoulder loop representing a military award, distinction, or membership in a unit.

Friendly Fire. Artillery, air strikes, and ground fire from our forces which inflict unintentional friendly casualties.

G-3/G-level Staff. A staff level at headquarters commanded by General Officers. The G-3 is the higher headquarters counterpart of the S-3, operations officer, at battalion and brigade level.

GP Small/Medium Tent. US Army general purpose tent that can nominally sleep 4 and 10 soldiers, respectively.

HAWK. Homing All the Way Killer. A US radar and missile medium altitude anti-aircraft weapon system.

Hamas. Palestinian political and military terror group, governing Gaza since 2006. Dedicated to destruction of Israel. Backed by Iran.

Happy Hour. Time set aside in military clubs for reduced-price drinks and other special attractions to encourage attendance and promote comradeship.

Headspace and Timing. Pre-firing adjustments to the M-2 machine gun bolt and firing pin assemblies to ensure proper functioning of the gun in automatic fire.

Hezbollah. Lebanese Shia Islamist political and military terror group, backed by Iran.

Honest John. A US Army surface-to-surface missile system.

Howitzer. A relatively high angle of fire artillery piece. Can be fired from behind a hill mass between it and the target.

Huey. Standard US UH-1 helicopter used in Vietnam to transport troops and supplies and serve as a fire support platform firing rockets.

Hump. Slang for trudging through the jungle (the **Bush**).

IG. Inspector General. Special staff office charged with addressing complaints and irregularities and assessing unit readiness.

Jump Master / JM. Paratrooper responsible for the proper execution of a parachute jump from an aircraft, Focuses on the proper performance of safety checks and jump procedures.

KP. Kitchen Police. A term describing various clean-up and serving duties in support of the cooks, assigned to (non-cook) soldiers on a roster basis to ensure fairness.

Laager. A type of night defensive position (NDP) for a battalion or larger unit in the field, from which to be resupplied by helicopter in preparation for continued operations at daybreak.

Leg. A term of derision for non-paratroopers. Referring to soldiers who have to walk, using their legs, to get to the fight, as opposed to paratroopers who jump into the fight.

Lensatic Compass. Standard army compass used for navigation and adjustment of indirect fires.

LZ. Landing zone. A natural or man-made clearing to accommodate helicopters.

M-1 Carbine. Standard light .30 caliber rifle/carbine carried in WWII and Korea. Capable of automatic fire. Used a smaller, less lethal round than the M-1 rifle and had a 20-30 round magazine. Replaced by the M-16 during the Vietnam War.

M-1 Rifle. Standard US Army .30 caliber semi-automatic rifle used in WWII and Korea, had an eight-round clip. Replaced by the M-16 during the Vietnam War.

M-2 Machine gun. Heavy US Army caliber .50 machine gun.

M-14 Rifle. Standard US Army 7.62mm rifle issued between the M-1 and M-16. Designed for use in European battlefield.

M-16. Rifle. Standard 5.56 mm rifle issued to soldiers in Vietnam. Capable of automatic fire and had a 20-round magazine.

M-17 Protective Mask. Standard US Army "gas mask." Worn on the left side, in a canvas case.

M-48. Standard medium US tank used in Vietnam.

M-60. Light, 7.62mm machine gun.

M-113. Standard US Army tracked tank-like armored personnel carrier (APC). Could carry upwards of ten soldiers (a squad).

M-1911 caliber .45 Colt pistol. Standard sidearm from WWI onward. Semi-automatic with a seven-round magazine.

MACV. Military Assistance Command, Vietnam. Established in 1962 to support all US military efforts in South Vietnam. Evolved into the highest military headquarters for all US forces.

Motor Pool. Parking area and maintenance bays for unit vehicles.

Mortar. A relatively simple high-angle fire weapon system capable of firing from behind a hill mass or other barrier between it and the target.

NCO. Non-Commissioned Officer. A soldier in the rank of corporal to sergeant major. Most commonly used as a generic term for any grade of sergeant.

Napalm. Jellied gasoline bomb fill. Highly combustible upon detonation.

Nike Hercules. A US radar and missile high altitude air defense weapon system.

NDP. Night Defensive Position. A temporary position for company-size units or smaller, from which operations will be resumed at daybreak.

OCS. Officer Candidate School. A training process to produce officers from the enlisted ranks.

OH-13. A light, two-man observation and command and control helicopter.

Officers Field Ration Mess. A dining facility for officers offering standard army-issue food, at a fixed rate.

Out. Radio brevity code word meaning, "I have nothing further to transmit."

PRC-25. Portable Radio Communications. The standard backpack FM field radio used in Vietnam.

PX. The Post Exchange. An on-base army facility offering clothing, toiletries, jewelry, furniture, garden, and other department store-like items.

Platoon. US Army formation containing 44 soldiers organized as four squads and a headquarters element.

Point Man / Slack Man. The Point Man is the first in line in a tactical formation, responsible for maintaining the compass direction and pace count (distance traveled). He must be able to "read" the environment for signs of the enemy. The soldier to his immediate rear is the Slack Man. He covers the Point Man, maintains a pace count, and provides over-watch security. These are the two most important and dangerous jobs for an infantry unit moving tactically.

RC-292. A man-portable FM radio antenna mounted on a sectioned mast.

ROTC Summer Camp. A six-week basic training camp for ROTC cadets between their junior and senior years.

RPG. A rocket-propelled grenade with a shaped charge warhead, used by the Vietcong to attack US vehicles, bunkers, and even hovering helicopters.

RTO. Radio-telephone operator. The soldier who carries the PRC-25 field radio commonly called the "Prick 25."

R&R. Rest and recuperation leave. A one-week leave granted to each soldier to such locations as Australia, Hong Kong, Thailand, The Philippines, and Hawaii.

Recoilless Rifle. A weapon system firing a relatively low-velocity projectile with a shaped charge warhead. Part of the propellant charge is allowed to exhaust at the breech end, producing a rearward momentum that counterbalances the forward momentum of the projectile. The net effect of this momentum balance is no recoil.

Registration. The process of adjusting artillery firing tables for local metrological conditions and variations in cannon/projectile velocity to produce the most accurate fires possible.

Roger. The brevity code word used on the radio meaning "I have received your message and understand."

SKS Carbine. A Russian-designed forerunner of the AK-47, subsequently manufactured by Communist China.

S-2. Intelligence Officer on a battalion or brigade staff. In combat, he is primarily responsible for collecting and disseminating information on the enemy.

S-3/S-3 Air. Operations Officer on a battalion or brigade staff. In combat, they are primarily responsible for preparing plans and managing their execution. The S-3 Air is one of his subordinates responsible for planning and managing the execution of air support operations. On division staff or in separate formations commanded by a general officer, these staff officers are designated G-3/G-3 Air.

Shaped Charge. A warhead formed around an inverted, copper conical liner. Upon detonation, the conical charge blows forward, forming a hot jet of gas and molten copper which can penetrate armored vehicles.

Snipe Hunt. A fool's errand, a prank. Named for the Snipe, a shorebird that is difficult to hunt/catch. The term, sniper, derives from one skilled enough to shoot this problematic quarry.

Spoon. The handle of a hand grenade.

Squad. US Army military formation containing 10 soldiers.

Stick. A row of parachutists on one side of the airplane.

Terry and the Pirates. An American action comic/newspaper comic strip series set in China with a wartime theme. Popular from the mid—1930s to the early 1950s.

Thompson-sub-machine gun. The .45 caliber "Tommy Gun."

Topographic Map. A map representing a depiction of the terrain as seen from above, indicating elevation and shape.

Tracer. A rifle or machine gun round with an incendiary charge in its base that produces a red glowing trail to mark the trajectory of the projectile as seen by the person firing it.

VRC-47. Vehicle Radio Communications. A configuration of the standard VRC-46 vehicular mounted FM radio used in Vietnam. The VRC-46 had a single transmitter and receiver. The VRC-47 had two receivers so that two frequencies could be monitored simultaneously.

WP. Spoken as "Willie Peter." White phosphorus. A shell or hand grenade filling that produces thick white smoke when exposed to air upon detonation.

WASP. White Anglo-Saxon Protestant.

Web Gear. The term for canvas harness and belt system used by soldiers to carry canteens, packs, holsters, first aid kits, etc.

XO. Executive Officer. Usually, the second in command in a company, battalion, or brigade. Usually one rank junior to the commander.

INDEX

Military Units

1-2 Infantry 172, 174, 175, 181, 185, 191
1-4 Cavalry 172, 174, 181, 183, 184, 210
1-16 Infantry 175, 187, 201, 204, 212, 215
1-26 Infantry 172, 175, 181, 183, 187, 188, 191
1st Brigade 172, 175, 178, 182, 187, 188, 197, 199, 208
1st Infantry vii, x, xi, 75, 79, 81, 92, 101, 117, 141, 154, 159, 173, 193, 195, 208, 212, 220
1st Infantry Division x, xi, 75, 79, 81, 92, 101, 117, 141, 154, 159, 173, 193, 195, 208
2-2 Infantry 210, 211, 215, 216, 217, 219, 222
2-28 Infantry xiv, xv, 175, 187, 190, 191, 213
2-33 Artillery xiv, 222
2d Brigade 92, 209
3rd Brigade 162, 175, 204, 208, 209
4th Infantry Division 208
8th Infantry Division 62
9th VC Division 153, 208
11th Armored Cavalry Regiment 209
25th Infantry Division 209
28th Infantry xiv, 86, 98, 118, 148, 194, 227
90th Infantry Division 61
173rd Airborne Brigade 208, 210
196th Brigade 208
273d Regiment 153, 159

A

Aachen, Germany 266
Airborne School 19, 41, 50, 51, 55, 56, 58, 60, 232
antisemitism xiii, 17, 18, 245, 247, 248-250, 255, 256, 259, 260, 269, 272-275

B

Beirut, Lebanon xii, 230-232
Berlin, Germany 117, 118, 242, 250, 265
Berry, Colonel Sid 181-183, 186
Billet, PFC Conrad 160
Blanford, Captain Raymond ix, 3, 4, 96, 99, 101, 106, 109, 110, 111, 114-122, 125-136, 138-140, 142, 145, 147, 155-161, 213, 220, 225, 226, 228
Blizzard, Sergeant 133
Bong Trang ix, 172, 181, 198, 199, 224
Bronx 8-11, 14, 19, 49, 54, 66, 112, 231, 234
Burch, Specialist Henry 139, 160
Bushey, First Lieutenant Peter 42, 236

C

Camp, Colonel Marlin 141, 207
Carolan, Lieutenant James 39

Caruthers, Colonel Lawrence, Jr. 207
CCNY (City College of New York) vii, 28-32, 34, 35, 37, 39, 40, 44, 45, 47, 50, 100, 136, 235, 236
Columbia University 26, 252, 253, 257, 260, 271, 272
communism 4, 5, 30, 34, 77
Contratto, SFC Robert 51, 55, 56, 58
Critical Theory 253

D

Daniel, Lieutenant Colonel Charles, Jr. 166, 167, 200-203
DePuy, Major General William E. 154, 155, 175, 192, 194, 195-197, 199, 210, 220, 225
Detroit, Michigan 6, 227, 228
Dobol, Ted 98
Dooley, Specialist Robert 6, 7, 108, 130, 138, 139, 141, 143-145, 149, 161, 204, 227, 228
Dresden, Germany 265, 267
Drzewiecki, Dr. Ted 37
Duster 239, 240

E

Eads, First Sergeant Troy 206, 207, 211, 216

F

Fort Bliss, Texas 48-50, 228
Frankfurt School 253
fraternities 38-42
Friedman, Mammie 26
Friedman, Max 26

G

Galvin, Lieutenant Tom ix, 196
Gaza 246, 253, 254, 256, 258, 259, 261-264, 266, 269, 271, 280
George Washington University 243, 258
German Army paratrooper 232
Gilbert, Major John 47
Gorman, Lieutenant Colonel Paul 183, 186, 187, 189, 190, 191, 194
Grimes, Specialist Harold 160

H

Hale, Sergeant First Class Loyal 99, 122, 124, 128-130, 142, 143, 145, 159
Hamas xiii, 242, 243, 245, 247, 251, 252, 254-256, 258-264, 273, 280
Hanson, Victor Davis 197
Harvard University 28, 30, 251, 254, 255, 260, 271
Hezbollah xii, 230, 231, 243, 280
Hill 150 ix, 3, 6, 46, 103, 105, 110, 111, 115, 124, 128, 129-136, 138, 140, 142, 144-146, 148-153, 156-161, 170, 188, 198, 201, 224-228, 236, 238
Hill 177 153
Hutcheson, Captain John 4, 6

I

intifada 258
Irish 6, 8, 14, 16, 17, 19, 31, 49, 71, 72

Israel xii, xiii, 100, 228, 231, 237, 238, 242, 243, 245, 247, 250-252, 254, 255-264, 267-275, 280

J

James, PFC Jimmy 160
Jezior, Major Tony 168-170, 175, 179, 180, 188, 190, 191, 198
Johannsen, Captain Nils 174, 181
Joulwan, Captain George 181

K

Kelley, Sergeant First Class Bernard 42, 236
Kessman, Bea Kurtz 223
Knight, Captain Peter 184-186
Kurtz, Bea 223
Kurtz, Carol vii, ix, 59, 228, 229, 234, 242
Kurtz Charles 237
Kurtz, Isidore 27, 237
Kurtz, Leslie 234
Kurtz, Libby 234
Kurtz, Mark 234, 237

L

Lai Khe 86, 89, 96, 99-102, 107, 148, 156, 170, 172, 175, 184, 192, 194, 207
Lindquist, First Sergeant 105, 110, 124, 126, 137, 145, 147, 161
Lithuania 19, 23, 26
Lithuanian 18, 19
Loc Ninh 2, 101-103, 105, 107, 109, 110, 112, 119, 121, 133, 148, 154-156, 157, 159, 161, 199, 224

Lyons, Second Lieutenant William 42, 236

M

Madden, Captain Jim 181, 193
Mainz, Germany 54, 60-63
Mamdani, Zohran 273, 274
Marshall, Brigadier General S. L. A. 158
Mavroudis, Major Antonio 42, 236
Meadows, Specialist Richard ix, 124, 131, 145
Miller, Corporal 176
Miller, Sergeant John 139
MIT (Massachusetts Institute of Technology) 255, 260
Moran, Captain 45, 80, 81, 86
Morton, Captain John 175
Mullen, Captain Bill ix, 172, 174, 175, 181, 185, 194, 199

N

Naval War College 230
Needels, Lieutenant Chris 175, 185, 190
Nelson, Specialist David 139, 160
New Left 246, 253
New York Times (NYT) 261, 262
Nicosia, Chief Warrant Officer 65
Nicosia, Rene 66
Northwestern University ix, 260

O

Operation El Paso II 101, 148
Operation Junction City 207, 212, 220
Operation Tucson 204

P

Pale of Settlement 23
Palestine Liberation Organization 231
Palestinian 254, 256-259, 262, 263, 269-273, 275, 280
Parkchester 8-16, 19, 29, 32, 49, 71, 72, 150
Pasco, Major Allen 42, 236
Pendleton, Elmer 194
Pitt, PFC Roy 139, 160
post-colonial 255, 271
Potsdam Conference 267
Prek Klok 210, 215, 218, 220, 224, 225, 239

R

Rabdau, Major Jim 119, 121, 122, 142
Rasmussen, Specialist Raymond 131
refugees 117, 266, 267, 270, 271
Rinker, Major 203, 212, 213
Rosenberg, Captain Kenneth 42, 236
Rosenberg, Julius & Ethel 35, 36
ROTC 19, 34-43, 46, 47, 52, 68, 80, 99, 118, 136, 138, 151, 225, 235, 283
ROTC Summer Camp 43, 45, 46, 52, 80, 136, 138, 283
Russian Army x, 22

S

Said, Edward 271
Saigon ix, 78, 86, 87, 95, 102, 172, 173, 195, 207, 225
Schneider, Major Robert 203, 204
Smith, Lieutenant Elvin 99, 122, 124, 128, 129, 139, 141-143, 160, 186
Stoczek, Poland 237, 238
Strickland, PFC Arthur 131
Sullivan, Specialist Curtis 160

T

Tactay, Specialist Eugene 160
Taylor, PFC Galen 160
Tulane University 201, 257, 260

U

UCLA 260
Uighurs 254
UN Partition Plan 268, 269

W

Wackernheim, Germany 63
Wallace, Lieutenant Colonel George M. III 163, 164, 166-168, 170, 175-180, 183-186, 188, 190, 191, 194, 197, 198
Walton, PFC Cleveland 160
Wergow, Poland 237
World War II 6, 18, 44, 50, 61-63, 65, 75, 77, 81, 83, 84, 102, 106, 107, 116, 123, 147, 157, 158, 215, 237, 247, 248, 249, 263-267

Y

Yariv, Israel Defense Force Brigadier General Eitan 242, 243
Young, Captain John 42, 236

Z

Zais, Major General Melvin 197
Zionism 259, 273, 274

www.ingramcontent.com/pod-product-compliance
Lightning Source LLC
Chambersburg PA
CBHW071150070526
44584CB00019B/2738